DATE DUE

DE 23 '94			
OO 9 '97			
MR			
DE 17 04			

Teaching American Indian Students

Teaching
American Indian Students

Edited by Jon Reyhner

Foreword by Ben Nighthorse Campbell

University of Oklahoma Press : Norman and London

Practices and Native Language

Indian Education (Billings, 1989)

This book is published with the generous assistance of the Wallace C. Thompson Endowment Fund.

Library of Congress Cataloging-in-Publication Data

Teaching American Indian students / edited by Jon Reyhner ; foreword by
   Ben Nighthorse Campbell.
          p.   cm.
      Includes bibliographical references and index.
      ISBN 0-8061-2449-0
      1. Indians of North America—Education.   2. Intercultural
   education—United States.   3. Indians of North America—Ethnic
   identity.   I. Reyhner, Jon Allan.
      E97.T37   1992
      371.97'97—dc20   92-54136
                                                                          CIP

Formerly published as *Teaching the Indian Child: A Bilingual/Multicultural Approach* (2nd ed.) © 1988 by Jon Reyhner.

The paper in this book meets the guidelines for permanence and durability of the Committee on Production Guidelines for Book Longevity of the Council on Library Resources, Inc. ∞

    2   3   4   5   6   7   8   9   10   11   12   13   14   15   16   17

Contents

Foreword

BEN NIGHTHORSE CAMPBELL

Nineteen ninety-two is the five hundredth year of contact between American Indians and Europeans, and it is an appropriate time to reflect on what we as a society have learned, examine where we have been, and chart a course for our future. In addition, I think it is appropriate to evaluate what we can and should be teaching Indian children to help them achieve the future they desire for themselves and their tribes.

American Indians have endured phenomenally rapid change, especially during the past two hundred years. Despite federal efforts to assimilate Indians, to terminate their nations, and even to exterminate them, they have tenaciously and sometimes perilously held on to their distinct ways of life. Unfortunately, the American education system has, at times, participated in these harmful policies to the detriment of American Indians.

Many people still remember the days when Indian children were forced to go to schools where their hair was cut upon entering and they were punished for speaking their native language. Armed with a better understanding of Indian children and their unique cultures, and working with enhanced pedagogical skills, teachers can help Indian students to overcome any alienation or apprehension they may feel about our present-day educational system.

In recent years, better communication has helped to bridge the gap between Indian and non-Indian cultures. Educators, and society in general, have given up the notion that everyone must look alike and learn alike. I believe we have made great strides in respecting the differences of people and cultures, but in many respects we still have a long way to go.

The dropout rate for Indian youths continues to be unbearably high. The matriculation rate to higher education is decisively low, and the high school completion level is abominable. According to the most current Department of Education data, the attrition rate for Indian youth is 35.5 percent at the sophomore level in high school—and that is for the ones who have made it as far as high school. Other minorities fare differently: 14.8 percent for whites, 22.2 percent for blacks, 8.2 percent for Asian Americans; only the dropout rate for Hispanics, 35.8 percent, is higher.

If we could only articulate to students the power of education. Education had a significant impact on my life. I literally came up from the streets to the halls of Congress by determining to get an education, to work and contribute to society so that I might make this world a better place for all people. That journey, though, from Sacramento to Washington, D.C., took many, many years.

My father, a Northern Cheyenne, left the reservation as a young man. He met and married my mother, a Portuguese immigrant, after getting out of the service. My mother became ill during my childhood and, unfortunately, spent twenty-two years in the hospital. My father, God bless him, suffered from alcoholism. He tried to do the best he could, but was unable to provide for me. I spent much of my youth in foster homes and in the streets. I remember distinctly the moment I decided I could and would do better than my father: I watched, powerless, as he was hit over the head with a bottle—a terrible experience for any child to endure. But as I stood there watching him, in pain and bleeding from his wound, I vowed to myself to get an education and make something of myself.

My education did not come easy. Many times I felt defeated and wondered if I could make it, but I was able to overcome my discouragement. The more I learned and then applied my new skills, the more I knew I could succeed. But we cannot teach children or instill in them any sense of hope or accomplishment if they are not in school, and I am afraid that we are losing some of the best and brightest too early for them even to become statistics. Your challenge, as an educator, is certainly clear for improving Indian education at many different levels.

As a member of Congress, I too am challenged to improve the

status of Indian education. The United States has a unique relationship of trust with the American Indian nations, and Congress is obligated to ensure that our responsibilities to the Indian tribes are carried out in a fair and honorable manner. Recent federal initiatives include passage of the Native American Languages Act, the 1992 White House Conference on Indian Education, and the secretary of education's Indian Nations at Risk Task Force. To promote Indian education, I support efforts toward achieving a better understanding of Indian culture and determining which methods work best in teaching Indian children, both for the student and for the teacher.

Without a doubt, teaching is one of the most important and worthwhile professions, and I commend you for taking on the challenge of teaching our Indian youth.

Preface

As a result of the civil rights movement, Indian activism, and liberal concern, in the late 1960s and early 1970s the United States demonstrated a new interest in American Indians, which resulted in legislation allowing Indians greater self-determination. Since then that interest has waned, but the seeds planted in the form of tribally controlled schools and colleges have managed to grow despite increasingly severe budget constraints and a decreased interest in civil rights.

Today, there are signs of a renewed interest in American Indians. The secretary of education's appointment in 1990 of the Indian Nations at Risk Task Force and the 1992 White House Conference on Indian Education indicate renewed federal interest, and the popularity of the Academy Award–winning motion picture *Dances with Wolves* demonstrates interest on the part of all Americans in the Indian experience. Even more important than popular and government interest, the increased strength of American Indians is evidenced by the preliminary 1990 census figures, which show that almost two million Americans identify themselves as American Indians (Johnson 1991). This is more than double the number the census reported in 1970 (Bureau of the Census 1988). New tribal colleges, tribal schools, and tribal industries give hope of a continued American Indian renaissance.

However, much still needs to be done. The Department of the Interior Inspector General's 1991 Audit Report found that Bureau of Indians Affairs "management of the Indian education program had experienced many deficiencies, resulting in children not receiving quality educational opportunities" (Office of Inspector

General, i). That report found that the bureauwide average for students ranged from a low of twenty-fourth percentile in third grade to a high of only the thirty-second percentile in twelfth grade, a high probably reached by the attrition of lower-scoring students (11). These findings and those of the Indian Nations at Risk Task Force clearly show that the "Indian problem" of the nineteenth century and the "national tragedy" of the 1960s are still with us.

While teaching a class during the spring of 1990 on the Northern Cheyenne Reservation, I asked teachers why Indian students were not doing well in school. After some discussion, they came to the agreement that it was because students were not interested in what the schools had to offer. The teachers remembered staying in school because their grandparents or parents continually reminded them of the importance of education.

The observations of those American Indian teachers and aides confirmed the results of the comprehensive *Navajo Area Student Dropout Study* (Platero Paperwork 1986), which found that the most common reason given by Navajo students for dropping out of school was boredom. This book is designed to help educators interest and involve Indian students in school and thus contribute to student success.

Whenever writing a book about people, terminology can be a problem. Various terms can be used to describe the indigenous people of the United States including *Indian, Native American, American Indian,* and *Alaska Native.* The contributors to this book have tried to use the names that this continent's indigenous people prefer while at the same time seeking clarity. In 1990 the Indian Nations at Risk Task Force chose to use *American Indian* and *Alaska Native,* or the shortened form *Native.* However, this book was well on the way to completion by that time, and it was decided to use the less inclusive term American Indian and Indian, even though some of the authors have worked extensively with Alaska Native peoples. Many of the ideas put forth in this book can be applied to indigenous minorities all over the world, and the editor wishes to apologize to Alaskan, Hawaiian, and other Native peoples for whatever slights they may feel for not receiving more specific mention.

The nineteen educators who contributed to this book draw on their extensive experience with Indian education to assist Indian school administrators, teachers, and teachers-in-training in improving the instruction of Indian children. Although this book includes work done at many Indian schools, colleges, and universities, it originated at the Indian Bilingual Teacher Training Program at Eastern Montana College.

My own experience in Indian education began in 1971 at Chinle, Arizona, teaching Navajo sixth graders. Since then I have worked in numerous schools, both public and Indian controlled, as an administrator on seven different reservations in three states. I would especially like to thank the Navajo and Chippewa-Cree school administrators for whom I have worked, Harrison Henry, Bert Corcoran, and Jimmie C. Begay, who gave me a chance to work in truly Indian-controlled schools.

Some of the authors of this edition are new to the book while others have contributed to previous editions. I would like to thank all the authors, old and new, for their support. In addition, I would like to thank the Newberry Library of Chicago and their D'Arcy McNickle Center for the Study of the American Indian for assistance provided through a short-term fellowship. I would also like to thank Margaret Connell Szasz, Robert Trennert, Wayne Holm, Tom Carron, and Almeda Sun for their helpful suggestions on individual chapters. Kathy Coleman has provided invaluable secretarial assistance. In addition my family, Marie, Deborah, and Tsosie, and my parents have given me the support over the years necessary to the completion of this book.

JON REYHNER

Billings, Montana

I
Multicultural Education

The Empowerment
of Indian Students

JIM CUMMINS

Indian students throughout North America have experienced dis-
proportional school failure in educational systems organized, administered, and controlled by members of the dominant group.
This pattern is common to indigenous groups in most western
countries who have been conquered, subjugated, segregated, and
regarded as inherently inferior by the dominant group. Educational failure is regarded by the dominant group as the natural
consequence of the minority group's inherent inferiority. With regard to the American Indian, this victim-blaming is legitimated
by pointing at high rates of alcohol abuse, poor hygiene, and lack
of middle-class child-rearing practices, all of which are viewed as
manifestations of the minority group's deficiency. It is not difficult to recognize in this picture the influence of racism, which is
embedded inextricably in the workings of the society itself. The
process of blaming the minority group for its own failure effectively screens from critical scrutiny the way in which the educational system causes school failure among minority students.

It is striking that in the United States context, the black, Hispanic, and Indian students, who most often experience school
failure, have all endured a long history of subjugation and overt
racism at the hands of the dominant white society. In schools, the
racism has often been expressed through physical violence. Chapter 3 describes the psychological and physical violence inflicted
by school personnel on Indian children, including the punishment
of children for speaking their native language and practicing traditional religions. We cannot understand the causes of minority
students' academic difficulties or plan effective ways of reversing

these difficulties unless we see that the issues are more complex than just a mismatch between the language of the home and that of the school or a lack of adequate English as a Second Language (ESL) teaching. The roots of school failure lie in the ways well-meaning educators inadvertently reinforce children's conflicting feelings about both their own culture and the majority culture. This "bicultural ambivalence" is the result of generations of overt racism. Minority groups that maintain a strong sense of pride in their own language and culture or who have not internalized mixed feelings about their own culture and the dominant group tend not to experience school failure (Ogbu 1978).

Two questions follow from this analysis. First, how is the historical pattern of overt racism continued in more subtle forms in our schools today? And second, how can this institutionalized racism be eliminated so that educational growth becomes a possibility for minority students? In schools today educators usually do not intend to discriminate against minority students; however, often in the name of equality, their interactions with minority students are controlled by unquestioned assumptions that reflect the values and priorities of the majority culture. It is in these interactions that minority students are educationally disabled.

Four Factors Affecting
Minority Student School Success

A considerable amount of data shows that power and status relations between minority and majority groups exert a major influence on school performance (Cummins 1984; Ogbu 1978). Minority groups that tend to experience academic difficulty (for example, Finns in Sweden; Hispanic, black, and Indian groups in the United States; and Franco-Ontarian, black, and Indian groups in Canada) appear to have developed an insecurity and ambivalence about the value of their own cultural identity as a result of their interactions with the dominant group. A central proposition of this chapter is that minority students are disempowered educationally in much the same way that their communities are disempowered by interactions with other societal institutions (see also Cummins 1986). The converse of this is that minority students will succeed educationally to the extent that the patterns of interaction in schools reverse those that prevail in the society at large. In short, minority students are empowered or disabled as a direct result of their interactions with educators. These interactions are mediated by the implicit or explicit role definitions that educators assume in relation to four institutional characteristics of schools. These characteristics reflect the extent to which

1. Minority students' language and culture are incorporated into the school program;
2. Minority community participation is encouraged as an integral component of children's education;
3. Instruction (pedagogy) is used to motivate students to use language actively in order to generate their own knowledge; and
4. Professionals involved in student testing (assessment) become advocates for minority students by focusing primarily on the ways in which students' academic difficulties are a function of interactions with and within the school context instead of locating the problem within the students.

Each dimension can be analyzed along a continuum, with one end reflecting an antiracist orientation and the other reflecting the more traditional assimilationist (Anglo-conformity) orientation. The overall hypothesis is that the assimilationist orientation often results in school failure while an intercultural, antiracist orientation allows students to develop the ability, confidence, and motivation that lead to academic success.

Of these four dimensions—cultural and linguistic incorporation, community participation, instruction, and testing—at least three are integral to most statements of multicultural education policy. Although the focus of much multicultural education policy has been on cultural preservation rather than on language, the language component is central to the present theoretical framework because a multicultural education policy that ignores linguistic diversity is empty. Considerable research shows the importance of language for school achievement. Instruction must be included as a central dimension of the framework because educators need to abandon the assumption that teaching focuses primarily on transmission of predetermined knowledge and skills if students' nonschool experiences, reflecting their community's culture, are to be incorporated into the school program. The four dimensions are explained below.

Cultural or linguistic incorporation. Considerable research data suggest that for minority groups experiencing above-average levels of school failure, the extent to which students' language and culture are incorporated into the school program constitutes a significant predictor of academic success (Cummins 1984). In programs where minority students' home-language skills are strongly reinforced, school success appears to reflect both the more solid cognitive or academic foundation developed through intensive first-language instruction and also the reinforcement of their cultural identity.

With respect to the incorporation of minority students' language and culture, educators' role definitions can be characterized along an additive-subtractive dimension (see Lambert 1975 for a discussion of additive and subtractive bilingualism). Educators who see their role as encouraging their students to add a second language and culture to supplement rather than supplant their native language and culture are more likely to create conditions in which students can develop a sense of empowerment. Educators who see their role as getting their students to replace their home language and culture with English and white values in order to assimilate them into the dominant culture are more likely to create the conditions for student failure. Students who develop skills in two languages have been found to have cognitive advantages over monolingual students (Hakuta and Diaz 1985).

Community participation.   Minority students' school performance is also helped when the children's communities (especially their parents and extended family) are involved with running their children's school. When educators involve minority parents as partners in their children's education, parents appear to communicate to their children a positive attitude toward education that leads to an improvement in the students' academic achievement (see, for example, Tizard, Schofield, and Hewison 1982; Ada 1988).

The educator role definitions associated with community participation can be characterized along a continuum from collaborative to exclusionary. Teachers operating at the collaborative end of the continuum actively encourage parents to participate in promoting their children's academic progress both in the home and through involvement in classroom activities (Ada 1988). A collaborative orientation may require a willingness on the part of the teacher to work closely with teachers or aides fluent in the student's first language in order to communicate effectively and in a noncondescending way with parents. Teachers with an exclusionary orientation, on the other hand, tend to regard teaching as their job and are likely to view collaboration with parents as either irrelevant or actually detrimental to children's progress. Parents may be viewed as part of the problem if they do not speak English with their children at home.

In the case of Indian students, it is obvious that our failure to build education around the enormously rich human heritage of this continent is depriving students of the sense of pride in their own cultures that is crucial to their academic growth. Students can become empowered only when education becomes a true community enterprise involving an equal partnership between educators in the school and educators in the home, the children's families. It is not enough to focus only on students' classroom experiences; expanding the focus is a central component of the change from an Anglo-conformity orientation. In addition, the collective historical experience of the community must be used as the context for all learning in the school. There are no easy formulas for implementing these changes; patience, ingenuity, and a spirit of committed experimentation are necessary.

Instruction (pedagogy).   Several investigators have suggested that the learning difficulties of minority students are often caused by the way we teach children designated "at risk." These students frequently receive intensive instruction that confines them to a passive role and induces a form of "learned helplessness" (see Cummins 1984, 1989, for reviews). In contrast, instruction that creates conditions for student environment, such as the Whole Language approach described in this book (chapter 12), aims to liberate students from dependence on instruction in the sense of encouraging them to become active generators of their own knowledge.

Two major orientations can be distinguished with respect to teaching. These differ in the extent to which the teacher retains exclusive control over classroom interaction as opposed to sharing some of the control with students. The dominant instructional model in most Western industrial societies has been termed a "transmission" model (Barnes 1976; Wells 1982, 1986). This model can be contrasted with an "experiential-interactive" model of teaching. The basic premise of the transmission model is that the task of teachers is to impart knowledge or skills they possess to their students who do not yet have these skills. This implies that teachers initiate and control the interaction, constantly orienting it toward the achievement of instructional objectives.

An experiential-interactive model of instruction focuses on giving students hands-on ("context-embedded") classroom experiences that provide students with a basis for understanding more abstract ("context-reduced") academic curricula. A transmission model of teaching contravenes central principles of language and literacy acquisition; a model allowing for reciprocal interaction between teacher and students represents a more appropriate alternative (Cummins 1984; Wells 1982, 1986). This interactive model incorporates proposals about the relation between language and learning made by a variety of investigators, most notably in recent years in the Bullock Report (1975) and by Barnes (1976), Lindfors (1987), and Wells (1982). Its applications with respect to the promotion of literacy conform closely to the psycholinguistic approaches to reading advocated by Goodman and Goodman (1977), Holdaway (1979), and Smith (1978, 1988).

A central tenet of the experiential-interactive model is that "talking and writing are means to learning" (Bullock Report 1975:50). The major characteristics of the interactive portion of the model are

genuine dialogue between student and teacher in both oral and written modalities,

guidance and facilitation rather than control of student learning by the teacher,

encouragement of student-student talk in a collaborative learning context,

encouragement of meaningful language use by students rather than correctness of surface forms,

conscious integration of language use and development with all curricular content rather than isolation of language from other content areas,

a focus on the development of higher-level cognitive skills rather than factual recall, and

task presentation that generates intrinsic rather than extrinsic motivation.

In short, instructional approaches that promote student empowerment encourage them to assume greater control over their own learning goals and to collaborate actively with each other in achieving those goals. These approaches reflect what cognitive psychologists such as Piaget (1954, 1966) and Vygotsky (1978) have emphasized about children's learning for more than half a century: learning is an active process that is enhanced through interaction. The stress on action (Piaget) and interaction (Vygotsky) contrasts with behavioristic learning models that focus on passive and isolated reception of knowledge.

The relevance of these two instructional models for multicultural education derives from the fact that a genuine multicultural orientation is impossible within a transmission model of pedagogy. To be sure, content about other cultural groups can be taught, but appreciation of other cultural groups can come about only through interaction in which experiences are shared. Transmission models entail the suppression of students' experiences and consequently do not allow for the validation of minority students' experiences in the classroom. The human resources represented by students' cultural backgrounds can be utilized in the classroom only when educators have (1) an additive orientation toward students' culture and language such that they can be shared rather than suppressed in the classroom, (2) an openness to collaborate with community resource persons who can provide insight about different cultural, religious, and linguistic traditions, and (3) a willingness to permit students' active use of written and oral language so that they can develop literacy and other language skills while sharing their experiences with peers and adults.

Testing (assessment). In the past, both classroom and psychological testing have disempowered or disabled minority students. Academic achievement and intelligence tests (such as IQ tests) located the causes of minority students' educational difficulties within the students, thereby screening from critical scrutiny the students' interactions with the educational system. This process led to massive overrepresentation of black and Hispanic students in classes for the educable mentally retarded until the early 1970s (Mercer 1973). Litigation and legislation during the 1960s and 1970s (such as Public Law 94-142) appeared, on the surface, to rectify this situation insofar as minority students are no longer overrepresented in classes for the retarded. However, the disabling structure has preserved itself simply by shifting the overrepresentation of minority students to classes for the learning disabled. Ortiz and Yates (1983), for example, reported that Hispanic students in Texas are overrepresented by a factor of three in learning disability classes. It seems implausible to conclude that three times as many

Hispanic as non-Hispanic white children suffer from intrinsic, neurologically based learning disabilities; rather, it is more plausible that these children's learning difficulties have been caused by the kind of educational interactions they have experienced.

Within the institutional structure in which psychosocial assessment takes place—in conformity with legal and policy requirements and training and certification programs—psychologists tend to locate the cause of academic problems in minority children themselves rather than in the school and its curriculum. Psychologists often are not conscious of the fact that minority children's culture-specific experiences affect their test results, and see minority languages as negative influences on children's lives. Specifically, psychological assessment has deflected attention away from the impact of schools' efforts to eradicate minority children's language and culture and the exclusion of minority parents from any meaningful role in their children's education. Unfortunately, the effect of both the curriculum—which has reflected, both overtly and covertly, the racist values of the dominant group—and restrictions on children's in-class expression of their own experiences has not been assessed.

Because the psychologist is only equipped with psychoeducational assessment tools, students' school problems are assumed to be psychoeducational in nature. The psychologist's training has resulted in a tunnel vision that does not take account of the experiential realities of minority children. However, a psychologist's professional credibility depends on satisfactorily interpreting children's difficulty and making reasonable placement or intervention recommendations. To admit that assessment reveals nothing about causes of minority students' academic difficulties would jeopardize the psychologist's status and credibility. Thus psychological testing may actually hide a variety of possible contributors to children's school failure.

The alternative role definition that is required to reverse the traditional legitimating function of testing is an advocacy role. The task of the psychologist, teacher, and special educator must be to "delegitimate" the traditional functions of academic and psychological testing in the educational disabling of minority students. In other words, they must be prepared to become advocates for the child in scrutinizing critically the cultural, social, and educational contexts within which the child has developed.

How can assessment play a role in challenging rather than legitimating the disabling of minority students within the educational system? The first step is to broaden the conceptual basis for testing so that it goes beyond psychoeducational considerations and toward focusing on the child's entire learning environment. It is virtually inevitable that assessment will contribute to the disabling of minority students when the only tools at the psychologist's disposal are psychological tests. Since tests focus only on psychological processes, minority children's educational difficulties will, of necessity, be attributed to psychological dysfunctions. To challenge the disabling of minority students, the assessment must focus on the extent to which children's language and culture are incorporated within the school program, the extent to which educators collaborate with parents as partners in a shared enterprise, and the extent to which children are encouraged to use language (both tribal and English) actively within the classroom to amplify their experiences in interaction with children and adults. In other words, the primary focus should be on remediating the educational interactions that minority children experience.

In order to broaden the focus of educational and psychological testing, it is necessary to reduce the territoriality between the roles of teachers and testing specialists. Formal testing has an important role to play, but its impact is considerably greater when combined with informal assessment. The longitudinal observation and monitoring of student progress throughout the school year by classroom teachers also yields valuable data. Teachers have more opportunity to observe children tackling academic and cognitive tasks than do psychologists, and teachers can also observe how children react to various types of intervention. In other words, the teacher has the opportunity to observe what Vygotsky calls "the zone of proximal development," defined as "the distance between the actual developmental level as determined by independent problem solving and the level of potential development as determined through problem solving under adult guidance or in collaboration with more capable peers" (1978:86).

It is important to note, however, that not all forms of instruction are equally capable of contributing to the assessment process. When the instruction is transmission-oriented—when the teacher views his or her task primarily as transmitting a body of knowledge and skills to the student—students are often limited to passive roles of responding to "display" questions (questions to which the teacher already knows the answer) and filling out worksheets focused on rote recall (memorization) or mechanical application. Typically, this type of instruction mirrors the biases of standardized tests. Instruction that creates conditions for empowerment, however, is experiential and interactive, and more likely to provide meaningful information for assessment.

Conclusion

Reversing the legacy of generations of subjugation and overt racism is a formidable challenge. Recent events in the United States and Canada in relation to the recognition of the rights of Indians do not encourage optimism about the dominant group's commitment to acknowledge or redress this legacy of racism. Thus, if the institutionalized racism in schools is going to be challenged, it can only be done by teachers and by Indian parents themselves. A first step is effective control by students and parents, or at least a genuine partnership with educators, in the operation of the school. The directions for change outlined above are obviously generic in that they are formulated to apply to a range of minority groups that have experienced systematic school failure. The appropriateness of these directions and the specific applications must be worked out by each community. The change process, however, will inevitably involve consciousness-raising on the part of the community; and insofar as community efforts for change represent a challenge to the status quo, they are likely to be strongly resisted by the dominant group.

2

Indian Education: Assumptions, Ideologies, Strategies

RICARDO L. GARCIA
JANET GOLDENSTEIN AHLER

Education for American Indian children should empower them to become full participants in their communities, the country, and the world. The contents of their education should provide them the full array of knowledge, skills, and attitudes necessary for participation as politically active, culturally viable, and economically prosperous citizens. This chapter lays a foundation for teaching Indian children. Basic operational assumptions and ideological perspectives are described to provide theoretical bases. The chapter ends with a discussion of strategies useful for applying the assumptions and some of the ideologies for teaching Indian children.

Educational Assumptions as Goals

In this book different perceptions about the educational needs of Indian children are presented. While many viewpoints are presented, there exists a fundamental consensus throughout the book: Indian children are unique individuals. Like all children, some are sad, glad, bratty, or cute; some are thin, rotund, agile, or clumsy. Some like to sleep at night, others during the day. Some are curious, bright, timid, or assertive. Some like to read, write, or do arithmetic. All are the progeny of the very oldest and most native cultures of North America. This is why some people label them *Native* American.

The fundamental consensus that Indian children are like most other children provides a foundation for one of the book's major assumptions: teaching Indian children is no different than teaching other children. This does not mean that Indian children are exactly the same as non-Indian children. Actually, teaching children as though they were the same robs children of their unique individuality. Good teaching requires that teachers understand and respect the individuality of all children. Neither appreciation nor respect are possible without knowing the children's cultural and environmental backgrounds. A child's culture and environmental background are what makes a child unique.

The idea of respect and appreciation is not a pie-in-the-sky, do-gooder attitude. Rather, it is an attitude that must pervade all of teaching regardless of the ethnic and cultural backgrounds of the students. So what? If all that is needed are respect and appreciation, then why a whole book on the topic of teaching Indian children? Why not a short article filled with platitudes on respect and appreciation? The answer is that true appreciation and respect do not come easily when teachers are not members of the culture to which their students belong. And even when they are members of the same culture, true appreciation and respect are attitudes that take a long time and a lot of effort to translate into behaviors. Appreciation and respect are the antecedent attitudes for teaching Indian children. The resulting behaviors needed to put the attitudes into effect are the efforts to provide Indian children a thorough foundation in the academic areas needed for school and occupational success. True appreciation and respect for the Indian child are teaching characteristics that will surmount a multitude of other shortcomings.

Another major assumption of this book is that the goals of Indian education are related to the historically validated goals of education elucidated by notable educators such as Horace Mann and John Dewey. Horace Mann is credited as the individual responsible for the establishment of the American common schools, the origin of our public school system. He argued in the 1840s that if education was left entirely to parents, only the children of the rich would get anything more than the simplest education, creating a society ruled by the wealthy. Mann promoted the notion that a free, public education should be the birthright of every child. Mann wrote,

> Education . . . is the great equalizer of the conditions of men—the balance wheel of the social machinery. . . . This idea . . . gives each man the independence and the means by which he can resist the selfishness of other men. (quoted in Noll and Kelley 1970, 213)

Education as the great equalizer is a vision of education as a liberating force that empowers individuals to take advantage of opportunities. At times, educated individuals can make their own opportunities. The idea that education should be a liberating force in the lives of Indian peoples is what Chief Plenty Coups, a noted leader of the Crow tribe, meant when he said, "Education is your most powerful weapon. With education you are the white man's equal; without education you are his victim" (quoted in Bryan 1985, 90).

But education has not always served as a weapon for liberating American Indians. Previous federal policies of assimilation have used education as a weapon to annihilate American Indian cultures and languages (for discussions regarding the policies, see chapter 3 and the "Educational Ideology" section of this chapter). While the assimilation policies are no longer an official position of the federal government, the attitudes of teachers and administrators in some reservation schools, as well as the teaching methods and textbooks used, still reflect the discarded policies. What is needed in all American Indian schools are practices and policies that align with John Dewey's notion of education in a democracy.

Dewey expanded the notion of education for individual empowerment to include education for sociopolitical empowerment. Education is necessary not only for the benefit of individuals, but also for the survival of democratic institutions. In his book *Democracy and Education,* Dewey (1916) described the interlocking character of democracy and education. Democracy without education cannot exist, a thesis rooted in the Jeffersonian principle that if "a nation expects to be ignorant and free . . . it expects what never was and never will be" (quoted in Padover 1946, 88).

Educated citizens are essential for the perpetuation of a democratic society. Just as education personally benefits individuals so does it benefit and empower individuals to be politically active citizens within their communities, states, and the nation. Democratic societies operate on the basis of a social contract in which individuals enter into an unspoken agreement with their human communities. As children, individuals should be given the protection of the community. The contract's quid pro quo is social responsibility. As adults, individuals should provide the next generation the same protection they received, which is only possible when adults are socially responsive citizens. Consequently, social responsibility to ensure the perpetuation of the human community within democratic institutions becomes a major task of adulthood.

The basic education of Indian children, specifically twelve or more years of schooling, should empower Indian students to be (1) capable of lifelong learning, (2) able to lead their individual lives in directions they desire, and (3) able to function as literate and politically active citizens. As an educational aim or outcome, lifelong learning refers to the students' ability to learn a vocation or pursue further education at colleges, universities, or technical-vocational institutes for economic gain or personal pleasure. The aim also refers to the students' ability to teach themselves by utilizing libraries, museums, computer data banks, or any other knowledge depositories. Consequently, schooling should provide Indian students an education with breadth and depth in the traditional areas of languages, literature, mathematics, sciences, the social sciences, the fine arts, health, and physical education. Depth and breadth should be especially evident in the teaching of language, literature, mathematics, science, and the social sciences so that students are enabled to use these academic disciplines to enhance their lives in meaningful ways. The social sciences—in particular those areas that teach responsible self-government—should permeate the school's curriculum in all grades. In the process, tribal languages, American Indian literature, Indian history and government, and contributions of American Indians to the sciences and mathematics must be included, as further indicated by the subject matter chapters in this book.

Self-direction, the second aim, refers to the students' ability to exercise options after high school graduation. The goal here is to create individuals who are autonomous and self-motivated, able to initiate action to fulfill their particular life aims. Twelve years of schooling should provide Indian students the ability to make a wide range of choices regarding avocations as well as vocations. Indian education should be structured to enable students, when they reach adulthood, to select vocational, technical, or professional career paths as well as cultural orientations.

The third aim, political literacy and activism, is a fundamental educational goal in a democratic society. The goal is especially relevant to Indian students. Only recently has the U.S. government granted American Indians the right of self-determination and self-government, a right most other Americans take for granted. The last one hundred years of American Indian history has been a chronicle of paternalistic control by the federal government (see chapter 3). Currently, American Indians are undergoing the first stages of a new phase of self-determination. They are relearning the hard lessons of self-rule. For example, most Americans are accustomed to the local control of their schools. In most communities, members of the local board of education are elected by the people in the community. The elected board members, who are supposed to represent the people's educational goals and values, hire a superintendent who in turn advises them on the hiring and firing of principals and teachers. Most communities do a reasonably good job of electing school board members and maintaining their schools largely because they are knowledgeable about and experienced in self-rule—they have been electing board members and maintaining their schools for a considerable number of years. Until the middle 1970s, the federal government through the Bureau of Indian Affairs would hire and fire school personnel in reservation schools, and public school districts on or near reservations had school boards dominated by non-Indians. Now, American Indians are learning the process of local control of public institutions, such as schools, with all of its difficulties. Problems are to be expected, but they will diminish in the future as Indian students learn how they can shape political affairs at tribal, state, and national levels.

Do lifelong learning, self-direction, and political activism appear to be assimilationist? If they are implemented within the context of the students' cultures and traditional ways, then the goals are integrative. The distinction is not merely semantic. Two examples of how the goals can be integrative rather than assimilative are found in the extended family and tribal government systems developed by American Indians.

Most American Indian tribes have extended family systems that provide the individual warmth, security, and self-esteem. It would be assimilationist folly to encourage American Indian students to abandon their extended families for nuclear families in the name of becoming self-directed and autonomous. It is possible to develop individual autonomy within a group context, as done in extended families. Also, on some reservations, American Indians have methods of local government reminiscent of a very old American tradition, communal life governed through a "town-meeting" type of government in which a tribal council is elected to represent various areas and people on a reservation. Communities acting as "committees of the whole" inform the council or council representatives of their desires. The council is responsible for administration of the tribe's wishes, but power to make policy is held by the tribe as a whole. Thus American Indians are not without experience in self-government, and they may want to integrate their traditional processes of local control into school management.

Do lifelong learning, self-direction, and political activism appear to be idealistic, unachievable aims? Consider the idea that all education is idealistic. Public education in the United States operates on the idealistic premise that all students are educable, as in Adler's maxim that "there are no unteachable children. There are only schools and teachers and parents who fail to teach them" (1982, 8). An education that is desirable for children in one state, or country for that matter, is desirable for children in another state or country; we live in one nation and in one world; all citizens need to be literate and politically active. While lifelong learning, self-direction, and political literacy and activism are idealistic goals, they are essential educational aims for all future citizens— Indian children included.

These goals are predicated on the faith that teachers and schools are committed to literacy. Literacy generally refers to the ability to speak, read, write, and comprehend American English in the United States. But literacy as conceived here refers to a hierarchically arranged complex of skills, attitudes, and knowledge. At the lowest level is functional literacy, which refers to the ability to speak, read, write, and comprehend standard American English; if the Indian student is taught bilingually, then functional literacy in the second language is also necessary. Functional literacy also refers to the ability to read technical literature, which entails an understanding of simple mathematical and scientific concepts. Functional literacy entails a basic knowledge of mathematics and scientific principles as well as the traditional language areas of comprehension, speech, reading. and writing.

At the second tier is cultural literacy, which expands functional literacy and refers to a knowledge of the literature, history, and grand traditions of the core American culture, including major scientific and technological accomplishments. Cultural literacy also refers to knowledge about a person's ethnic or cultural heritage. While it is important that Indian children know the values and beliefs of the core American culture as embodied in its literature and history, *it is equally important* that Indian children be taught the content of their tribal cultures, including, if their parents desire, a knowledge of the tribe's language and oral tradition, which constitute the literature and history of many tribes. Last, cultural literacy refers to a knowledge of cultures and events on a global scale. While knowledge of the American core culture and knowledge of one's own heritage are basic to cultural literacy, global awareness and appreciation of the peoples of the world are essential for the humanistic education of American Indian students.

At the highest tier is critical literacy, which refers to the ability to think analytically and creatively. Specific abilities here are

1. the ability to analyze and evaluate oral and written expression, including the ability to detect a writer's or speaker's biases;
2. in the area of mathematics, rather than rote memorization of formulas, the ability to reason quantitatively with mathematical concepts and formulas and apply that reasoning to real world situations;
3. in the area of science, the ability to propose tentative explanations of phenomena, to gather data systematically and examine them to check the correctness of those explanations, and to evaluate scientific theories in relationship to empirical data;
4. in the fine arts and the performing arts, the ability to understand the disciplined routines or forms used by artists to express ideas or emotions or to produce a desired response.

Critical literacy is the highest level of cognitive development because it requires that students learn to use the knowledge, concepts, and skills gained at the functional and cultural levels of literacy as tools for molding and shaping their lives. More than the memorization and repetition of places, events, dates, names, formulas, and scientific maxims is required to achieve critical literacy. Rather, critical literacy requires students to analyze, synthesize, evaluate, and infer using data or other forms of knowledge.

Behind philosophic assumptions and goals there exist many educational ideologies. An educational ideology is a cluster of values and beliefs pertaining to appropriate instructional goals for particular conceptions or views regarding the nature of the general American society. What follows is a description and evaluation of selected educational ideologies as they pertain to the education of American Indian children.

Educational Ideologies

An educational ideology that is multicultural relates well to the foregoing assumptions and goals. Multicultural education offers an alternative to the old assimilationist ideology of the "melting pot." American Indians as well as later immigrants to this country have long been subjected to an education that values and promotes conformity to an Anglo-dominated American mainstream culture, an ideology that came under attack as the political and social consciousness of the relatively powerless minorities was raised during the civil rights movement of the 1960s. Multicultural education rejects the conformity notion; it responds to and provides for the cultural pluralism and diversity of our nation and world.

A variety of multicultural education models have been developed (Banks 1987; Garcia 1991; Gibson 1976). They respond to different situations and are aimed at different student populations, but all embrace two major goals. The first of these is to meet the educational needs of culturally diverse students by recognizing that their cultural knowledge is worthwhile and by reinforcing and expanding on that knowledge in the classroom so as not to force assimilation processes on those students who are not members of the American mainstream. This goal is a direct response to the demands by American minority groups for educational opportunities historically denied them. There is no reason to presume in meeting this goal that students who are not members of the American mainstream are culturally deficient or deprived.

Another, more encompassing goal of multicultural education is to promote cultural awareness and sensitivity among all students, which will lead to the appreciation of and respect for one's own and others' cultures. This can be achieved primarily by reducing ethnocentrism and eliminating racism and other negative attitudes about others (such as stereotyping, bigotry, and resulting discrimination). Initially, this goal was aimed especially at American mainstream students, who would have to learn to appreciate the minority cultures in order for equity in education to be realized.

However, it has become clear that this goal is appropriate for all cultural groups of students.

Commitments toward achieving these two goals through multicultural education in teacher training programs stem from a variety of sources. Most national educational organizations have encouraged the implementation of multicultural education, and the National Council for Accreditation of Teacher Education (NCATE), which evaluates teacher education institutions for accreditation, has mandated the inclusion of multicultural education in the training of all new teachers since 1980. In addition, several states have certification requirements that stipulate some training in multicultural education, sometimes specifically including American Indian studies. The rationale for these requirements is that new teachers of Indian students will get enough acquaintance with the content area to be able to meet their students' needs. But content knowledge alone will not serve to improve some teachers' attitudes toward Indian students. A combination of training in Native American studies and multicultural education will better equip teachers to attain both multicultural education goals.

What does multicultural education mean for American Indians, especially in reservation schools? McKenna alleged that

multiculturalism, with its presumed liberal, humane acceptance, even sponsorship, of cultural difference is for the Indian a Potemkin village— a facade—to mask the real agenda for American Indians. That agenda is the acceleration of domestic dependency or internal colonialism, the major features of which are political destabilization, economic exploitation, cultural annihilation, and the destruction of the spirits and persons of Indian nations. (1981, 2)

In other words, McKenna views multicultural education as an extension of the centuries-long assimilationist, melting-pot policies of the United States government toward native peoples. Perhaps McKenna's suspicions are historically well founded, but it must be recognized that any ideology can be subverted and misapplied. Proponents of multicultural education expressly foster individual choice in cultural affiliation and reject any semblance of forced assimilation.

In a study of teacher and parental attitudes toward multicultural education on her own reservation, Swisher (1984) found that although teachers' attitudes were more positive overall than parents' attitudes toward multicultural education and its implementation in their reservation schools, specific results within groups of parents and teachers were significant. Parents who had lived away from the reservation for more than ten years had a more positive attitude than those who had lived away fewer years or who had lived all their lives on the reservation. The more educated the parents were, the more positive their attitudes. Parents who were designated as "full bloods" and parents who were enrolled members of that reservation expressed less positive attitudes than others. Younger teachers and teachers with fewer years of teaching experience on the reservation had more positive attitudes toward multicultural education. While the study is descriptive, we might speculate, nevertheless, that those parents who have less positive attitudes may possess the type of skepticism expressed by McKenna above—the belief that any educational ideology is potentially more of the same assimilationism. Moreover, the older, more experienced reservation teachers may still be influenced by the earlier institutional expectation of assimilation for their American Indian students.

Despite the misgivings of some educators and reservation residents, the initial stages of multicultural education have become a reality in many reservation schools. The multicultural education goal that is most often and singularly addressed is the attempt to meet the needs of students who are not part of the American mainstream. The response to these needs in reservation schools has typically been to introduce American Indian content, representing the traditional aspects of the dominant reservation culture, in the form of arts and crafts, music, traditional stories and histories, and native language vocabulary. Much of this information is a mere addition to the regular curriculum, which remains representative of the American mainstream culture. The focus on this one goal does have several justifications. Learning more about one's own culture in school allows for the development of a more positive self-concept among American Indian students, a prerequisite for broader cultural awareness. It is also appropriate to redress the historical exclusion of American Indian culture content in reservation schools as part of the attempted assimilation process. Further, meeting this goal would serve to protect and preserve the cultural continuity and integrity of the reservation cultures. The result, however, is a bilingual or bicultural exposure, not a truly multicultural education.

It might be argued that this exposure is a promising beginning for a multicultural curriculum, but Indian culture in reservation schools must do more than scratch the surface of the mainstream curriculum. Basic values and practices of the reservation cultures should be added to the present content. Native language should be treated as a serious aspect of language learning and include speaking, reading, and writing. Even the particular goal of meeting Indian students' needs will not be realized as long as American mainstream standards continue to be imposed through such means as standardized testing and as long as native cultural content is a minor addition to the core curriculum rather than an integral part. Reservation school standards should represent the cultural values, experiences, and aspirations of the populations being served. American mainstream cultural content could be reduced in the core curriculum in favor of American Indian cultural content without sacrificing commitments to teaching "basic skills." Indeed, the definition of "basic skills" might be subject to revision by the population served.

There is further need to look at multicultural education for American Indians in terms of the other major goal, to increase the cultural awareness and sensitivity in all students. First, it should be pointed out that the assessments and recommendations that follow are intended to concentrate on American Indians only because that is the purpose of this book, not because American Indians need to address these issues more than any other group. This multicultural education goal is aimed at everyone from all cultural groups. In order to meet this goal, cultural diversity and pluralism must be recognized. Navajo educator Dillon Platero, writing about cultural pluralism with regard to Indian education in 1973, stated

> Cultural pluralism and its implications for teaching in the nation's public and private schools is a phenomenon which has become almost a fad. To members of other clearly defined cultural groups, such as many American Indians, there is more than a touch of irony in observing the non-culturally differentiated mass clamor about the desirability of multicultural facility. (39)

Platero would probably admit now, nearly two decades later, that this issue is more than a mere fad. More important is the need to recognize that the group to whom he refers as the "nonculturally differentiated mass" is indeed a diverse group in many respects. There appears to be a tendency to ignore cultural diversity among those of European descent. In fact, few Euro-Americans identify so strongly with the American mainstream culture that they have no ties to or identification with a specific European culture or a combination of European cultures. A Norwegian American may be as different from a Polish American as an Arikara is from a Cheyenne. Cultural diversity within a reservation population must also be recognized. In addition to tribal and band group differences, there are varying degrees of affiliation with traditional and modern reservation cultures.

Understanding processes such as those involving cultural transmission is critical in multicultural education. Cultural transmission refers to education generally and more broadly than just schooling. One specific process is enculturation, the lifelong learning of one's own culture. For American Indians this may include learning aspects of their groups' traditional culture as well as the ever-changing modern culture of the reservation. Most of this learning occurs through contact with the family, peers, and community members. Until recently, little of this enculturation process was reinforced in the reservation classroom. In contrast, American mainstream students are firmly enculturated through schooling because the formal school is designed for and represents the mainstream culture. Potentially, multicultural education could alter this rigid model of American schools.

Another type of cultural transmission process is acculturation—a process that affects Indians so profoundly that understanding its complexities may be fundamental for cultural survival. Acculturation refers to the cultural change that occurs when two or more cultures are in persistent contact. In this process, change may occur in each of the cultures in varying degrees, and sometimes new, hybrid cultures evolve. A particular kind of acculturation is assimilation, in which one culture changes significantly more than the other culture and, as a result, comes to resemble it. This process is often established deliberately through force to maintain control over conquered peoples, but it can occur voluntarily as well.

Although American Indians are certainly familiar with these processes, multicultural education can lead to greater insight regarding them. Reservation schools can teach about assimilation through examples of other indigenous cultures of the world that have experienced similar colonial take-overs. Knowledge about the Bushmen of South Africa, the Maoris of New Zealand, and the Australian aborigines would contribute invaluable comparisons with the experiences of American Indians. Awareness that the world colonialists themselves have been conquered and colonized in the distant past is enlightening as well: examples are the Saxon and Norman conquests of England, the Moorish colonization in Spain, the Roman settlements in ancient Germanic territories. Other conquests such as the British invasion and domination of Ireland, the Spanish conquests in the Americas, and Japanese imperialism in Asia and the Pacific can add to cross-cultural knowledge, which will enhance rather than detract from cultural self-understanding for American Indians. This knowledge will give American Indian students the power to gain more control over their own destinies. They can change their lives, allowing them to modify the path of their own future, and they can also band together with other individuals to gain political strength to change the course of both their tribe's and their nation's future.

Educational Strategies

Educational strategies are broad-based approaches for teaching Indian students. Specific methods and materials for teaching different academic subjects are the topics of many of the text's remaining chapters. This chapter ends with a description of strategies that show promise for teaching American Indian students. Effective strategies are easily thwarted by potent sociocultural forces endemic to American life, including the forces of ethnocentrism and racism. These forces pervade all sectors of American life and are found on and off Indian reservations. For instance, reservation schools continue to reinforce the confusion between the concepts "culture" and "race" by using them interchangeably. American Indian students (as much as any other students) should be engaged in learning the complexities of the concept "culture," which is defined as the shared and learned ways of feeling, thinking, and acting among a particular group of people (Harris 1975). Reservation schools can enhance their students' understanding of culture by exposing them to different cultures and languages in the nation and the world. Language is an integral facet of culture and should be treated with a seriousness beyond vocabulary learning. "Race" refers to physical, observable traits associated with ancestry (Hunter and Whitten 1976). The criteria for determining racial categories are arbitrary and culturally defined; many human geneticists and physical anthropologists seriously question if there is a scientific basis for racial categories (see Montagu 1974). American Indian students should be encouraged to question the criterion of "blood quantum," which is fundamental to the legal definition of an American Indian used by the United States government.

To date, no one has been able to demonstrate a direct link between a person's inherited physical characteristics and the way he or she thinks, feels, and acts. The one does not directly determine the other. A "white-skinned," blue-eyed person who is raised from birth by Chinese in China will likely behave like a Chinese person, not a European. People who "look like" Indians will not necessarily exhibit any specific Indian cultural behavior unless they have been raised in an Indian culture. Reservation schools can promote their students' cultural awareness by making them aware of these concept distinctions. For instance, references to "white" versus "Indian" behavior mistakenly suggest a direct link between the two concepts. That the term "Indian" has come to imply either a cultural or a racial classification complicates the situation further. The words "American Indian," "Indian," or "Native American" are used appropriately to denote individuals defined in cultural terms, but none of these terms is a completely accurate description of the first inhabitants of the American continents. The term "Indian" is a misnomer; when Christopher Columbus came to America, he thought he had reached India and so called the people he saw "Indians." "Native American" is an accurate description of the first inhabitants, but is also suitable for anyone born on the American continents.

Attitudes play a major role in the development of cultural appreciation and awareness. There are two types of prejudice, each associated with both culture and race, which warrant examination. The first, "ethnocentrism," is a prejudice based on culture and is defined as "a preference toward one's own way of life versus all others, and judgment of other groups' life-styles (usually negative) in terms of the value system of one's own lifestyle" (Hunter and Whitten 1976, 147). Many social scientists argue that feeling good about the life-style of one's own cultural group is

necessary to the group's cohesiveness and survival; but the negative, judgmental extremes of ethnocentrism impede cultural appreciation and awareness. We need not lose our own cultural values and practices by learning to view others' life-styles simply as
different. This latter approach, referred to as "cultural relativism," is in favor of understanding others' beliefs and practices
within their own cultural contexts.

Ethnocentric barriers between and among American Indian
groups can be recognized and minimized. This would facilitate
the development of an understanding of mutual circumstances,
needs, and goals, which in turn would reverse some of the divisive-
ness that exists among various tribes and reservations. That divi-
siveness has been fostered by the government on occasion in order
to maintain powerlessness among Indians. Reservation schools
might begin reducing ethnocentrism by engaging students in studies of other tribes for whom there has been traditional mistrust
and by opening communication between traditional "enemies."
Likewise, direct communication between American Indians and
Euro-Americans might lead to mutual respect through positive interaction. Too often, superficial differences and stereotypes are
stressed. Through contact, both groups would probably discover
that there are more similarities than previously assumed, and that
many differences follow lines of "traditional" versus "modern"
cultural adaptations. For example, many traditional European
cultures, especially before the Industrial Revolution, valued and
maintained extended family arrangements similar to those of
many traditional American Indians. European descendants who
are part of the modern American mainstream have had to adopt
other, less extended forms of family; and this has also happened
to American Indians who have become members of the modern
mainstream American culture.

"Racism," the second type of prejudice, is, of course, based
on the concept of race. It is the belief that one race is superior to
another in ways related to biological inheritance and, therefore,
innately determined. The very idea of race and the criteria for determining racial categories are arbitrary and culturally defined.
For instance, Forbes (1990) documents how many Mexican Americans, the majority of whose ancestors lived in the Americas before 1492, are not classified as American Indians in the 1980
United States census, and points out that there was no way for

United States citizens of Mexican origin to indicate if their ancestry was American Indian. Racism makes open communication impossible, and it is considered to be ultimately self-destructive as well. Many social scientists would argue that the American (United States) racial classification system is in itself racist. Implicit in the system is the notion that in order to be classified as white, one must be "pure" white. Racism also reaches into designations between "full bloods" and "mixed bloods" among American Indians.

Within reservation schools that have mixed populations, there is often a specific denial of racism. Yet, at the same time, there are individual reports of occasional incidents of racial strife, and there are observable patterns of in-school segregation. This tension can exist between the so-called full bloods and mixed bloods as well as between Indians and non-Indians. Tensions based on racial categories will not disappear by ignoring or denying them. Schools should explore the use of more constructive forms of group classifications. Racial issues can be confronted in schools without increasing tension by dealing with racism in the abstract and involving students in creating means for eliminating it.

Ethnocentrism and racism are the root causes for the many stereotypes and biases pertaining to American Indians. To discourage these prejudices, the following generalizations should be kept in mind: Indian groups are (1) similar, (2) different, (3) diverse, and (4) on-going social realities. Their political, economic, and aesthetic histories are evident in their folkways and arts. Each group is different in many ways. For example, both Navajos and Crows are considered American Indians, but their regional cultures, climatic adaptations, and languages differ vastly.

Teachers need to be aware of stereotypes about American Indians. A stereotype is an exaggerated image or generalization of a group of people. Stereotypes lump people together as though they all had the same qualities or characteristics. In spite of the linguistic, tribal, and regional diversity of American Indians, they have been stereotyped into at least three general images: (1) the noble savage, (2) the conquered savage, and (3) the savage (Garcia 1982; see chapter 11 for a discussion of stereotyping in literature).

The Iroquois people are a model for the noble savage stereotype. They have been portrayed as good, honest, and fair ("noble") but nevertheless uncivilized and savage. Though the Iroquois were "good" Indians, they were viewed as uncivilized because they refused to adopt Anglo ways. Henry Wadsworth Longfellow's "Song of Hiawatha" uses the word *savage* more than fifty times to describe Indians.

The Cherokee people are a model for the conquered savage stereotype. They have been portrayed as a conquered people who have assimilated partly but not entirely into the mainstream, non-Indian culture. They were the "almost civilized" people who were conquered and divested of most of their ways.

The Sioux people are a model for the savage stereotype. They have been portrayed as warriors on the warpath. According to this stereotype of the Indians, they were neither noble nor civilized. Their main objectives were to wage wars and to massacre. This stereotype was used to justify overt hostility toward Indians, as in the expression "The only good Indian is a dead one."

Keep in mind that these are only three of the many stereotypes about American Indians. What is important to understand is that stereotypes divest people and groups of their diversity and their basic humanity. People tend to stereotype groups of individuals and then to behave as though the stereotypes were accurate images of the whole group. Using the four generalizations stated above should help to counter cultural stereotyping. When stereotyping does appear it should be identified so that students will be sensitized to its pernicious effect rather than victimized by it.

To reduce ethnocentrism, racism, and stereotyping thinking, teachers can use the concept of cultural relativism. Cultural relativism favors viewing cultural groups from their own vantage point. This approach can assist teachers with the awesome task of teaching Indian students who come from many different cultures. The basic premise of cultural relativism is that cultures are different but not necessarily inferior or superior. Actually, cultural differences develop to accommodate unique ecological, demographic, and economic situations. Cultural relativism necessitates that we perceive cultures from their unique perspectives rather than from the perspective of mainstream American, the cultural viewpoint most common in schools. Using our own culture as the standard or model, we tend to compare other cultures to our own. After the comparison we may conclude that the other cultures are "better" or "worse," "civilized" or "savage." Cultural relativism asks us to view other cultures from their viewpoints, and when they differ from ours, to accept that they are merely different—neither superior nor inferior.

Cultural relativism does not mean that anything in the name of culture is acceptable. The purpose of cultural relativism in this book is to assist educators to develop more objective attitudes about Indian cultures in the United States. Cultural relativism can provide a climate of acceptance for the cultures of Indian children and gives public schools a way to incorporate these cultures into the classroom. Cultural relativism allows teachers to approach a new culture with an open mind. Yet, cultural relativism should not be perceived as nihilism, where "anything goes," but rather as a way of building acceptance toward the cultures of Indian children.

Cultural Continuity as a Strategy

Teachers can use cultural continuity as a means of ameliorating more basic problems that confront most cultures. These problems—poverty, hunger, ignorance, and disease—are powerful enemies of Indian children that can discourage even the most optimistic teachers; teacher turnover in Indian reservation schools is quite high primarily because these problems, especially those caused by poverty, may overshadow the more positive and viable aspects of Indian culture.

As discouraging as this may sound, teachers have very little direct control over poverty and its consequences. Teachers do have control over their classrooms, the materials used in their classrooms, and the knowledge and skills learned in their classrooms. Although they cannot control poverty, teachers can equip themselves with the knowledge that education, and their attempts to educate American Indian students, can be a liberating force in students' lives. Teachers can empower their students to use creative intelligence to break free from the bindings of poverty. Continuity between the culture of the home and the culture of the school will help to unleash creative intelligence by smoothing the transition between students' lives at home and their lives in school.

As Swisher and Deyhle discuss in chapter 5, classroom experiences should be compatible with the students' learning modalities. Experience reveals that competitive learning modalities dominate in most classrooms. While competition plays a role in the academic development of students, cooperative learning modalities have been underutilized, to the detriment of children who are disinclined toward competitive learning modalities. Yet, the research of Slavin (1983) and Johnson, Johnson, and Holubec (1986) has yielded positive results when students were allowed to learn within a cooperative modality. Our experience in reservation schools that have used cooperative learning approaches indicates the approaches increase American Indian students' academic achievement. Teachers should be careful, however, about the use of either competitive or cooperative learning modalities. Indian children who are reared in extended families in traditional tribes may be socialized toward cooperation rather than competition as a modality for action, but this is not to say that Indian children are not competitive. Rather, teachers should keep in mind that Indian children's behavior will tend toward either cooperation or competition depending on their family and tribal environments and socialization practices. This is why knowledge of the Indian child's home and cultural background is so important.

Summary

Education should be a liberating force in the lives of Indian children. Twelve years of schooling should empower Indian students to be lifelong learners who are self-directed and politically active tribal members and citizens able to participate and prosper in their communities, their states, the nation, and the world. Teachers committed to functional, cultural, and critical literacy should be able to effectuate the previously mentioned educational goals, but teachers should be aware of ideologies and social forces that affect schooling, especially "assimilation," "ethnocentrism," "racism," and "multicultural education." The effects of these ideologies on teacher and student thinking can aid or impede the best-laid strategies for teaching American Indian students.

Effective strategies for teaching American Indian students include the reduction of ethnocentrism and racism and the use of culturally compatible curricular materials and teaching methods, such as cooperative learning, to achieve cultural continuity. Teachers can make a difference in the lives of their students, especially if teachers realize that all cultures have in common the enemies of ignorance, poverty, disease, and hunger. While teachers cannot have a direct impact on poverty, disease, or hunger, they can have an impact on ignorance. Teaching is a noble pursuit precisely because it serves the cause of reducing ignorance, which in turn reduces the impact of poverty, disease, and hunger. To make a difference, teachers need to commit themselves to the reduction of ignorance and the empowerment of their students.

3

A History of Indian Education

JON REYHNER
JEANNE EDER

To understand the state of Indian education today requires an understanding of its past history. European immigrants to what is now the United States first wanted to obtain Indian lands by purchase or force and remove the Indians westward to lands thought to be either not needed or unsuitable for white settlement. Little need was seen for educating Indians that were far away except by missionaries interested in serving their God by saving souls. As it became apparent that colonization would extend across the continent after the California Gold Rush of 1849 and the building of western railroads, Indian reservations were established through treaty negotiations throughout the West.

Whenever there was close contact between white settlers and Indians, Indians were pressured to conform to white ways of behaving, including the adoption of Christianity, "civilized" dress, and farming. Education was seen as a way of assimilating young Indians into the dominant society. It was cheaper to convince Indians in school that whites had their best interests in mind than to "convince" them on the battlefield. School attendance was enforced, students were not allowed to speak their tribal languages, and tribal traditions were labeled first "works of the devil" and later "enemies of progress."

Had the goal of coercive assimilation been reached, there would be no culturally recognizable Indian people today. However, many Indian children did not succeed in schools that did not recognize their language and culture, and many older Indians worked strenuously to preserve their heritage. Despite the fact that whites have usually tried to force Indians to conform to white ways, there have been relatively short periods of time when Indian languages and cultures received some support. Because neither coercive assimilation nor missionary efforts were completely successful, the goal of cultural obliteration and complete assimilation was questioned over the years and has now been moderated.

While colonial charters and missionary activities expressed the altruistic aims of civilizing and Christianizing America's native inhabitants, baser human motivations often prevailed. Indian education has been a moneymaking business. It gave John Eliot a steady income in the seventeenth century from missionary funds collected in England; in the eighteenth century it allowed Eleazar Wheelock to start Dartmouth college for mostly white students with funds collected in England by Samson Occom, a Mohegan, for the benefit of Indians; and in the nineteenth century corruption in the Bureau of Indian Affairs (BIA) was notorious. When civil service reforms brought corruption under control at the turn of the century, rapid growth of the budget for Indian education seemed to give the bureaucracy that administered it a life independent of the students served. Boards of education and superintendents, once not interested in having Indian students, became interested when Congress authorized payments to replace the lack of property taxes from Indian trust land. In 1989 a United States Senate Special Committee on Investigations concluded that "paternalist federal control over American Indians has created a federal bureaucracy ensnarled in red tape and riddled with fraud, mismanagement and waste" (U.S. Senate 1989, 5).

The continued problems with Indian education over the centuries, resulting in a lack of success for large numbers of Indian students in BIA and public schools over the years, has led to a number of investigations, including those by Meriam (1928) and by Kennedy (U.S. Senate 1969). Reports on why Indian students do not learn to read and write as well as non-Indian students became ammunition for reformers who used them over the years as evidence to support the passage of a variety of special programs funded by the federal government. Some, such as those authorized by the Johnson-O'Malley Act (first authorized in 1934) and Indian Education Act (first authorized in 1972), are for Indian students only; others, including Chapter I, Bilingual (Title VII), and Special Education, are for any students who meet the achievement, language, or handicap criteria of the laws.

For educators to understand today why the programs in their schools exist and to understand why certain types of curriculum and teaching methodologies are considered more likely to lead to success, they must know about the past failures and successes of Indian education. This chapter summarizes the history and present conditions of Indian education. Other sources of information on the history of Indian education include Szasz's *Education and the American Indian* (1977) and Reyhner and Eder's *A History of Indian Education* (1989).

Missionary Activity and Paternalism (1492–1870)

The original idea behind Indian education was to "civilize" and assimilate Indians into the mainstream of the dominant culture brought from Europe. The Spanish after 1492 sought both to exploit Indians through forced labor and to convert them to Catholicism. When Pánfilo de Narváez took possession of the coast around Tampa Bay, Florida, he had with him four Franciscan fathers who came to start missions. In 1568, the Jesuits established a school in Havana, Florida, for Indian youths. Catholic and Protestant religious groups dominated non-Indian attempts to educate Indian children for the next three hundred years (Layman 1942; U.S. Senate 1969).

Protestants were not far behind the Catholics. King James in 1617 asked Anglican clergy to collect money for the erecting of "churches and schools for ye education of ye children of these Barbarians in Virginia" (*Report on Indian Education* 1976, 26). In 1631, Reverend John Eliot arrived in America and established a school in Roxbury, Massachusetts. Five years later he instructed some Pequot war captives "in the habits of industry." He developed a plan to bring Indians together in small, self-governing "Indian praying towns" where they could be instructed in Christian ethics and arts. In order to become accepted by the Puritans in these praying towns, Indians had to give up totally their old way of life, including long hair for men and short hair for women. Harvard was founded in 1636 in part to provide education for Indian youth. Later using funds collected for missionary work in England, Eliot published an Algonquian translation of the Bible (*Report on Indian Education* 1976; Salisbury 1986).

In the 1630s Jesuits reported that Indians "love their Children above all things" (Szasz 1988, 8) and that they could not "bear to have their children punished, nor even scolded, not being able to refuse anything to a crying child" (Layman 1942, 21). These parents resisted sending their children to be educated by missionaries in schools where play was often considered sinful. Pettitt (1946) in a careful study of Indian child-rearing practices found numerous commonalities between tribes and concluded that the lack of discipline noted by most European commentators was more apparent than real. Indian communities used a number of methods to ensure the proper behavior of children, however physical (corporal) punishment was deemed inappropriate because children needed to learn to endure pain and hardship with courage. Several books including Mari Sandoz's *These Were the Sioux* (1961) and Morey and Gilliam's *Respect for Life* (1974) give good descriptions of Indian child-rearing practices.

Over the next three hundred years white educators advocated boarding schools for Indian students because they felt that Indian families were a negative influence on their children's "education." However, Indian parents seldom agreed to have their children taken away. In 1744 the Six Nations of the Iroquois Confederacy, as reported by Benjamin Franklin, rejected an offer to send their sons to the College of William and Mary:

but you, who are wise must know that different nations have different conceptions of things; and you will therefore not take it amiss, if our ideas of this kind of education happen not to be the same with yours. We have had some experience of it; Several of our young people were formerly brought up at the colleges of the Northern Provinces; they were instructed in all your Sciences; but, when they came back to us, they were bad runners, ignorant of every means of living in the woods, unable to bear either cold or hunger, knew neither how to build a cabin, take a deer, or kill an enemy, spoke our language imperfectly, were therefore neither fit for hunters, warriors, nor counsellors; they were totally good for nothing. We are however not the less obliged by your kind Offer, though we decline accepting it: And to show our grateful sense of it, if the Gentlemen of Virginia will send us a dozen of their sons, we will take great care of their education, instruct them in all we know, and make *Men* of them. (Franklin 1784, 21–22)

Because of the expense of Indian wars and the desire to preserve a profitable trade in furs, King George issued a royal proclamation in 1763 closing the West to white settlement in an attempt to reduce friction between colonists and Indian tribes. Taxation of colonists to pay for the cost of Indian wars and of a standing army to enforce the provisions of the 1763 proclamation was one of the causes of the American Revolution.

While the new government actively sought the support of Indian tribes against the British, many remained neutral or saw the British as more likely to represent their interests. The fact that George Washington complained to Congress about his new governments inability to prevent the "commission of outrages upon the Indians" along the frontier suggests the tribes supporting Britain may have been right in their assessment of the rebellious colonists (Richardson 1910, 119).

The new Continental Congress made conciliatory gestures toward Indians, such as the appropriation in 1775 of five hundred dollars to educate Indians at Dartmouth. Congress approved its first Indian treaty with the Delaware tribe in 1778. When a new constitution was adopted in 1787, Congress received the sole power to regulate commerce with Indian tribes and make treaties. From the first treaty in 1778 till 1871, when treaty making with Indian tribes was ended, the United States entered into almost 400 treaties, of which 120 had educational provisions. Almost a billion acres of land were ceded to the United States in these treaties (U.S. Senate 1969; *Report on Indian Education* 1976). Article III of the Northwest Ordinance of 1787 declared,

The utmost good faith shall always be observed toward the Indians, their lands and property shall never be taken from them without their consent; and in their property, rights and liberty, they never shall be invaded or disturbed, unless in just and lawful wars authorized by Congress. (Vogel 1972, 74)

The 1789 treaty with the Oneida, Tuscarora, and Stockbridge Indians was the first to contain education provisions (*Report on Indian Education* 1976). Treaties often had provisions for general education, teachers' salaries, school construction, supplies, and so forth. Starting in 1793, trade and intercourse acts were passed incorporating plans to civilize Indians including providing social and educational services to Indians. In 1802, up to $15,000 per year was authorized "to provide Civilization among the aborigines." The money from this fund went mostly to missionary groups, with the Protestant American Board of Foreign Missions getting the largest amount. As more treaties were negotiated, the provisions for educational and civilization purposes increased, sometimes at the request of the tribes who saw they would have to change to survive. In 1819 Congress established a civilization fund, which lasted until 1873, to provide financial support to religious groups and other interested individuals who were willing to live among and teach Indians.

In 1820, Congress began to develop plans to move eastern tribes, including the Cherokees, west of the Mississippi. In 1830 the Indian Removal Act was passed authorizing President Jackson to exchange lands in the West for those held in the eastern states. In *Cherokee Nation v. Georgia,* Chief Justice John Marshall opinioned that Indians have an "unquestioned right to the lands they occupy, until that right shall be extinguished by a voluntary cession to our government" and that they were "domestic dependent nations . . . in a state of pupilage. Their relation to the United States resembles that of a ward to his guardian" (5 Pet. 1, 12 [1831]).

The next year in *Worcester v. Georgia,* the Supreme Court struck down an attempt by Georgia to keep missionaries and white friends off the Cherokee Nation. Again, Chief Justice John Marshall held,

The treaties and laws of the United States contemplate the Indian territory as completely separated from that of the states; and provide that all intercourse with them shall be carried on exclusively by the government of the Union. . . .

The Indian nations had always been considered as distinct, independent political communities, retaining their original natural rights, as the undisputed possessors of the soil, from time immemorial. (6 Pet. 500 [1832])

He went on to affirm that "the words 'treaty' and 'nation' " when applied to Indians had the same meaning as when applied "to the other nations of the earth" (6 Pet. 500–501 [1832]). President Jackson supported the state of Georgia's effort to keep missionaries and white friends off Cherokee land and to force their removal west of the Mississippi. He is reported to have remarked, "John Marshall has made his decision, now let him enforce it" (Vogel 1972, 124).

In the 1830s the Cherokees, using a syllabary invented by a tribal member, Sequoyah, started their own educational system, which developed literacy in Cherokee as well as English. They also published a Cherokee language newspaper. Despite their moves toward civilization, they were forced to move west of the Mississippi River by Congress in 1838. Assembled at bayonet point and marched west, an estimated 4,000 of the 11,500 Indians who started on the "Trail of Tears" died of dysentery, malnutrition, exposure, or exhaustion before they reached Oklahoma (Woodward 1963, 218). The "Five Civilized Tribes" of Oklahoma built a system of district and seminary schools. Within ten years the majority of their teachers had changed from eastern-educated missionaries to locally trained teachers. However, their schools were closed by the federal government in the late 1890s (Fuchs and Havighurst 1983).

Alexis de Tocqueville, in his book *Democracy in America,* described the great evils in the young republic's treatment of Indians. He wrote that the tribes stood in the path of the greediest nation on earth, a nation destitute of good faith. He described watching Choctaws crossing the Mississippi River in 1831 as part of the forced western removal of the Five Civilized Tribes:

It was then the depths of winter, and that year the cold was exceptionally severe; the snow was hard on the ground, and huge masses of ice drifted on the river. The Indians brought their families with them; there were among them the wounded, the sick, newborn babies, and old men on the point of death. They had neither tents nor wagons, but only some provisions and weapons. I saw them embark to cross the great river, and the sight will never fade from my memory. Neither sob nor complaint rose from that silent assembly. Their afflictions were long standing, and they felt them irremediable. ([1835] 1966, 198–199)

To deal with the removed and other tribes, the position of commissioner of Indian affairs was created in 1832 within the War Department. By 1838, the United States government was operating six manual training schools with eight hundred students and eighty-seven boarding schools with about 2,900 students (U.S. Senate 1969). In 1839, Commissioner T. Hartley Crawford, formalized the development of manual labor schools to educate Indian children in farming and homemaking (*Report on Indian Education* 1976). Ten years later the Office of Indian Affairs was transferred from the War Department to the Department of the Interior. This transfer had little effect on Indian education, and missionaries continued to be the major influence on Indian children. In 1851 the period of reservation settlement began and did not end till the 1930s. Schools set up on the reservations were designed to devalue the traditional culture and religion of Indian people and coercively to assimilate Indian youth into the dominant society. The forced settlement on reservations caused an almost total dependence on the federal agent for food, shelter, and clothing. This was especially true for the plains tribes who were dependent on the buffalo, which were rapidly decimated in the third quarter of the nineteenth century.

Americans in the nineteenth century saw their country expanding across the continent. They began to feel that their continued success was God's will and that their "manifest destiny [was] to overspread and possess the whole continent which providence ha[d] given" them (Sullivan 1845). United States government officials saw themselves as trading education for land. Teachers in mission schools were expected to promote government policy, including the policy of removing eastern tribes west of the Mississippi River. President Monroe's secretary of war, John C. Calhoun, declared in 1819 that it was the duty of employees in government-funded missions, even if these missions were funded with tribal annuities or trust money,

to impress on the minds of the Indians the friendly and benevolent views of the government towards them and the advantages to them in yielding to the policy of the government and cooperating with it in such measures as it may deem necessary for their civilization and happiness. (Layman 1942, 123)

Native Language Use and Repression

In its early years a northeast mission school used only books written in the Ojibwa language. When missionaries later switched to instruction in English, the quality of education is reported to have declined (Layman 1942). A missionary to the Sioux, Stephen R. Riggs, found teaching English in the 1830s "to be very difficult and not producing much apparent fruit." It was not that the students lacked ability that prevented them from learning English, but rather their unwillingness. However, "Teaching Dakota was a different thing. It was their own language" (Riggs 1880, 38). A Cherokee told the Baptists in 1824, "We want our children to learn English so that the white man cannot cheat us" (McLoughlin 1984, 155).

To alleviate corruption and maintain peace with the Indians after the Civil War, President Grant appointed a commission on Indian affairs in 1869 to supervise the appointment of Indian agents, teachers, and farmers as well as the buying of supplies. This Board of Indian Commissioners continued to operate until 1933. In its first annual report, the board found,

The history of the Government connections with the Indians is a shameful record of broken treaties and unfulfilled promises.

The history of the border white man's connection with the Indians is a sickening record of murder, outrage, robbery, and wrongs committed by the former as the rule, and occasional savage outbreaks and unspeakable barbarous deeds of retaliation by the latter as the exception. (Board 1870, 7)

However, as an alternative to the westerner's call for actual genocide, a Peace Commission (established in 1867) appointed by President Grant called for cultural, and specifically linguistic, genocide. They felt that language differences led to misunderstandings and that

Now, by educating the children of these tribes in the English language these differences would have disappeared, and civilization would have followed at once. . . .

Through sameness of language is produced sameness of sentiment, and thought; customs and habits are molded and assimilated in the same way, and thus in process of time the differences producing trouble would have been gradually obliterated. . . . In the difference of language today lies two-thirds of our trouble. . . . Schools should be established, which children should be required to attend; their barbarous dialect should be blotted out and the English language substituted. (Report of Indian Peace Commissioners 1868, 16–17)

Under Secretary of the Interior Carl Schurz, the Indian Bureau issued regulations in 1880 that "all instruction must be in English" in both mission and government schools under threat of loss of government funding (Prucha 1973, 199). Again in 1884 a specific order went out to a school teaching in both Dakota and English that

English language only must be taught the Indian youth placed there for educational and industrial training at the expense of the Government. If Dakota or any other language is taught such children, they will be taken away and their support by the Government will be withdrawn from the school. (Atkins 1887, xxi)

It was felt by J. D. C. Atkins, commissioner of Indian affairs from 1885 to 1888, that "to teach Indian school children their native tongue is practically to exclude English, and to prevent them from acquiring it" (1887, xxiii). The ethnocentric attitude prevalent in the late nineteenth century is evident in Atkins's 1887 report:

> Every nation is jealous of its own language, and no nation ought to be more so than ours, which approaches nearer than any other nationality to the perfect protection of its people. True Americans all feel that the Constitution, laws, and institutions of the United States, in their adaptation to the wants and requirements of man, are superior to those of any other country; and they should understand that by the spread of the English language will these laws and institutions be more firmly established and widely disseminated. Nothing so surely and perfectly stamps upon an individual a national characteristic as language. . . . No unity or community of feeling can be established among different peoples unless they are brought to speak the same language, and thus become imbued with like ideas of duty. . . .
>
> The instruction of the Indians in the vernacular is not only of no use to them, but is detrimental to the cause of their education and civilization, and no school will be permitted on the reservation in which the English language is not exclusively taught. (Atkins 1887, xxi–xxiii)

Atkins's Indian school superintendent optimistically predicted in 1885,

> if there were a sufficient number of reservation boarding-school-buildings to accommodate all the Indian children of school age, and these buildings could be filled and kept filled with Indian pupils, the Indian problem would be solved within the school age of the Indian child now six years old. (Oberly 1885, cxiii)

Despite patriotic and optimistic announcements like the ones above, observers in the field such as General Oliver O. Howard (1907) reported that successful missionary teachers learned the tribal language so that they could understand the children and the children could understand them. Luther Standing Bear, a former Carlisle student who started teaching in 1884, reported,

> At that time, teaching amounted to very little. It really did not require a well-educated person to teach on the reservation. The main thing was to teach the children to write their names in English, then came learning the alphabet and how to count. I liked this work very well, and the children were doing splendidly. The first reading books we used had a great many little pictures in them. I would have the children read a line of English,

and if they did not understand all they had read, I would explain it to them in Sioux. This made the studies very interesting. (1928, 192–193)

Standing Bear complained that new teachers sent to the reservation knew only books. In other words, they knew nothing of the children they were to teach. Enforcement of the English-only regulations were usually strict. Lawrence Horn, a Blackfoot, who attended the government school at Heart Butte, Montana, recalled students getting a stroke of a leather strap with holes in it every time they spoke "Indian" (Parsons 1980).

Missionaries were in favor of ending tribal traditions, but they were more willing than the government to use tribal languages in their education efforts. For example, the mission schools for the Santee Sioux, including the Santee Sioux Normal School started in 1970 to train Sioux teachers, made extensive use of the Dakota language. A correspondent who visited schools with Secretary of the Interior Schurz reported that the educational facilities "were perhaps better than those of any other of the northern tribes." At Alfred L. Riggs's mission school the elementary books and the Bible were in Dakota. After the children were taught to read in Dakota, they were given a book with illustrations explained in Dakota and English. Based on his experience, Riggs found that children who learned to read and write Dakota could then master English easier. A child whose instruction included a four-year course in Dakota would be further advanced in English at the end than a child who received exclusive instruction in English (*Report* 1880, 77, 98).

Some teachers and administrators, faced with the irrelevancy of both their teacher training and textbooks, advocated to Commissioner of Indian Affairs Atkins the development of special textbooks appropriate for Indian students (Oberly 1885). However, no special textbooks were developed until well into the twentieth century.

Reformers also attempted to improve Indian education through civil service reform. However, Luther Standing Bear, based on his teaching experience from about 1884 to 1890, complained that the civil service examination was not necessary for primary teachers and that his students did better than the students of white teachers who got all their knowledge from books "but outside of that, . . . knew nothing." Standing Bear felt,

The Indian children should have been taught how to translate the Sioux tongue into English properly; but the English teachers only taught them the English language, like a bunch of parrots. While they could read all the words placed before them, they did not know the proper use of them; their meaning was a puzzle. (1928, 239)

A white teacher, Estelle Brown (1952), who took the civil service examination around 1901, found the examination had nothing to do with teaching Indians.

Government Control and Dependency (1870–1923)

From an estimated number as high as ten million before Columbus's arrival, the Indian population was rapidly declining as a result of diseases from Europe to which Indians lacked natural immunity and to increased warfare—which was becoming increasingly deadly owing to guns—caused by the pressures of the growing white population. Even starvation took its toll as buffalo and other game disappeared. Predictions of the Indians' ultimate demise led to the popularity of the term "Vanishing American." By 1900, the Indian population of the United States had declined to 250,000 (Thornton 1987). In 1871 Congress, no longer recognizing tribes as independent powers, ended all treaty making with Indian tribes. Many humanitarians saw education and the life of a farmer as the only hope for the now conquered and vanishing Indians, despite the fact that much of the land they had been left with was, at best, suitable only for ranching. Of course, many of the policymakers in Washington had never been west of the Mississippi.

In his second inaugural address in 1873, President Grant pleaded for leniency toward the American Indian, declaring "the wrong inflicted upon him should be taken into account, and the balance placed to his credit" (Richardson 1910, 4176). Grant's Board of Indian Commissioners divided up the reservations among the various religious groups. The Catholics, who had expected thirty-eight agencies based on their previous missionary efforts, got only eight from the all-Protestant board.

Congress appropriated $100,000 in 1870 for the support of industrial and other schools among the Indian tribes. This moved education for Indians directly under the control of the Bureau of Indian Affairs. Emphasis was on day and boarding schools teaching such skills as speaking, reading, and writing English and basic arithmetic along with a half-day of vocational training.

The discovery of gold in the Black Hills in 1873 set the stage for the conflict between the United States and the Sioux and Cheyenne nations. Contemporary Westerners often had a dim view of Indians, the Indian Bureau, and eastern government officials. One advocate of the western point of view wrote that the Indian Bureau was

responsible for arson, murder and rape; it is a refuge of incompetents and thieves. . . . From the Indian agent the savage obtains his supplies of food to enable him to make his raids; from some creature of the agent, he obtains his supplies of ammunition and improved arms, that make him more than a match for the raw recruit, that the American government enlists from the city slums, dignifies by the name of soldier, and sends out to meet these agile warriors.

The whole system of Indian management is a fraud: the Indian Department rotten from the outmost edge to the innermost core. . . .

[Putting the Indian Bureau back under the army] would do away with our junketing peace commissions, composed of low-browed, thick-lipped, bottle-nosed humanitarians, the inferiors of the savages in every manly trait, and objects of unlimited contempt by these shrewd marauders. (Triplett 1883, 347)

Before the institution of Civil Service reforms in the BIA in the 1890s, ongoing scandals involved selling rotten beef and other substandard supplies to the government to become part of annuities owed by treaty to Indians. In addition, Indian agents often got their jobs based on their support of the winning presidential candidate rather than on their abilities. They saw their positions as sources of income to recoup their campaign contributions and become wealthy. Indian agents often hired friends and relatives to teach in Indian schools regardless of their abilities (Reyhner and Eder 1989).

With the repeal of the Civilization Fund in 1873, the federal government became more involved in the direct operation of Indian schools. In the words of J. D. C. Atkins, Commissioner of Indian Affairs, the goal of education was to take Indians who were in "blind ignorance, the devotees of abominable superstitions, and the victims of idleness and thriftlessness" and turn them into farmers because

the civilization of the Indian race [is] . . . naturally deductible from a knowledge and practice upon their part of the art of agriculture; for the history of agriculture among all people and in all countries intimately connects it with the highest intellectual and moral development of man. (1885, iii)

Indian students saw little relevance for the education they received. One teacher reported that at the boarding school where he taught

Few of the pupils had any desire to learn to read, for there was nothing to read in their homes nor in the camp; there seemed little incentive to learn English, for there was no opportunity to use it; there seemed to be nothing gained through knowing that "c-a-t" spells cat; arithmetic offered no attraction; not one was interested in knowing the name of the capital of New York. (Kneale 1950, 52–53)

Another teacher from the same era found the Indians she worked with to have a universal dislike of English, "the tongue of their despised conquerors" (Golden 1954, 10).

In order to better separate the Indian child from the "savagery" of their parents, the first government-run off-reservation Indian boarding school was opened at Carlisle, Pennsylvania, in 1879, under the directorship of Capt. Richard Henry Pratt. Pratt saw the purpose of boarding schools for Indians as taking the "Indian" out of his Indian students. In 1902, the BIA was operating twenty-five boarding schools in fifteen states for 9,736 students (Reyhner and Eder 1989). One of these schools, Haskell Institute, was established in 1884 at Lawrence, Kansas. Over the years Haskell has been changed from a secondary manual training school to its present status as a junior college still operated by the Bureau of Indian Affairs.

In addition to taking children away from their parents, other regulations were forced on Indian adults in order to suppress Indian cultures. Presidentially appointed Indian agents were virtual dictators, with authority to control all aspects of reservation life. In 1881 in an attempt to force change among Plains Indian tribes the religious practice of the Sun Dance was banned. In 1885 this ban was extended to a general policy forbidding traditional Indian religious ceremonies and all aspects related to such ceremonies. In 1886 Indian men were ordered to cut their hair short. Eventually Indians began to feel that the government owed them a living of annuities and rations in return for the land that was taken and the game that was killed. Many treaties specifically provided for annuities, but only for a transitional period as the Indians were expected to learn to be farmers. However, the marginal quality even for grazing of much reservation land and the lack of desire among most Indians to become farmers frustrated the government's attempts to make Indians self-sufficient on their reservations. A demoralizing situation of dependency developed on many reservations that continues to this day.

The General Allotment (Dawes) Act was passed by Congress in 1887 in an attempt to end this growing dependency and to destroy the traditional Indian tribal life. The Dawes Act granted 160 acres to each family head and 80 acres to single persons over eighteen and orphans under eighteen. Fee patent title was issued to each allottee to be held in trust by the government for twenty-five years. Indians were given four years to decide what land they wanted; if they did not decide then the secretary of the interior would decide for them. All allottees would be given citizenship, and land left over after allotment was to be sold to the U.S. government, with the profits to be used for "education and civilization." Allotment over the next forty-seven years reduced tribal holdings from about 140 million acres to 50 million acres. Three goals of the supporters of the Dawes Act were to break up tribal life, to enable Indians to acquire the benefits of civilization, and to protect their remaining land holdings (*Report on Indian Education* 1976). Not all reservations were allotted, with the Navajo Reservation being the largest exception. When oil was found on the Navajo Reservation in the late 1920s, an attempt was made to allot their lands; but the Teapot Dome scandal in Wyoming discredited Secretary of the Interior Albert B. Fall and his policies, and soon after the Dawes Act was repealed.

Along with the Dawes Act, the federal government stepped up its effort to educate Indians. By 1887 Congress was appropriating more than a million dollars a year for Indian education. About half the appropriations went to missionaries who were contracted to educate Indians. However, feuding between Protestants and Catholics, aggravated because the Catholics were much more successful in establishing schools, led the Protestants to support funding only government-run schools, which at that time still included Bible reading (Utley 1984). With the appointment in 1889 of General Thomas J. Morgan, a Baptist minister, as commissioner of Indian affairs, the Republicans made a systematic effort to stop government funding of all missionary schools, and by 1900 all direct funding was ended. Morgan's educational plan also called for compulsory attendance, standardized curriculum, textbooks, and instruction. Congress passed laws permitting Morgan to enforce school attendance through withholding rations and annuities from Indian families who did not send their children to school (Prucha 1976).

The continued failure of boarding schools and English-only education to make over Indians into white people in a few years (as the "friends of the Indians" had optimistically and naively predicted in the 1880s) led to disillusionment at the turn of the century and a lowering of expectations. Increasingly, Indians were seen as blacks then were: as a permanent underclass who needed to receive a second-class, nonacademic, and vocational education (Hoxie 1984).

However, as the reformers were becoming disillusioned, others led by the new science of anthropology were gaining an appreciation of traditional Indian cultures. In the words of historian Francis Paul Prucha, "the old view that Indian cultures had nothing to offer American society, that the sooner they were destroyed and replaced the better, gave way little by little to an interest in Indian ways and then to a positive appreciation of Indian art and other contributions" (1985, 58). This change in attitude was due in part to the new scientific outlook, which went beyond the ethnocentric view that all cultures were inferior to the dominant culture, and in part to such books as Helen Hunt Jackson's *A Century of Dishonor* (1881), which described the mistreatment of American Indians. Jackson chronicled broken treaties and stolen land, and emphasized that Indians had no legal rights in state courts since they were not citizens. The anthropologist Franz Boas wrote in 1911,

> It is somewhat difficult for us to recognize that the value which we attribute to our own civilization is due to the fact that we participate in this civilization, and that it has been controlling all our actions since the time of our birth; but it is certainly conceivable that there may be other civilizations, based perhaps on different traditions and on a different equilibrium of emotion and reason, which are of no less value than ours, although it may be impossible for us to appreciate their values without having grown up under their influence. (208)

Francis E. Leupp, commissioner of Indian affairs during Theo-
dore Roosevelt's second term, reported to the House of Representatives in 1905 that

> The Indian is a natural warrior, a natural logician, a natural artist. We
> have room for all three in our highly organized social system. Let us not
> make the mistake, in the process of absorbing them, of washing out of
> them whatever is distinctly Indian. Our aboriginal brother brings, as his
> contribution to the common store of character, a great deal that is admi-
> rable and which needs only to be developed along the right line. Our
> proper work with him is improvement, not transformation. (quoted in
> Prucha 1985, 58–59)

Albert Yava, a Hopi who started in school around 1893 or 1894,
described in his autobiography how Hopi communities were split
apart over the issue of education when police officers were sent
into homes to enforce school attendance:

> Many people felt that the Government was trying to obliterate our cul-
> ture by making the children attend school. And if you want to be honest
> about it, the schooling the children have been getting over the past
> seventy-five or eighty years has educated them to the white man's ways
> but made them less knowledgeable about the traditional ways of their
> own people. . . . Something important is being gained, but something
> important is being lost. (1978, 10)

For the majority of Indians boarding schools did not seem to
work. Kluckhohn and Leighton reported that 95 percent of Navajo children "went home rather than to white communities, after
leaving school, only to find themselves handicapped for taking
part in Navajo life because they did not know the techniques and
customs of their own people" (1962, 141). They also rejected education because it often was an unpleasant experience. Entering
students were often not allowed to speak the only language they
knew; schools were often underfunded and employed harsh disciplinary measures. Hoke Denetsosie, a Navajo, wrote that conditions were terrible at the boarding school he attended: students
were constantly hungry, were always marched around, and were
slapped and whipped by the disciplinarian (Johnson 1977).

Moves to Reform Indian Education (1924–1944)

With the start of the twentieth century, the trend began to place
Indian children in public schools. Tuition payments were autho-

rized by Congress in 1890 to some public schools enrolling Indian children. By 1912 there were more Indian children in public schools than in government schools and the number of government schools for Indian children began to decline. The use of federal funds to support instruction in church schools was made illegal in 1917. In 1924, with the passage of the Indian Citizenship Act, all Indians became citizens of the United States.

In 1924 the secretary of the interior called together a "committee of One Hundred Citizens" to discuss how Indian education could be improved. The committee recommended better school facilities, better trained personnel, an increase in the number of Indian students in public schools, and scholarships for high school and college. The committee's recommendations helped bring about reservation day schools offering a sixth-grade education and reservation boarding schools providing an eighth-grade education (*Report on Indian Education* 1976).

Reformers, most notably John Collier, increasingly criticized the BIA's treatment of Indians. This criticism led to a government-sponsored study in 1927 headed by Lewis Meriam. Meriam's 1928 report condemned the allotment policy and the poor quality of services provided by the BIA, urged protection for Indian property, and recommended that Indians be allowed more freedom to manage their own affairs. In the area of education it pointed out shocking conditions of boarding schools, recommended not sending elementary age children to boarding schools at all, and urged an increase in the number of day schools. It stated,

> The philosophy underlying the establishment of boarding schools, that the way to "civilize" the Indian is to take Indian children, even very young children, as completely as possible away from their home and family life, is at variance with modern views of education and social work, which regard the home and family as essential social institutions from which it is generally undesirable to uproot children. (1928, 403)

A number of fictionalized accounts with characters who went to boarding schools exist. Most interesting are Oliver LaFarge's Pulitzer Prize–winning *Laughing Boy* ([1929] 1971) and his *The Enemy Gods* (1937), Ruth Underhill's *Hawk Over Whirlpools* (1940), and Frank Waters *The Man Who Killed the Deer* ([1941] 1971). Autobiographical accounts of Indians who attended boarding schools show the schools in a more favorable light since the unsuccessful students were not likely to write much. Of particular interest are Francis La Flesche's *The Middle Five: Indian School-boys of the Omaha Tribe* ([1900] 1963), Charles A. Eastman's *From the Deep Woods to Civilization* ([1916] 1977), Albert Yava's *Big Falling Snow* (1981), Polingaysi Qoyawayma's *No Turning Back* (1964), and Luther Standing Bear's *My People the Sioux* (1928). All the above books can be used in the classroom either as independent reading for students or to be read aloud by the teacher.

The effects of World War I and the Great Depression caused people to question whether or not the United States was progressing toward an earthly utopia of wealth and plenty. In their doubts some people looked to the close-knit, nonmaterialistic world of the American Indians for an alternative to what they saw as wrong with modern society. After the inauguration of Franklin D. Roosevelt in 1933, the BIA's leading critic, John Collier, became commissioner of Indian affairs. He immediately sought to implement the recommendations of the Meriam Report. The result was the Indian Reorganization (Wheeler-Howard) Act of 1934, which ended allotment of Indian lands and provided for Indian religious freedom, a measure of tribal self-government, and Indian preference in hiring Bureau of Indian Affairs employees.

Also in 1934, the Johnson-O'Malley (JOM) Act was passed, authorizing the secretary of the interior to enter into contracts with state or territories to pay them for providing services to Indians. The JOM Act allowed the federal government to pay states for educating Indians in public schools. Originally this money went into the general operating fund of the school districts and could in fact be used to support the education of non-Indian students. Today, much changed, the JOM Act still provides money to public schools educating Indian children. However, current JOM programs must be supplemental programs like special counseling, tutoring, or native culture programs. They must also be approved by an Indian parent advisory committee (PAC).

Besides the effects of what was called the "Indian New Deal," Indians also benefited from the many other mainstream New Deal employment programs such as the Works Progress Administration (WPA) and the Civilian Conservation Corps (CCC). These public works programs gave many Indians their first introduction to wage labor and began the creation of a cash economy, which gradually transformed the old reservation trading.

Under Collier's Indian New Deal the government built more

day schools and closed some boarding schools. A few native language textbooks were written and a greater emphasis was placed
on Indian culture in the classrooms of BIA schools. Summer institutes were held to give teachers special training in teaching Indian students. Most of the gains made in the schools were quickly
wiped out as funding dried up with the start of World War II.
However, the education that was lost in the schools was more than
made up in the field. More than twenty-four thousand Indians
served in the armed forces. The most famous of these were the
Navajo "code talkers" in the South Pacific who provided a communications code based on their native language that the Japanese
could not break. Thousands of other American Indians found
work in cities. According to Szasz, "given the comparatively
short time span of the conflict . . . [World War II] affected some
tribes more than any other major event in the four centuries of
Indian-white relations" (1977, 107).

The Termination Era (1945–1968)

At the end of the war there was a renewed call to "set the American Indians free." The argument was made and accepted in Congress that the Indian Reorganization Act had forced a collectivist
system upon the Indians, with large doses of paternalism and
regimentation, and that "tribal control and governmental regulations constantly remind the Indian of his inferior status" (Armstrong 1945, 49, 51). The "final solution" Congress came up with
for the Indian problem was to let the Indians become "free" by
terminating their reservations. In 1953 six termination bills were
passed. As part of termination, states were to assume responsibility for the education of all Indian children in public schools. In
1954 the Menominee became the first tribe to have their reservation terminated by Congress. Much quicker than the allotment
policy, the termination policy of the 1950s was judged a failure.
Land still owned by the Menominee tribe was put back into federal trust status in 1973. Other terminated tribes were not so
lucky. Another termination program involved the relocation of Indians from reservations to the cities. Many Indians had great difficulty adjusting to urban America and returned home.

   One bright spot in the otherwise bleak picture for Indian tribes
in the termination period was the passage in 1946 of the Indian
Claims Commission Act. This act allowed Indians to file claims

against the United States for lands illegally taken over the years. Millions of dollars have been paid out under this act, however there is no way that money can replace land and the traditional way of life that use of that land represented.

The typical reservation school of the termination era—bureau, mission, or public operated—has been described by Murray L. Wax:

> The situation almost appears colonial, or at the least caste-like: between Indian community and schools there is a strong social barrier, typified by the fences which surround the [school] compound. Parents rarely visit the schools; teachers rarely visit the homes; each side finds interaction with the other uncomfortable.
>
> The consequence of this barrier [between the school and the community] is that by the intermediate grades Indian children have begun to develop a closed and solidary peer society within the walls of the school. (Wax, 1971, 83)

Ralph Nader testified before the Special Senate Subcommittee on Indian Education in 1969 that cultural conflict in Indian schools was inevitable:

> The student, bringing with him all the values, attitudes, and beliefs that constitute his "indianness" is expected to subordinate that Indianness to the general American standards of the school. The fact that he, the student, must do all the modifying, all the compromising, seems to say something to him about the relative value of his own culture as opposed to that of the school. (Nader 1969, 49)

In addition, Nader stated that English was a second language for half the Indian children entering school, but no attempt was made to modify the curriculum for these children; by the time the child "has begun to understand English, he has already fallen well behind in all the basic skill areas. In fact, it appears that his language handicap increases as he moves through school" (U.S. Senate 1969, 51).

The effort to get Indians into public schools, which was advanced by funding provided through the Johnson-O'Malley Act, got another boost from Impact Aid. First passed in 1950, Public Laws (P.L.) 874 and 815 authorized funds for public schools with students who lived on tax-exempt federal land, such as military bases. These acts were designed to ensure that the cost of educating these children did not represent a financial burden for public schools. In 1953 the Impact Aid laws were amended to include

Indians living or working on reservations or other federal trust land. P.L. 874 provides a large part of the operating expenses of many reservation public schools today while many reservation schools were built using P.L. 815 funds.

In 1959 the Center for Indian Education was established at Arizona State University. The center began publishing the *Journal of American Indian Education,* which remains today one of the very few journals solely devoted to publishing information and research on Indian education.

The Move Toward Self-Determination (1969–present)

Over the years, through education, involvement with federal programs, and generally increased experience working with white America, Indian tribes had been developing a core of leadership capable of telling the federal government what the tribes wanted. This leadership was almost unanimous in opposing termination. The alternative put forward was self-determination; letting Indian people through their tribal governments determine their own destiny. With *Brown v. Board of Education of Topeka* (347 U.S. 483 [1954]), "separate but equal" schools for blacks were outlawed. The treatment of all minorities in the United States received increased attention in the 1960s. In 1970, President Nixon sent a message to Congress, stating,

the story of the Indian in America is something more than the record of the white man's frequent aggression, broken agreements, intermittent remorse and prolonged failure. It is a record also of endurance, of survival, of adaptation and creativity in the face of overwhelming obstacles. It is a record of enormous contributions to this country—to its art and culture, to its strength and spirit, to its sense of history and its sense of purpose.

It is long past time that the Indian policies of the Federal government began to recognize and build upon the capacities and insights of the Indian people. Both as a matter of justice and as a matter of enlightened social policy, we must begin to act on the basis of what the Indians themselves have long been telling us. *The time has come to break decisively with the past and to create the conditions for a new era in which the Indian future is determined by Indian acts and Indian decisions.* (quoted in Fuchs and Havighurst 1972, 1)

Two major studies of Indian education were made at the end of the 1960s. The National Study of American Indian Education was carried out from 1967 to 1971 and was directed by Robert J. Havighurst of the University of Chicago. The results of the study were summarized in *To Live on This Earth* (Fuchs and Havighurst 1972). The second study was by the Special Senate Subcommittee on Indian Education. The testimony from hearings held by this committee fill seven volumes, and the subcommittee produced a summary report titled *Indian Education: A National Tragedy, a National Challenge* (U.S. Senate 1969). In the introduction to this report Senator Edward Kennedy wrote that Indian dropout rates were twice the national average, Indian students lagged two to three years behind white students in school achievement, only one percent had Indian teachers, one-fourth of teachers of Indian students preferred not to teach them, and that "Indian children more any other minority group believed themselves to be 'below average' in intelligence." This report, also known as the Kennedy Report, led to the passage of the Indian Education Act, Title IV of P.L. 92-318, in 1972. This act authorized funding for special programs for Indian children in reservation schools and, for the first time, urban Indian students. As amended in 1975, it required committees of Indian parents to be involved in planning these special programs, encouraged the establishment of community-run schools, and stressed culturally relevant and bilingual curriculum materials (Szasz 1977). In 1974, parent committees were required for Johnson-O'Malley Act programs.

During the 1960s Indian educators became increasingly active, and at the end of the decade they formed the National Indian Education Association (NIEA). In 1971 the Coalition of Indian Controlled School Boards was formed. While the more mainstream Indian leadership testified before congressional committees and lobbied Congress, the more radical young urban Indians followed the lead of the Black Panthers. In 1969 Alcatraz Island in San Francisco Bay was seized by a group called "Indians of All Tribes," which demanded that the island be turned into an Indian cultural and educational center. In 1972, the American Indian Movement (AIM) damaged the BIA headquarters in Washington, D.C. The next year, AIM took over the village of Wounded Knee and fought gun battles with the Federal Bureau of Investigation (Burnette and Koster 1974; Deloria 1974; Prucha 1985). On a more local level, AIM, insisting on more Indian culture and his-

tory and more Indian involvement in school administration, organized a number of sit-ins and walkouts in high schools.

On the whole, the new tribal leadership did not find schools,
whether public or BIA, responsive to their demands for greater
local control and Indian curriculum. In 1964, the Economic Opportunity Act was passed, establishing the Office of Economic
Opportunity (OEO) and authorizing programs such as Head Start,
Upward Bound, Job Corp, and Vista. In an attempt to have a
school they could call their own, in 1966 a group of Navajos
started an experimental school at Rough Rock, Arizona, funded
by the Bureau of Indian Affairs and the OEO. Over the next seven
years, eleven additional contract schools were started. In 1975 the
Indian Self-Determination and Education Assistance Act (P.L. 93-
638) required the BIA to contract as many of its services to tribes
as those tribes desired. The purpose of the act was "to promote
maximum Indian participation in the government and education
of Indian people" and "to support the right of Indians to control
their own educational activities" (*Indian Education* 1982, 120).
By 1988 there were 65 tribally controlled contract schools.

Matching the successful growth of tribally controlled elementary and secondary schools was the even more significant growth
of tribally controlled colleges. The first such college, Navajo
Community College (NCC), was founded in 1968 under the leadership of Guy Gorman. By 1989, there were twenty-four such colleges located in ten states. Montana leads the nation with seven
tribal colleges—one on each of its seven reservations. While
poorly funded by the United States government, these colleges
play an integral role in improving the quality of life for Indian
people on and off reservations. Sinte Gleska University in South
Dakota has taken the lead by expanding to a four-year college and
even offering master's degrees in education. Through its four-year
education program Sinte Gleska has produced forty-three teachers
(Bordeaux 1991; Boyer 1989).

In addition to the tribally controlled schools and colleges, the
1970s saw the establishment of Native American studies departments at many universities and colleges across the nation, including Eleazor Wheelock's Dartmouth College. Faculty in these departments developed courses focusing on American Indians and
provided support for Indian students in their struggle to learn the
"white man's way."

Conclusion

The preliminary 1990 census figures show almost two million people in the United States identifying themselves as American Indians. This is an increase of almost a half million people in each of the past two decades. The catastrophic decline in American Indian population that characterized the first three centuries of European contact with this continent's native inhabitants has in the past century reversed itself in an increasingly rapid revival. The policies of cultural tolerance that began at the turn of the century and helped make this revival possible are now taken for granted.

The policies of John Collier's Indian New Deal and the current policy of self-determination are taking hold. Self-determination in education has led to an increased number of tribally controlled schools, a more active role by tribal councils in education, and reservation public schools with all-Indian school boards. Many reservation schools have large numbers of Indian teachers, however efforts to modify seriously the curriculum have not really taken place except in a few schools such as the Navajo Nation's Rock Point Community School (Reyhner 1989).

After years of BIA control, American Indians have had to relearn self-government. This relearning process, often hampered by reservation poverty, has not always gone smoothly. The board of the first locally controlled school at Rough Rock gave more attention to providing local employment than quality education (McCarty 1989; Szasz 1977). The high unemployment rate on most reservations, the lack of educational expertise on the part of local school boards, and instability of funding created many pressures and problems for locally controlled schools. The third director of Rough Rock Demonstration School, Ehelou Yazzie, graphically described in 1976 the shaky government financing of tribally controlled schools that continues with only a little improvement to this day:

It is June:
The BIA contract is not signed. We have no idea what our budget for fall will be. No teacher is certain that his/her job will be funded. . . .
This is the way it is at Rough Rock. We expect a crisis a month, and we are never disappointed. . . .
The system is a monumental fake and hoax. It is a political game in

which the community or school that refuses to lie down and die wins just enough to stand up for the next punch. (Task Force Five 1976, 259).

However, despite numerous problems, the policies of self-determination and local control have led to the training and certification of Indian teachers and the development of local leadership through elected parent committees, school boards, and tribal councils (McCarty 1989). As the federal government tries to cut funding to all programs, the question becomes whether or not schools will be able to turn out Indian graduates who are self-assured, employable, and able to provide leadership in making reservations and urban Indian communities self-sufficient.

4

Bilingual Education

JON REYHNER

Educators and politicians commonly assume that American Indians who retain their traditional cultures oppose having their
children schooled. That was one reason why reformers in the late
nineteenth century separated Indian children from their parents
and made the children give up their tribal languages and cultures,
as described in the previous chapter. With this separation accom-
plished through boarding schools and the breakup of reservations,
Indians could "leap into the mainstream of American life" (Utley
1984, 211).

However, there is evidence that, when given a chance, Indian
parents and grandparents often saw the value of the "white
man's" education while still wanting to maintain their Indian heritage. They did oppose having their children taught that all that
their ancestors had believed in was useless, or worse yet evil, and
to be forgotten. Fuchs and Havighurst (1972) in their comprehensive national study of Indian education found that most Indians
approved of the schools their children attended. However, Indian
community leaders were "overwhelmingly in favor of the school
doing something to help Indian students learn about their tribal
culture" (187). The most common parental suggestion was that
"schools should pay more attention to the Indian heritage" (170).
Rosalie and Murray Wax's research (1968) on the Pine Ridge Reservation showed that tribal elders and students' extended families
encouraged students to stay in school and that the forces causing
students to drop out of school were those of cultural disintegration, exemplified by alcohol abuse, dysfunctional families, and
high rates of unemployment—forces similar to those that cause

non-Indian students to drop out. Lin found that Crow boys expressed a "concern for and motivation toward education" equal to that of white students (1985, 9) and that Indian college students with a "traditional" rather than "modern" orientation reported better grades (1990).

The history of Indian education as described in the preceding chapter shows that government efforts to force rapid assimilation through separating Indian children from their families and schooling them were a failure. Rapid erosion of traditional culture caused by "submersing" students into an all-English environment in off-reservation boarding schools often led to cultural disintegration, not cultural replacement. As early as 1928, an investigation of the Bureau of Indian Affairs called for curriculum based more on "local Indian life, or at least written within the scope of the child's early experiences" (Meriam 1928, 33). The anthropologist Clyde Kluckhohn, describing the impact of the white culture on the Navajos wrote, "Navajo culture is becoming an ugly patchwork of meaningless and unrelated pieces, whereas it was once a finely patterned mosaic" (1962, 340).

Many Indians see the loss of their language as "one of the most critical problems" facing Indian people today. The loss of language leads to a breakdown in communication between children and their parents and grandparents and separates them from their past (Ahenakew 1986). Tribal heritage is not outdated in modern society as it provides a sense of group membership and belonging that is badly needed in an overly individualistic and materialistic modern society. Franklin D. Roosevelt's commissioner of Indian affairs, John Collier (1947, 17), thought modern society had lost the "passion and reverence for human personality and for the web of life and the earth which the American Indians have tended as a central sacred fire."

Tribal and National Language Policies

Since the 1970s the official policy of the U.S. government has been that of self-determination, a reversal of the assimilationist policies of the late nineteenth and early twentieth centuries and the termination policies of the 1950s. Self-determination is a continuation of the policies of John Collier and the "Indian New Deal" of the late 1930s and early 1940s. The policy of self-determination allows Indian people and their tribes rights to determine their future directions and represents an admission by the United States government that past assimilationist policies have failed.

In recognition of the importance of tribal language and culture, several tribes have gone on record supporting native language instruction. The Northern Ute Tribal Business Committee passed resolution 84-96 in 1984, declaring,

the Ute language is a living and vital language that has the ability to match any other in the world for expressiveness and beauty. Our language is capable of lexical expansion into modern conceptual fields such as the field of politics, economics, mathematics and science.

Be it known that the Ute language shall be recognized as our first language, and the English language shall be recognized as our second language. We assert that our students are fully capable of developing fluency in our mother tongue and the foreign English language and we further assert that a higher level of Ute mastery results in higher levels of English skills. (Northern Ute 1985, 16)

The Northern Ute tribe requires Ute language instruction preschool through twelfth grade, encourages "pre-service training in Ute language theory and methodology for teachers," and requires three credits of in-service training in Ute language for teachers within one year of employment (Northern Ute 1985, 16–18).

In a Preface to the 1985 Navajo Tribal Education Policies, Navajo Tribal Chairman Peterson Zah declared, "We believe that an excellent education can produce achievement in the basic academic skills and skills required by modern technology and still educate young Navajo citizens in their language, history, government and culture" (Navajo Division of Education 1985, vii). The Navajo Tribal Education Policies support local control, parental involvement, Indian preference in hiring, and instruction in the Navajo language. The code declares,

The Navajo language is an essential element of the life, culture and identity of the Navajo people. The Navajo Nation recognizes the importance of preserving and perpetuating that language to the survival of the Nation. Instruction in the Navajo language shall be made available for all grade levels in all schools serving the Navajo Nation. Navajo language instruction shall include to the greatest extent practicable: thinking, speaking, comprehension, reading and writing skills and study of the formal grammar of the language. (1985, 9)

Courses in Navajo history and culture are also required.

The Pascua Yaqui Tribal Language Policy holds that "Our ancient language is the foundation of our cultural and spiritual heritage" and declares that "all aspects of the educational process shall reflect the beauty of our Yaqui language, culture and values" (Pascua Yaqui Tribal Council 1984, 1).

In 1990, with the help of Senator Inouye of Hawaii and an intensive campaign by Indian people, the Native American Languages Act (Title I of Public Law 101-477) was passed by Congress. This act states that "the status of the cultures and languages of Native Americans is unique and the United States has the responsibility to act together with Native Americans to ensure the survival of these unique cultures and languages" and declares it the policy of the United States to "preserve, protect, and promote the rights and freedom of Native Americans to use, practice, and develop Native American languages." The act recognizes "the right of Indian tribes and other Native American governing bodies to use the Native American languages as a medium of instruction in all schools funded by the Secretary of the Interior" and establishes that "the right of Native Americans to express themselves through the use of Native American languages shall not be restricted in any public proceeding, including publicly supported education programs."

Bilingual Education

Jim Cummins (1986, 1989), summarizing the research on bilingual education, concluded that subtractive educational programs that seek to replace native language and culture with English language and culture cause students to fail while additive programs that teach English language and culture in addition to the native language and culture create conditions that enable students to succeed in school. His research indicates that (1) minority language use at home does not handicap children academically (1981, 32), (2) "bilingual children are more cognitively flexible in certain respects and better able to analyze linguistic meaning than monolingual children" (37), and (3) bilingual education can reinforce students' cultural identity and reduce their mixed feelings about the dominant society (35). Cummins found no group of students for whom bilingual education would not work. The "enrichment potential of bilingual education is accessible to all students" (1981, 42).

Numerous types and subtypes of bilingual instructional programs to provide the enrichment Cummins details have been identified (Trueba 1979). For the purposes of this chapter, three basic program types are described in terms of how they affect Indian children's ability to use tribal languages and English. These programs are all in contrast to what has been called "submersion" education for non-English speaking children, which involves the common practice of placing them into a regular all-English classroom with little or no special attention and letting them "sink or swim." Under the administration of John Collier in the late 1930s and 1940s some preliminary work was done to provide native language instruction in Bureau of Indian Affairs (BIA) schools, but after Collier left the BIA, it was not until the civil rights movement of the 1960s that bilingual education became an issue again for Indian children.

In response to pressure by Hispanics and other groups for bilingual education, Congress passed in 1968 the Bilingual Education Act as Title VII of the Elementary and Secondary Education Act. This act was amended in 1978 to include specific funding for programs for limited-English-proficient Indian children. In the 1974 case of *Lau v. Nichols* (414 U.S. 563), the Supreme Court found that the historically common practice of submersing students in a regular classroom did not provide non-English-speaking students with educational opportunities equal to those of English-speaking students, as was required by the Civil Rights Act of 1964. This case concerned Chinese-speaking students in the San Francisco public schools who were not offered any special educational programs even though the students did not speak English. The Supreme Court mandated that they get some form of special bilingual or English as a Second Language (ESL) instruction until they could speak English well enough to succeed in a regular classroom.

Most recently, the Bilingual Education Act was reauthorized for five years as Title VII of the Elementary and Secondary Education Act of 1988 (P.L. 100-297). In 1989, Congress appropriated $200 million to fund Title VII programs. For the first time programs of family English literacy were funded, recognizing the importance of parental involvement in bilingual education. The new act continued to fund, but at reduced levels, maintenance (described in the act as developmental) and transitional bilingual education programs while increasing funding for immersion (described in the act as special alternative) bilingual programs. The names "maintenance" and "transitional" refer to the long-term role of the first language in a school's educational program whereas "immersion" refers to the way in which the second language is taught. However, in the United States, immersion programs with respect to the teaching of English tend to be specifically designed, English-only, programs for non-English-speaking students. All three types of bilingual programs can use various ESL teaching methods for the English language portion of the instructional program.

Maintenance bilingual programs place the most emphasis on developing children's native as well as English language abilities. They are designed to teach reading, writing, and some other subjects in the native language of the child while adding English language skills and instruction in some subjects. The maintenance bilingual program at Rock Point Community School on the Navajo Reservation in Arizona graduates students who can read and write in Navajo and who also score higher on English language standardized achievement tests than do comparable Indian students who have not had a bilingual education (Holm 1985; Reyhner 1990; Rosier and Holm 1980). Bilingual education has effects beyond increased English and mathematics achievement scores. In Chicago's bilingual-bicultural Little Big Horn High School the student dropout rate was reduced (Hakuta 1986). Maintenance bilingual programs can also be called "two-way" programs when students speaking only English are taught a tribal language at school.

Transitional bilingual programs are designed to teach English to language-minority students as quickly as possible. While children are taught extensively in their native language during their first year of school, instruction in English is quickly phased in so that by about fourth grade all instruction is in English. Transitional programs do little to promote native language skills. Even though they are the most common form of bilingual programs in the United States, Cummins (1981) found no educational justification for transitional bilingual programs and found that "quick exiting" students from transitional programs after only two or three years was educationally unsound.

Immersion bilingual programs were designed to teach French to English-speaking children in Canada. Immersion programs use the second language extensively, "immersing" students in the second language. Immersion teachers should be bilingual, but they speak to the students only in the language to be learned. Students are allowed to speak their native language to the teacher and among themselves, especially during the first two years of the program. This type of program has been found to be very effective in teaching French and Spanish to middle-class English-speaking students and has had no long-term negative effects on children's English skills (Ovando and Collier 1985).

Whether a child should learn a second language by immersion or by a maintenance bilingual program is dependent not only on the language spoken at home, but also on the child's socioeconomic and cultural background, the social status of the child's native language, and the language preferences of the child, the parents, and the community (Cummins 1981). Students who come from a middle- or upper-class background and who are members of the dominant society (language-majority students) do well in immersion programs where they hear and are encouraged to speak only the new language in the classroom. However, such programs were never intended to replace the home language, and English language instruction was continued in school or was brought back after an initial period of instruction in only the second language (*Studies in Immersion Education* 1984).

Often students whose families have below-average incomes and who have minority group cultural backgrounds (language-minority students), such as Indian students, tend to lose their first language skills in immersion programs. For Indians, English language immersion programs can reinforce feelings of inferiority and worthlessness as a result of their ignoring the home language and culture of the child. However, immersion has been found an effective way to renew aboriginal (tribal) languages (Fleres 1989). Bernadine Featherly (1985), after an extensive study of the literature and research on the Crow Reservation, concluded that native-language-speaking parents should not try to "teach" their children to speak English and that Crow-speaking children should be taught to read in Crow before they are taught to read in English.

Exposure to television, schooling, and English-speaking children can get American Indian students speaking English fairly well in about two years, as can transitional bilingual programs, which usually are found in the first three or four grades. However, speaking skills acquired in these ways are "context-embedded,"

meaning that language is connected to the situation that is being
talked about, which is familiar to the student. Many classroom
situations after grade four, especially those involved with reading
textbooks, are "context-reduced," meaning that all information
must be gained from words or the text. It takes an average of five
to seven years for a student to acquire the academic competence
needed to understand English in a context-reduced situation (Collier 1989; Cummins 1981, 1989). Under the old submersion, newer
transitional, or most recent immersion approaches, Indian students often experienced so much failure in school that they tend to
give up and drop out, never catching up to their white peers.

A frequent criticism of bilingual education is that it delays the
learning of English. However, Stephen Krashen has found the reverse to be true:

The proper use of the first language can help the acquisition of English a
great deal; well-organized bilingual programs are very effective in teaching English as a second language, often more effective, in fact, than all-
day English programs that "submerse" the child in English. (1985, 69)

In fact the older grammar-based ESL programs have been found
boring by students and teachers (Spolsky 1978). ESL instruction
has been seen as a quick fix to the shortage of bilingual teachers,
but ESL teachers need extensive training that involves knowledge
of the structure of the native language of their students and a
background in the students' culture. No generic ESL training can
provide competent teachers for all minority language groups or all
Indian tribes.

The result of traditional English-only "submersion" programs
for Indian students is that while the Indian students learn at the
same rate as white students, they never close the gap and catch up
with white students of their same age (Office of Inspector General
1991). When test scores are reported in grade equivalents rather
than in percentiles or normal curve equivalent (NCE) scores, Indian students actually seem to fall further behind white students
as they progress in school, but this is an artifact of the way grade
equivalent scores are calculated. An analogy could be made to
runners in a race. Toward the finish line (high school graduation),
the racers get more spread out, some further behind and some further ahead. Non-Indians who start behind Indians, on average, do

not catch up to Indian students, and the majority of white students who started school (speaking standard English fluently and knowing both the behavioral norms and content of middle-class white culture) ahead of Indian students remain ahead.

The 1966 study *Equality of Educational Opportunity* (Coleman et al.) reported the reading achievement scores of Indian students in sixth grade to be 1.8 grade levels behind the average scores of whites, by ninth grade that figure became 1.9, and by twelfth grade they were 2.6 years behind. Mathematics achievement and verbal ability scores were very similar. At the twelfth-grade-level the Indian students were 2.5 years behind in English verbal ability and a full three grade levels behind in mathematics. Blacks and Hispanic Americans were either as far behind or further behind whites in achievement than were Indians, while Asian Americans were either equal to or slightly behind white students. Using an intelligence test not requiring knowledge of the English language (the Goodenough Draw-A-Man Test), the average intelligence quotients (IQs) of a sample of 867 Indian and Eskimo children were 103 for boys and 108 for girls, scores above the averages for white students (Fuchs and Havighurst 1972).

A Sample Maintenance Bilingual Program

The Rock Point Community School on the Navajo Reservation in Arizona began a program of bilingual education in 1967. At Rock Point most students enter school speaking mostly or only Navajo, and they are taught to read first in Navajo. The Rock Point School Board felt it was very important to build on the linguistic strengths of incoming students. Since almost no non-Navajos speak Navajo and since relatively few Navajos are college graduates, it was necessary at Rock Point to hire non-degreed teachers. The establishment of an on-site training program with college-level courses at Rock Point eventually led most of the teachers to earn degrees and Arizona teacher certification. Hiring teachers locally allowed Rock Point Community School to avoid the heavy teacher turnover that plagues many reservation schools. All but one of the elementary teachers during the 1987–88 school year were Navajo.

At Rock Point some teachers teach only in English and others only in Navajo. In kindergarten about two-thirds of the instruction is in Navajo; the rest of the class time is spent teaching oral

English through math and social studies lessons. By second grade students receive half of their instruction in English and half in Navajo. English reading instruction begins in second grade. In the upper grades one-sixth to one-fourth of the instruction is in Navajo and the rest is in English. In the early grades, mathematics is taught first in Navajo and then the specialized English vocabulary is taught later (Reyhner 1990; Rosier and Holm 1980). By teaching content area subjects in the early grades in Navajo, Rock Point students are not held back in those subjects until they learn English. The concepts they learn in Navajo are retained and usable by the student later in either language, and almost all basic reading skills learned in the Navajo reading program transfer into the English reading program.

Teachers were required to produce many of their own materials to teach in Navajo. In 1973 Bernard Spolsky found a "good bit" of Navajo language material on the nation's largest reservation, but not enough "to fill out a first grade year of reading" (Spolsky 1973, 31). Although there is now considerably more material, most schools must also rely on teacher- and student-made materials.

The community, teachers, and administrators at Rock Point were concerned that bilingual education lead to greater academic achievement in English as well as reading and writing skills in Navajo. Standardized tests are used to evaluate how well Rock Point students do in comparison with students in surrounding schools, in the state, and in the nation (Rosier and Holm 1980). In 1983 Rock Point students by eighth grade outperformed Navajo students in neighboring public schools, other Navajo-speaking students throughout the reservation, and other Arizona Indian students in the reading section of the California Achievement Test. On the grammar (written English) portion of the test the results were much the same. In mathematics, the Rock Point students did even better, outperforming the comparison groups and approaching or exceeding national averages (Holm 1985). The 1988 school evaluation reported similar results (Reyhner 1990).

Bernard Spolsky of the University of New Mexico summed up the results of the Rock Point School's educational program:

> In a community that respects its own language but wishes its children to learn another, a good bilingual program that starts with the bulk of instruction in the child's native language and moves systematically to-

ward the standard language will achieve better results in standard language competence than a program that refuses to recognize the existence of the native language. (Spolsky 1980, vi)

The soundness of the Rock Point bilingual program is further supported by its close resemblance to the successful Spanish-English programs found in California. Rock Point and these successful bilingual programs share the following characteristics:

1. High quality subject matter teaching in the first language, without translation.
2. Development of literacy in the first language.
3. Comprehensible input in English. Ideally, comprehensible input in English is provided directly by high quality English as a second language classes, supplemented by comprehensible, or "sheltered" subject matter teaching in English. (Krashen and Biber 1988, 25)

Additional indications of the success of Rock Point's bilingual program were staff and administrative stability, high community involvement, and low student absenteeism (Reyhner 1990).

One of the biggest problems in developing any kind of successful educational program on reservations has been the high turnover of teaching staff (Bureau 1988b; Fuchs and Havighurst 1972; Latham 1989). A necessary condition for long-range planning is school board and administrative stability. School boards and administrators can learn from the Rock Point School experience that extensive curriculum planning and long-term effort are needed to raise student achievement test scores.

In the recent book *Forked Tongue: The Politics of Bilingual Education,* Rosalie Pedalino Porter (1990) has attacked bilingual education as politically motivated and detrimental to the poor. She especially attacked transitional bilingual education programs for providing insufficient ESL instruction while barely mentioning maintenance programs such as the one at Rock Point. Unlike the transitional programs criticized by Porter, Rock Point's bilingual program provides extensive ESL instruction starting in kindergarten (one-third of class time) and quickly moving to half-day English instruction in grades one through three. It is hard to understand why Porter advocates in her book two-way bilingual programs for monolingual English-speaking students to learn to speak, read, and write Spanish while deploring instruction in the same skills for Spanish-speaking children. Other than maintaining that Indian languages will naturally die out, Porter has nothing to say directly about Indian bilingual education.

Ingredients of Successful Bilingual Programs

Teachers in successful bilingual programs know the children's home language and culture, rely on trained linguists for assistance, and utilize culturally appropriate curriculum and teaching methods.

Involving Indian teachers from the students' home community is a key to the success of programs teaching native languages, greater staff stability, and better academic achievement for Indian students. It is simpler to enroll native speakers of a tribal language in college and train them to be teachers than to teach a tribal language to a non-Indian teacher. In an Arizona study of Bureau of Indian Affairs and Indian-controlled contract schools, Lois Hirst (1986) found that Indian students who had Indian teachers did better on standardized achievement tests in reading and language arts.

Fuchs and Havighurst concluded that research suggests "teachers of Indian children should be systematically trained to take account of the sociocultural processes operating in the community and classrooms where they work" (1972, 305). The Rock Point school administration concluded that most "college trained teachers" are not prepared to teach in a situation like that at Rock Point (Rosier and Holm 1980, 110).

Most campus-based teacher training programs do not adequately prepare teachers to use tribal languages as vehicle for instruction (as does the Title VII–funded Indian Bilingual Teacher Training Program at Eastern Montana College), and even with bilingual teacher training, teachers still need professional support. A maintenance bilingual program that seeks to use the children's native language as a bridge to academic success in English schoolwork requires teaching reading and writing in the native language. Writing systems (orthographies) have only recently been developed for many of the estimated 206 Indian languages still spoken in the United States (Leap 1982a). Robert St. Clair (1982) has outlined the needs of bilingual programs. He feels that while professional linguists tend to develop sophisticated orthographies that reflect the grammatical structure of the language, literacy programs for elementary schools need simple, practical writing systems similar to the Initial Teaching Alphabet (i.t.a.). The experiences of the Dene Standardization Project in Canada provide a model for Indian communities interested in developing a practical writing system (Biscaye and Pepper 1990).

A linguist with an educational background is to be preferred in developing a simplified orthography suitable for use with children. Watahomigie and Yamamoto (1987) describe the "action linguist," who will work with both the community and schools to preserve and restore native languages, in contrast with the typical academician, who is most interested in doing pure research for the benefit of his professional advancement. Sources of linguistic help for schools and tribes include university linguistic departments, the Wycliffe Bible Translators who are found on many reservations, and a number of Indian linguists who have been trained at the Massachusetts Institute of Technology, the University of Arizona, and other schools with linguistic departments that have shown an interest in Indians and Indian languages.

In addition to simple, practical (most often phonetic) orthographies, St. Clair sees the need for simple classroom dictionaries of frequently used words—an "experience based dictionary," which includes only common definitions of words and uses them in sample sentences (1982, 11). He does not see a problem with competing tribal dialects since the same orthography can be used with different dialects. St. Clair feels that tribal elders have an important role to play in a bilingual program:

> If there are any tribal members who can really save the program [of language renewal], they are the elders. These are people who may be in the sixty- to eighty-year old range who have actually spoken the language fluently as children and who fully participated in the ways of the tribe. They still know the ceremonies and are the most valuable elements in any language renewal program. The secret is to get them to work with young children. They can teach them to speak the language and, if circumstances permit, the children can teach them how to read and write in the new system. This program, then, requires parental as well as communal support. (1982, 8)

In addition to teachers who know the children's home culture and language, and the help of professional linguists, effective bilingual instruction needs native language materials. Without teaching materials a bilingual program will fail, and it is pointless to teach reading in an Indian language if only a few books are available in that language. Commercial publishers are not interested in the small markets that even the largest tribes represent. However, there is a long history of missionary interest in translating religious works into Indian languages. In 1663 John Eliot, with the assistance of Indian translators, had fifteen hundred copies of the Bible printed in the Massachusetts dialect of the Algonquian language. Among the other Algonquian books Eliot had printed was an Indian primer (Salisbury 1974). Christian missionaries have researched and published dictionaries such as the Franciscan Fathers' (1910) *Ethnologic Dictionary of the Navajo Language,* which still serve as basic sources of information on Indian languages. The Wycliffe Bible Translators are very active on a number of reservations and have freely provided help to school bilingual programs.

In the 1970s and 1980s bilingual materials development centers funded by Title VII (Bilingual Education Act) produced curriculum materials that were not available through commercial sources. These centers printed materials in many Indian languages which are still in use in schools, but the Bilingual Education Act is no longer funding such centers and little new material is being produced.

Native language curriculum material can be produced locally. Community people such as elders can dictate or write native language materials, which are then used in the classroom; or students can use the language experience approach in which students with their teachers help write their own stories, which students then use to learn to read. As a director of a bilingual program on the Blackfeet Reservation, I arranged for the videotaping of elders telling traditional and historical stories in the Blackfeet language. These stories were transcribed by a Blackfeet linguist working with the Blackfeet Dictionary Project at the University of Lethbridge. A selection was then made from these stories to make up a booklet of Blackfeet stories for use with intermediate grade students (Reyhner 1984b). A tape recorder would work as well as a videotape for gathering materials.

As an approach to language experience, kindergarten students can draw pictures and provide picture captions, which the teacher then writes down; or photographs can be taken of the community and made into a book, with a text based on students' answers when asked, "Tell me about this picture." Older students can take pictures, interview elders and other community members, and write their own books. An example of materials that can be produced with the help of younger students is *Heart Butte: A Blackfeet Indian Community* (Reyhner 1984a). An example that includes work of older students at Rock Point Community School is *Between Sacred Mountains: Stories and Lessons from the Land* (Bingham and Bingham 1984).

As the bilingual program director on the Havasupai Reservation, I encouraged linguists involved in a Bible translating project who volunteered to do a three-day workshop with the bilingual teacher aides. Using the language experience approach, the aides wrote stories about their childhood and school days (*Gwe Gnaavja* 1985). The poet Mick Fedullo (1990) has developed a teaching guide to help teachers to get Indian students to write imaginatively. His techniques are the result of years of working with Indian students all over the western United States. Some teachers did not believe that their students had the ability to write expressive poetry in English until they observed Fedullo work with their classes. While this poetry was in English, the same expressive language activities can be done in the native language. A good example is the booklet *Hman Qaj Gwe Tnuudja,* done in Havasupai at Havasupai Elementary School in 1985 with the assistance of Akira Yamamoto, a Yuman language linguist.

For primary grade children, self-made books, hand printed and student illustrated, work fine and are appreciated by parents. For older children, more elaborate books are also useful. Only a few years ago, to publish such language experience books would have required expensive professional typesetting and printing. The special characters required by most Indian language orthographies added to that expense. Today with microcomputers and laser printers, excellent material can be produced in school at a fraction of the former costs, and, using photocopying machines, an unlimited number of copies can be made relatively inexpensively.

The American Indian Studies Center at the University of California at Los Angeles (3220 Campbell Hall, 405 Hilgard Avenue, Los Angeles, CA 90024-1548) publishes bibliographies of language arts materials in native North American languages and ESL materials for the period 1965 to 1976 (Evans, Abbey, and Reed 1977; Evans and Abbey 1979).

A note of caution for teachers who want to publish native language material with cultural content: Some tribes require prior approval of such material by a tribal cultural committee before it can be printed. In all cases, local people should be involved in producing and editing traditional stories.

Language Renewal

For many Indian groups, only a few elders still speak the group's native language. In this case, bilingual education means language renewal. Successful efforts toward language renewal are to be found around the world. Examples are to be found among the Gaelic, Welsh, and Irish of Great Britain (Baker 1988), the Maori of New Zealand (Fleres 1989; Nicholson 1990), and the Dene of Canada (Blondin 1989). Baker (1988) emphasizes the importance of native language maintenance programs being voluntary in nature, while Littlebear (1990) emphasizes the importance of family involvement in these efforts.

In New Zealand, Maori grandparents are volunteering to run day-care centers that feature an immersion program in the Maori language. These "language nests" were started in 1982. With grassroots support these nests expanded rapidly; by 1988 there were 521 centers with 8,000 children—15 percent of Maoris under five years old. In the centers' informal extended family, child-care setting, Maori preschoolers are saturated with Maori language and culture (Fleres 1989). A similar Hawaiian language program is being run in Hawaii with help from the University of Hawaii at Hilo. In New Zealand, language renewal among adults is also being carried on through the use of week-long immersion classes at Maori cultural centers (Nicholson 1990).

Brandt and Ayoungman (1989) give practical advice on renewing aboriginal languages in a special issue of the *Canadian Journal of Native Education* on language renewal. They warn parents and educators not to " 'teach' their children 'Indian' by giving them isolated words such as the names of foods, colors, or numbers." Instead they recommend that family members simply talk to their children "all the time in the language . . . using the normal strategies of talking to children, asking them questions, telling them what to say in natural functional situations, such as 'Ask your grandma to give you some food,' or expanding their productions" (1989, 45).

Teachers seeking ideas on how to restore native languages or to teach English as a second language would do well to study Krashen and Terrell's "Natural Approach" to language acquisition because the translation approaches used in the past have shown little success (Krashen and Terrell 1983; Leap 1982). While McLaughlin (1987) criticized the theoretical backing for the Natural Approach, he agreed that the classroom practices suggested by Krashen and Terrell are the most promising to date.

The first principle of the Natural Approach is that "comprehension precedes production." This implies that

1. the instructor always uses the target language (the language to be learned);

2. the focus of the communication is on a topic of interest to the student; and

3. the instructor strives at all times to help the student understand.

The second principle is that language production, whether oral or written, is allowed to emerge in stages, first by nonverbal communication, second by single words such as yes or no, third by combinations of two or three words, fourth by phrases, fifth by sentences, and finally by more complex discourse. In the beginning students use a lot of incorrect grammar and pronunciation. Krashen and Terrell emphasize in their method that "the students are not forced to speak before they are ready" and that "speech errors which do not interfere with communication are not corrected" (1983, 20).

The third principle is that the goal of language acquisition is communication. Each classroom lesson is organized around an activity rather than a grammatical structure. Possible activities include field trips, science projects, and games. For example, students can play a game such as Red Rover in the language to be learned, or, better yet, an Indian children's game that involves both language and movement. Students need to do more than just talk about a topic, they need to participate as well. "Young people learn best from their own and not other people's experiences" (Cantieni and Tremblay 1979, 248).

Krashen and Terrell's fourth principle is that classroom activities must lower the "affective filter of the students." This means that

Activities in the classroom focus at all times on topics which are interesting and relevant to the students and encourage them to express their ideas, opinions, desires, emotions and feelings. An environment which is conducive to acquisition must be created by the instructor—low anxiety level, good rapport with the teacher, friendly relationship with other students; otherwise acquisition will be impossible. Such an atmosphere is not a luxury but a necessity. (1983, 21)

It is easy to see that the above principles apply equally to teaching a native language or English. By not focusing on vocabulary (such as memorizing the names of numbers and colors) or grammar, students acquire language skills they can use. Only if students use the language skills they acquire will they remember them. It is important that the environment both inside and outside of school allows students to use newly acquired language skills. The home is an obvious place to use the native language, but some tribes have also started radio and television stations with native language programming. Students must also have environments where they can use English in conversation. One of the important factors in the success of the Rock Point Community School curriculum is that students are encouraged and required to talk and write a lot in both Navajo and English.

Conclusion

Kenji Hakuta concluded a historical study of bilingual education with this thought:

Perhaps the rosiest future for bilingual education in the United States can be attained by dissolving the paradoxical attitude of admiration and pride for school-attained bilingualism on the one hand and scorn and shame for home-brewed immigrant [and Indian] bilingualism on the other. The goals of the educational system could be seen as the development of all students as functional bilinguals, including monolingual English-speakers. The motive is linguistic, cognitive, and cultural enrichment. (1986, 229)

It is important to remember that native language instruction is not being promoted as a substitute for English language instruction but as a supplement. Speaking at the Native American Language Issues Institute in 1989, Dick Littlebear saw "our native languages nurturing our spirits and hearts and the English language as sustenance for our bodies" (1990, 8). William Leap could find no tribe that had let native language restoration outrank the importance of teaching English (1982). Malcolm McFee (1968) pointed out that assimilation is not a one-way street to progress and that American Indians can learn to participate successfully in white society while, at the same time, retaining their language and traditional Indian values to become what he has described as the "150 percent man." This 150 percent person is the goal of bilingual education.

II

Instruction, Curriculum, and Community

5

Adapting Instruction to Culture

KAREN SWISHER
DONNA DEYHLE

Our Indian students feel inferior. They are passive in the classroom. A white kid can ask a question in the classroom. The Indians cannot ask questions because they don't understand. And they don't learn as much.
—Navajo counselor, personal communication, 1984

For decades educators and educational researchers have attempted to find reasons for the high rate of academic failure among minority youth. Genetic characteristics, racial segregation and discrimination, and cultural deprivation have been offered as explanations for low achievement. Some researchers viewed the school as a panacea for bringing about educational equity; others viewed it as not making a difference.

In the late 1960s and early 1970s the cultural difference hypothesis was presented as an alternative explanation for low achievement. This hypothesis attributed poor academic performance to differences between children's home learning methods and environments and those of the school. Researchers such as Ramirez and Castaneda (1974) and Philips (1972) suggested that the school culture was alien and often conflicted with the home culture, and that creating a congruity between the school culture and the home culture would help ethnic minority youths to grow academically and emotionally. Researchers in the mid-1970s also began to look

This chapter is an adaptation of the article "The Styles of Learning Are Different, but the Teaching Is Just the Same: Suggestions for Teachers of American Indian Youth," published in the August 1989 Special Issue of the *Journal of American Indian Education,* and an earlier article, "Styles of Learning and Learning of Styles: Educational Conflicts for American Indian/Alaska Native Youth," published in 1987 in the *Journal of Multilingual and Multicultural Development.*

81

at classrooms ethnographically, to investigate the interactional structure of schooling—that is, the interactional context in which students from different minority group cultures prefer to learn and demonstrate what they have learned.

In addition to the examination of the cultural differences affecting the learning process in the 1970s, there emerged a powerful theoretical model that looked outside the schools at historical factors that formed and shaped minority responses to schools. According to Ogbu (1978, 1987), minority school achievement needed to be examined in relationship to the minority group's experiences in the postschool opportunity structure (job market) and the group's responses to the perception of dismal future opportunities. This is not to ignore language and cultural differences, for it is within the context of the larger structural factors that language and cultural differences lead to oppositional cultural responses within the classroom. We agree with Ogbu's theory, but for the purpose of this chapter, we focus on the in-school factors that teachers can affect and change in their interaction with their students.

In the 1980s educational researchers and practitioners continued to search for instructional methods that addressed the relationship between how children learn to learn and the ways in which they are expected to demonstrate learning in the classroom. This chapter illustrates with specific classroom examples the differences in learning style of various groups of American Indian and Alaska Native youths. Each example is followed by a summary of the literature, including research studies, concerning different cultural patterns of behavior. The chapter concludes with suggestions for teachers to consider as they adapt their teaching styles to styles of learning and interaction that students bring with them to the classroom.

Learning Style: The Acquisition of Knowledge and How It Is Demonstrated

People perceive the world in different ways, learn about the world in different ways, and demonstrate what they have learned in different ways. An individual's approach to learning and demonstration of what he or she has learned is influenced by the values, norms, and socialization practices of the culture in which that individual has been enculturated. Differences and similarities in learning to learn and in the demonstration of learning among several American Indian groups are presented and discussed in this section.

Learning to Learn

When I make an assignment my Indian students are reluctant to finish quickly or to correct other peers' papers. My Anglo students are quick to jump into the task. The Indian students seem to need time to think about things before they take action on their assignment. It is almost like they have to make sure they can do it before they try. Or, on the other hand, they seem to just not care about doing their assignments. (teacher, personal communication, 1987)

It is generally accepted in the literature that the ways in which children have learned to learn prior to entering the formal education environment are influenced by early socialization experiences (John 1972; Philips 1972; Cazden 1982). Different sociocultural environments cause behaviors to differ from culture to culture.

Differences between the home learning style and the school learning style are often manifested when an Indian child goes to school. Wax, Wax, and Dumont described one such conflict, in which performance does not precede competence:

Indians tend to ridicule the person who performs clumsily: an individual should not attempt an action unless he knows how to do it; and if he does not know, then he should watch until he has understood. In European and American culture generally, the opposite attitude is usually the case; we "give a man credit for trying" and we feel that the way to learn is to attempt to do. (1964, 95)

Werner and Begishe (1968) presented evidence from the Navajos to illustrate how home culture affects styles of learning. They reported that Navajos seem to be unprepared or ill at ease if pushed into early performance without sufficient thought or the acquisition of mental competence preceding the actual physical activity. This philosophy suggests, "If at first you don't think, and think again, don't bother trying." In contrast, the white culture's approach, which stresses performance as a prerequisite for the acquisition of competence, is summed up in the philosophy "If at first you don't succeed, try, try, again" (1968, 1–2).

Longstreet (1978) also reported how Navajo children have learned to learn. She observed that Navajo children watch an activity repeatedly before attempting any kind of public performance. They do not have an adult close by helping and correcting them; instead, they observe and review the performance in their heads until they can perform the task well in front of an audience.

Brewer, in describing learning at home and school for Oglala Sioux children, said that observation, self-testing in private, and then demonstration of a task for approval were essential steps in learning. "Learning through public mistakes was not and is not a method of learning which Indians value" (1977, 3).

In pointing out how culturally influenced styles may conflict with one another, Appleton (1983), in a report titled "Culture: A Way of Reading," described differences in Yaqui Indian learning style. In the typical public school classroom, Appleton wrote, Yaqui children avoid unfamiliar ground, where trial and error or an inquiry method of reasoning was required. Instead, they come to school believing that a respectful attitude toward any task includes doing the task well. For Yaquis, doing an activity according to recommended or correct form is as important as the purpose or goal of the activity, and if it cannot be done well, there is little reason to engage in the activity at all.

These Navajo, Oglala Sioux, and Yaqui examples exhibit home socialization practices that influence the way these Indian children learn to learn. These children preferred to learn privately and to gain competence before publicly performing. Although each group was different and distinct from the others in language and other aspects of their particular culture, a similar approach to learning seems to be prevalent.

Experiencing the World:
A Visual Approach to Learning

I study like this. The teacher lectures and then I take notes. And then I read them over. I study them. And then when I take a test I see the study notes in my mind (her hands quickly outline a rectangular shape). I see the paper and then I know where the answers are when I see the paper in my mind. (Navajo student, personal communication, 1988)

Within the last two decades researchers have investigated the visual approach that many Indian groups use as a method by which they come to know and understand the world. John suggested that there is considerable agreement among social scientists, educators, and others "that the Indian children of the Southwest are visual in their approaches to their world" (1972, 333). Impressions formed by careful observation are lasting impressions. She reported that Navajo children learn by looking: "They scrutinize the face of adults; they recognize at great distances their family's livestock. They are alert to danger signs of changing weather or the approach of predatory animals" (1972, 333). Appleton, in describing Yaqui children, said they are encouraged to learn by watching and modeling; "learning the correct way to do a task by watching it being performed repeatedly by others is highly reinforced" (1983, 173).

Indian children of the Northwest also exhibit the same sort of visual strength in how they view their world. For example, Kwakiutl children apparently have learned to learn by observation (Philion and Galloway 1969; Rohner 1965; Wolcott 1967). Rohner (1965) found that in their homes, Kwakiutl children learned by observation, manipulation, and experimentation, but in school the learning experience was limited to verbal instruction, reading, and writing. Philion and Galloway (1969), in their research with Kwakiutl children and the reading process, stated that the children displayed remarkable ability in visual discrimination. By imitating the behavior of others, very young children (ages four or five) were able to perform complicated sets of actions without verbal directions.

Kleinfeld (1973) described the extraordinary accuracy of Eskimos in memory of visual information. Their figural and spatial abilities enabled them to draw maps of the terrain that were accurate in significant detail and in spatial arrangements.

The visual strength of Indian children in the Southwest has also been the subject of reports by Cazden and John (1971) and John-Steiner and Osterreich (1975). Philips (1972) added to the literature on observations of visual strength from her work with Warm Springs Oregon Indian children. When viewed as cultural strengths and not weaknesses or deficiencies, the natural skills and abilities of Indian children contribute to a total picture of that child's learning style.

Field Dependence and Field Independence: The Influence of Culture

Yeah, when I think about this field dependent/independent stuff, my Indian students seem to be more field sensitive. They do better when they understand the total picture. (teacher, personal communication, 1988)

Although field dependence/independence is the most thoroughly researched dimension of cognitive style (Cazden and Leggett 1981), there are few reports devoted to study of this dimension with American Indian students. The work of Ramirez and Castaneda (1974) with Mexican American children has provided a framework for looking at the impact of culture on learning styles of Indian children. Ramirez and Castaneda examined field dependence/independence in light of cultural differences among Mexican Americans and postulated that Mexican American youth tend to grow up in a culture in which family organization tends to produce primarily field dependent or, as they term it, field sensitive learning styles. Conversely, children reared in formally organized families that promote strong individual identity tend to be more field independent (Cohen 1969). It has been speculated that viewed from this paradigm, Indian children tend to be more field sensitive. However, in one study of field dependence/independence in Navajo children, Dinges and Hollenbeck (1978) found that their Navajo sample scored significantly higher in a field independent direction than did the white sample. Their findings contrast with previous research and hypothesized results, which suggested that there is a direct relationship among family organization, cultural isolation, and field dependence/field independence for cultures of the United States and in other cultures of the world. They attempted to determine that a similar relationship also holds for other American Indian groups but found contrasting data. They suggested a multi-factor explanation comprising genetic, environmental, experiential, and linguistic factors unique to the Navajo to account for the outcomes.

In summary, the body of research, although small, on learning styles of American Indian students presents some converging evidence that suggests common patterns or methods in the way these students come to know or understand the world. They approach tasks visually, seem to prefer to learn by careful observation preceding performance, and seem to learn in their natural settings experientially. Research with other student groups has clearly illustrated that differences in learning style (whether they be described as relational/analytical, field dependent/independent, or global/linear) can result in "academic disorientation." While it is not clear where Indian students fit on this continuum, it is clear from the research summarized in the previous section that American Indian students come to learn about the world in ways that differ from those of non-Indian students.

Showing Competence: Public and Private Talk

I have noticed that when I asked a question, the [Pima] students would not respond; there was dead silence. But when I made a comment without questioning, they were more likely to respond and join in the discussion. (teacher, personal communication, 1988)

The way in which people prefer to demonstrate learning is an important corollary to the way in which they prefer to learn. As Mehan has described,

To be successful in classroom lessons, students must not only know the *content* of academic subjects, they must know the appropriate *form* in which to cast their academic knowledge. Although it is incumbent upon students to display *what* they know during lessons, they must also know *how* to display it. (1981, 51)

There is evidence that the ways in which children acquire and demonstrate knowledge are influenced by accustomed cultural norms and socialization practices (Cohen 1969). A body of recent research on minority children has produced studies that show different reactions to cooperative versus competitive situations, questioning techniques, classroom pace, and classroom organization. Included in this research is considerable ethnographic evidence on children's responses to different interactional situations in school and in their home and community. Classroom studies of Indian children's interactional styles or demonstration of knowledge have come to focus on the continuity/discontinuity spectrum as it relates to a child's home and school environments. The interactional style of the home environment sometimes conflicts or interferes with the interactional style required for successful participation in the classroom (Cazden 1982; Dumont 1972; Erickson and Mohatt 1982; Philips 1972, 1983; Van Ness 1981).

In particular, recent studies point to the different cultural orientation Indian children experience when participating in classroom learning. One of the most extensive studies was done by Philips (1972). Examining participant structures and communicative competence with children from the Warm Springs Indian Reservation in Oregon, Philips observed that Indian children were reluctant to participate in structures that required large and small group recitations. However, they were more talkative than non-Indian children in the last two structures, in which students initiated the interaction with the teacher or worked on student-led group projects. She noted that Warm Springs Indian children failed to participate verbally in their classrooms because the norms for social performance in their community did not support public linguistic performance, although the school environment demanded it. Philips's study revealed that observation, careful listening, supervised participation, and individualized self-correction or testing were modes of learning in the Warm Springs Indian community. She concluded that this process of competence acquisition may help to explain the Warm Springs Indian children's reluctance to speak in front of their classmates. An incongruity exists in that the processes of acquisition of knowledge and demonstration of knowledge in the classroom are "collapsed into the single act of answering questions or reciting when called upon to do so by the teacher, particularly in the lower grades" (1972, 388).

Other ethnographic research suggests that the communication difficulty experienced by the Warm Springs Indian children when participant structures are teacher dominated and require public recitations may be generalized to other groups of American Indian children as well as other minority group children. Dumont (1972) found a similar situation in a study that contrasted two Cherokee classrooms. In one classroom, teacher-dominated recitations were a predominant structure and the children were silent. In the other classroom the children were observed to talk excitedly and productively about all of their learning tasks because they could choose when and how to participate and the teacher encouraged small group student-directed projects. The landmark research conducted by Philips and Dumont presents frameworks for analyzing the interactional structure that exists in schools attended by children from other tribal groups. This research indicates that some Indian children are more apt to participate actively and verbally in group projects and in situations where they volunteer participation. Conversely, these Indian children are less apt to perform on demand when they are individually "put on the spot" by teachers who expect them to answer questions in front of other students.

Cooperating and Competing:
The Individual and the Group

You put them out on the basketball court and they are competitive as can be. But in the classroom they don't want to compete against each other. I can ask a question and when a student responds incorrectly no other student will correct him. They don't want to look better than each other or to put another student down. The Anglo students are eager to show that they know the correct answer. They want to shine, the Indian students want to blend into the total class. (teacher, personal communication, 1988)

There is evidence that Indian children are predisposed to participate more readily in group or team situations. While much of the evidence on cooperation versus competition is anecdotal, Miller and Thomas (1972) and Brown (1977) conducted studies with Blackfeet and Cherokee Indian children, respectively, using the Madsen Cooperation Board to examine cooperative and competitive behaviors. Miller and Thomas found dramatic differences between Canadian Blackfoot children and Canadian white children while playing a game that permitted either competitive or cooperative behavior, but rewarded cooperative behavior. White children behaved competitively even when it was maladaptive to do so, while Blackfoot children cooperated. Brown found Cherokee children to be more cooperative and less competitive than white American children. There was a negative relationship between the cooperative behavior of Cherokee children and their school achievement. In other words, the students' cooperative behavior produced lower achievement. In the Cherokee classroom society, children closely followed traditional Cherokee norms such as maintaining harmonious relations and, more important, held fast to standards of achievement that all children could meet (Brown 1977). High-ability students, who did not want to violate this norm, did not display their competence, and the result was lowered achievement for many Cherokee students.

The implications of this research are that if Indian children have learned to learn in a cooperative way, they may experience conflicts when they enter the competitive world of the classroom. It also confirms the findings of ethnographic studies that suggest that many Indian students avoid competition when they view it as unfair (Dumont 1972; Wax, Wax, and Dumont 1964).

It is apparent that many Indian children tend to avoid individual competition, especially when it makes one individual appear to be better than another. In fact, in many Indian societies an individual's humility is something to be respected and preserved. Havighurst observed that "Indian children may not parade their knowledge before others nor try to appear better than their peers" (1970, 109).

In looking at competition and the peer society of Indian youth, Wax stated that

It has frequently been observed that Indian pupils hesitate to engage in an individual performance before the public gaze, especially where they sense competitive assessment against their peers. Indian children do not wish to be exposed as inadequate before their peers, and equally do not wish to demonstrate by their individual superiority the inferiority of their peers. On the other hand, where performance is socially defined as benefitting the peer society, Indians become excellent competitors (as witness their success in team athletics). (1971, 85)

What the literature suggests is that for Indian children from certain groups, public display of knowledge that is not in keeping with community or group norms may be an unreasonable expectation. It may be an experience that causes Indian children to withdraw and act out the stereotype of the "silent Indian child."

Teaching Style: Adaptation to Learning Style

The teaching style or method one chooses to transmit learning can have a significant effect on whether students learn or fail. As John suggested,

Styles of teaching are, in part, an expression of the goals of education. When working with Indian children, educators choose methods of instruction that zero in on what they wish to accomplish instead of methods that reflect the developmental stages of children or respond to the specific features of tribal life. (1972, 332)

There are many variables to consider in choosing teaching methods that will lead to optimal learning in a particular situation. Among those variables, the culture of the learner has only recently been considered anything other than a deficiency to be remedied. As Burgess pointed out, "Unfortunately, many instructors ignore culture and its impact on learning both in 'content' and 'style,' rather than devising methods and techniques through which culturally diverse individuals approach problem solving" (1978, 52).

Leacock (1976) provided a strong argument for understanding culture and its influence on instruction. She believed that "true cultural insight" enables one to look beyond differences that are superficial and socially determined to the integrity of the individual; it prevents misinterpretation of behaviors that do not follow an accustomed pattern. Leacock cited as an example teachers' misinterpretation of the pervading "cooperative spirit" in Indian societies and a reluctance of Indian children to compete with peers as a lack of desire and motivation. In essence, she was saying that cultural differences are often misinterpreted and that the lens through which the teacher views behavior is colored by the ways in which atypical behaviors were characterized during the teacher-training process. For example, "timidity" is often interpreted as lack of initiative, motivation, or competitive spirit; but viewed through a more culturally relativistic lens, timid behavior might reveal a reluctance to compete with one's peers or to display learning in a way not congruent with the child's life-style. Wax, Wax, and Dumont reported similar conflicts when teachers misinterpret cultural behavior. They concluded,

When Indian children err, their elders "explain," which as we understood it means that they painstakingly and relatively privately illustrate or point out the correct procedure or proper behavior. However . . . teachers in school do not understand this. Their irate scolding becomes an assault on the child's status before his peers. (At the same time, the teacher diminishes his own stature, inasmuch as respected elders among Indians control their tempers and instruct in quiet patience.) (1964, 95)

Mohatt and Erickson's (1981) study of cultural differences in teaching styles in an Odawa school supports the differences between participant structures Philips (1972) found in Warm Springs and illustrates that teachers who viewed cultural differences as strengths were able to create the type of atmosphere that motivates learning. In this study an Odawa Indian and a non-Indian teacher were observed to see if there were differences in their teaching styles. Although both teachers were effective and experienced, they varied as to their teaching strategies. The Odawa teacher's strategies reflected Odawa cultural patterns of what is appropriate in ordinary social relations between adults and children, which were then manifested in the pacing of classroom activities and interactions with students.

In most classrooms teachers tend to introduce almost all new concepts and give all instructions verbally (Rohner 1965; Appleton 1983). This teaching style conflicts with the traditional cultural patterns reinforced in many Indian communities, where visual perception is encouraged. As John speculates, "If the description of the ways in which young Navajo children learn is correct, that is, that they tend to approach their world visually and by quiet, persistent exploration, then a style of teaching stressing overt verbal performance is alien to such a child" (1972, 338). This is not to say that Indian children should not be expected to respond to verbal instructions or perform verbally, but, rather, that new concepts might be presented through alternative modes or teaching styles and that Indian children might be invited to display their learning in alternative interactions. For example, Cazden and Leggett (1981) recommended that because children differ in sensory modality strength, their learning may be limited by overly verbal environments, and therefore schools should deliberately plan more multisensory instruction. While Cazden and Leggett were referring to children in bilingual classrooms, they do use the term "bilingual classrooms" to refer to any classroom that includes minority children. Their recommendation makes sense for teachers of Indian children.

In the Classroom: Translating Theory into Practice

The premise of this chapter is that although Indian students come to school with an approach to learning which is culturally influenced and often different from those of mainstream American students, the styles that teachers use to deliver instruction are essentially the same for everyone. Philips capsulized this attitude when she said,

Surprisingly little attention has been given to the teaching methods used in teaching ethnic minority students in this country. Particularly when the notion of culturally relevant curriculum materials has been around as long as it has. It is as if we have been able to recognize that there are cultural differences in what people learn, but not in how they learn. (1983, 132–33)

The best research intentions are often challenged by teachers with the "But what do I do on Monday morning?" syndrome. Educators have wrestled for years with the difficulty of translating theory into practice. Teachers who are empathetic and want to change do not do so simply because they have not had time to reflect, research, and restructure their teaching style.

In addition to the practical implications discussed in this chapter, the multicultural literature is replete with general suggestions and guidelines on how to incorporate learning style aspects in teaching. Bennett (1985) encourages teachers to know their own teaching and learning styles and determine how far they can stray from these strengths and preferences and still be comfortable. She cautions teachers to build classroom flexibility slowly, adding one new strategy at a time. Her encouragement to use all modes (visual, auditory, tactile, and kinesthetic) when teaching concepts and skills is compatible with Cazden and Leggett's (1981) suggestion that teachers plan for multisensory instruction.

Cox and Ramirez (1981) recommend that direct observation and classroom experience be used in assessing and planning for learning style differences. They have summarized a field-tested process into six points:

1. Assess students' preferred ways of learning and the way(s) in which student behaviors change from situation to situation.
2. Plan learning experiences that address conceptual goals or skills or other objectives that incorporate the students' preferred ways of learning using teaching methods, incentives, materials, and situations that are planned according to student preferences.
3. Implement the learning experiences that were planned.
4. Evaluate the learning experiences in terms of attainment of conceptual or other goals as well as in terms of observed student behaviors and involvement.
5. As the year progresses, plan and implement student participation in learning experiences that require behaviors the student has previously avoided. Incorporate only one aspect at a time of the total experience from the less familiar behaviors—focusing on only the reward, the materials, the situation, or the task requirements—so that the student utilizes what is familiar and comfortable or motivating as support for the newer learning experience aspects.
5. Continue to provide familiar, comfortable, successful experiences as well as to gradually introduce the children to learning in new ways. (1981, 64–65)

Following this process, teachers can implement specific methods and strategies that will communicate to Indian students an attitude of understanding and caring while demanding high performance. Kleinfeld (1979b) has referred to this type of teacher as a "warm demander"—in other words, one who can balance humanistic concerns with high expectations for achievement. The suggestions that we have outlined are distilled from many sources. Certainly, the authors whose work we have reviewed are to be given credit, but so are countless teachers who have shared workable ideas with us in workshops. The following suggestions have special significance for teachers of Indian students:

Discuss students' learning styles with them; help them to understand why they do what they do in the learning situation.

Be aware of students' background knowledge and experiences.

Be aware of the pacing of activities within a time framework that may be rigid and inflexible.

Be aware of how questions are asked; think about the discussion style of your students.

Remember that some students do not like to be "spotlighted" in front of a group.

Provide time for practice before performance is expected. Let children "save face," but communicate that it is "ok" to make mistakes.

Be aware of proximity preferences, how close is comfortable.

Organize the classroom to meet the interactional needs of students and provide activities that encourage both independence and cooperation.

Provide feedback that is immediate and consistent; give praise that is specific.

We urge teachers to consult the materials cited in this chapter. No one source can provide all the answers to the complex questions facing teachers of Indian students. The community in which one chooses to teach will provide the most comprehensive resource for perplexing sorts of questions. Teachers must become participants in the community; they must observe and ask questions in a way that communicates genuine care and concern. Teachers are learners too, and must let students (and their parents) know this. An excellent source of guidelines generated by beginning teachers of Indian youth is provided by a program operated by the Division of Teacher Education at Indiana University. In this program, student teacher volunteers over several years have been placed on Indian reservations in the Southwest. The teachers' observations were organized into an article, which emphasized that "anyone attempting to teach children of another culture should be as fully aware as possible of the language, customs, traditions, and taboos of that culture so that he or she can avoid classroom and community misunderstandings and become an effective teacher" (Mahan and Criger 1977, 13).

Conclusion

In summary, it seems appropriate to end this chapter with an observation by a historian who participated in a conference about multicultural education and American Indians:

Schools, in general, can never hope to perfectly mirror the society they represent. Likewise, American Indian society . . . can never be a perfect instrument within the format of the schools which came to us from Europe. But, the schools can do a lot more than they have done in the past! Furthermore, the time for them to do that something has long since passed. (O'Neil 1979, 154)

6

Adapting Curriculum to Culture

JON REYHNER

The previous chapter dealt with adapting teaching methods to the way Indian children learn to learn in their homes. This chapter looks at the other key aspect of teaching in our schools: the textbooks that form the basis of the curriculum of most American schools. Textbooks, especially basal readers, are examined to document that their content is often inappropriate for Indian children.

Despite a long history of criticism, textbooks continue to play an important role in American schools. "In the nineteenth century, a heavy reliance on textbooks was the distinguishing mark of American education," according to Frances Fitzgerald, who concluded that textbooks "were substitutes for well-trained teachers" (1979, 19).

Cronback, in a 1955 study of textbooks, found them central to the educational scene, taking a "dominant place" in most schools. Summarizing three National Science Foundation studies in 1979, Shaver, Davis, and Helburn found that "Teachers tend not only to rely on, but to believe in, the textbook as the source of knowledge. Textbooks are not seen as support materials, but as the central instrument of instruction by most social studies teachers" (151).

The negative effect of textbooks written from a Eurocentric point of view on Indian children was reported by George Wharton James in 1908:

Again and again when I have visited Indian schools the thoughtful youths and maidens have come to me with complaints about the American history they were compelled to study . . . "When we read in the

United States history of white men fighting to defend their families, their homes, their corn-fields, their towns, and their hunting grounds, they are always called 'patriots,' and the children are urged to follow the example of these brave, noble, and gallant men. But when Indians—our ancestors, even our own parents—have fought to defend us and our homes, corn-fields, and hunting-grounds they are called vindictive and merciless savages, bloody murderers, and everything else that is vile." (25)

Cronback reported that "the latent function" of textbooks was "to transmit the myths and the mores, the traditions and the legends, and the folkways and superstitions" of the culture producing them, and that textbook writing in the United States was a white middle-class activity, with the textbooks reflecting the values of that class (1955, 105). Margaret Gribskov (1973) and Rupert Costo (1970) criticized social studies textbooks for their unbalanced treatment of American Indians.

The use of textbooks in all curricular areas needs to be deemphasized and more attention needs to be placed on using other kinds of books and giving kids real world, hands-on, experiences in all subject areas. In the past these hands-on activities, then called "projects," were used successfully with Indian students (MacGregor 1946). Frank Smith (1988) uses the term "enterprises," while Freeman and Freeman refer to an "explorer classroom" (1988, described by T. L. McCarty and Rachel Schaffer in chapter 8 of this volume). Teachers' overreliance on textbooks that ignore the American Indian experience causes problems in all subject areas, but in the interest of brevity and because the success of Indian students in school hinges on their ability to learn to read, this chapter focuses on the use of textbooks in reading instruction.

Most Indian children today, like other children in the United States, are taught reading using basal reading textbooks (Austin and Morrison 1963; Goodman et al. 1988). In the past, there have been two major problems with using basal readers with Indian students. First, Indians, along with other minorities, were largely absent from basal reading textbooks (Klineberg 1963). The second problem, shared by Indian and non-Indian students, is that the stories in these texts tend to be boring, bland, and unrealistic (Bettelheim and Zelan 1982; Bowler 1978; Henry 1961; Yarington 1978). As early as 1885, teachers and school administrators were commenting to Washington and the director of Indian schools was suggesting that the government develop textbooks appropriate for Indian students with "stories which they [Indian students] can comprehend and which interest them" (Atkins 1885, cxxii–cxxiii, 240). However, little was done then and only a bit more today to produce culturally appropriate teaching material for Indian children. Some of the material that is available is described in the reading and content-area chapters in this book and in appendices B and C.

Research indicates the importance for American Indian students of books with Indian themes and characters. Simpson-Tyson concluded from a review of research and a study of Crow Indian children that reading and language activities for Indian students in the first grade "should be laden with Native American cultural experiences" (1978, 801). Cummins, reviewing recent research on bilingual education, concluded that schools need to build on the entry-level characteristics of students and to "validate" their "cultural identity" in order to give them the best chance for success (1981, 42). In *What Works: Research About Teaching and Learning* the U.S. Department of Education states, "students read passages more deftly when the passages describe events, people, and places of which the students have some prior knowledge" (1986, 53). The conclusion of recent research is not that much different from the conclusion of the 1928 Meriam Report that educational material, especially for the primary grades, "must come from local Indian life, or at least be written within the scope of the child's early experience" (33).

A Short History of
Reading Textbooks and Their Use

The adequacy of basal readers for providing beginning reading material has been questioned as long as the books have been in use. Charles Eliot, president of Harvard University for forty years, criticized late nineteenth-century reading textbooks for being at best "mere scraps of literature" and at worst "ineffable trash" (Hardy 1891, 145–46). In 1918 Edmund Burk Huey commented on how the illustrations in reading textbooks "had far more attention" than the story content (276).

William S. Gray, the senior editor of Scott, Foresman's "Dick and Jane" reading series, consciously left out the "sordid surroundings" and "family conflict" found in the lives of "deprived children" so that in school these children could "live vicariously in a pleasant, attractive home" (Gray et al. 1951, 23–24). Psychologists have disagreed with Gray's escapist philosophy. Bruno Bettelheim found a lack of significant content in reading textbooks and that the readers lead children to have unrealistic expectations as to how families lived. Parents never argued, mother was always ready to play with the children, father was never tired after work, and children never experienced sibling rivalry. Bettelheim felt the content of basal stories aggravated rather than alleviated emotional problems children might have by making them seem abnormal in terms of the world the textbook stories portrayed (1961). The effect of these stories on one Indian child from Cochiti Pueblo has been described by Joseph H. Suina:

> The Dick and Jane reading series in the primary grades presented me with pictures of a home with a pitched roof, straight walls, and sidewalks. I could not identify with these from my Pueblo world. However, it was clear I didn't have these things and what I did have did not measure up. . . . I was ashamed of being who I was and I wanted to change right then and there. Somehow it became so important to have straight walls, clean hair and teeth, a spotted dog to chase after. I even became critical and hateful toward my bony, fleabag of a dog. I loved the familiar and cozy surroundings of my grandmother's house but now I imagined it could be a heck of a lot better if only I had a white man's house with a bed, a nice couch, and a clock. In school books, all the child characters ever did was run around chasing their dog or a kite. They were always happy. As for me, all I seemed to do at home was go back and forth with buckets of water and cut up sticks for a lousy fire. "Didn't the teacher say that drinking coffee would stunt my growth?" . . . "Did my grandmother really care about my well-being?" (1988, 298)

Psychologists have criticized basal stories for lacking a variety of content, which can be labeled under the general category of realism. Child, Potter, and Levine (1946, 45) found an "unrealistic optimism" in 913 third-grade basal stories they studied, while Bettelheim (1961, 388) found "unrealistic images of life and people." Klineberg (1963) found a white middle-class world of abundance and fun with no non-white Americans, while Blom, Waite, and Zimet (1968, 318) found a predominance of "neutral 'Polyanna' stories."

More recently Bettelheim and Zelan (1982) have found first-grade reading textbooks to be "boring," an "insult to the child's intelligence," "uninteresting," and "without merit." They felt,

If, rather than concentrating on developing reading skills, educational efforts from the very beginning were concentrated on developing the desire to become literate—essentially an inner attitude to reading—then the final result might be that a larger segment of the adult population would be literate. (21)

Reading Textbooks and the Real World

In recent years many changes have taken place in basal reader stories. Reading specialists such as Aukerman (1981) have found more realism in recent basal reading textbooks. However, there are economic forces preventing making textbooks more realistic. Textbook publishers, with millions of dollars riding on the success of their reading textbooks, fear that including unpleasant but truthful stories might reduce sales (Yarington 1978). They do not want to offend any special interest group that might oppose the adoption of their textbook in any part of the United States.

Goldhammer felt that children, after reading primers describing an idealized middle-class family that never was and never will be, would think that "the school is attempting to perpetrate a hoax, and that, consequently, the teacher, who is a liar, and the school, which promulgates the lie, are not to be trusted" (1969). Children may mistakenly doubt their own perceptions of reality rather than doubt the authority of the text, the teacher, and the school. This hidden curriculum can lead children to depend on authority. Learned reliance on authority has been given as a reason why older students have trouble understanding the scientific method of discovering reality (Child, Potter, and Levine 1946).

The child who mistrusts the world and has a poor self-concept often is not only a poor reader but also not well socialized. Jahoda found a steadily growing body of empirical evidence to show that "inadequate reality testing is characteristic of many who feel hostile to racial out-groups" (1960, 13). Hiding the faults of the dominant group—or other ethnic groups—does not lead to a healthier attitude toward life or to out-groups. Research on adolescent prejudice indicates that teachers should not try to hide the existence of group differences, even negative stereotypes about various groups. Hiding negative feelings

is undoubtedly well motivated and practiced because it is thought that the acknowledgement of group differences may breed prejudice, but its more likely consequence is to compromise the integrity of the teacher [or textbook] and, in the process, either mute his or her potential or produce a boomerang effect by making it seem to the discerning youngster that there is some justification after all for prejudice. (Glock et al. 1975, 175)

The forthright acknowledgment of group differences, "whether they appear to reflect on a group positively, negatively, or neutrally," will bring prejudices into the light of day, where they can be explored so that children will not feel deceived (Glock et al. 1975, 175). In sum, the research on story content leads to the conclusion that censorship should be avoided and that stories should realistically mirror the world in which they are set. Even folktales should not be watered down as they contain symbolic truths (Livingston 1974; Bettelheim 1977).

Indians in Basal Readers

Despite tremendous gains in the last twenty years in introducing minority characters into previously all-white basal reading series, basals still are predominantly about whites, and even stories with minority characters often do not reflect minority cultures. Only 1 percent of the stories in first-grade basal readers have American Indian characters. At the third-grade level, 7 percent of the stories have major characters who are Indian; 15 percent of fifth-grade-level stories do (Reyhner 1986). In a random sample of one-fourth of basal reader stories from eight basal reading series, only two of the sixteen stories with identifiable Indian characters dealt with urban Indians, even though half of the Indians in the United States live in metropolitan areas, including 21 percent in central cities, according to the 1980 census.

American Indian stories in basal reading textbooks are set for the most part in the rural American Southwest. Such activities as pottery making, rug weaving, sheepherding, silversmithing, and basketmaking are overemphasized in these Indian stories. The proportion of rural settings for all basal reading stories increased with grade level. Blom, Waite, and Zimet in 1968 reported a lack of urban settings in basal stories in proportion to the number of children living in urban areas. The fact that only a fourth of all Indians live on reservations and that many live in cities would indicate that teachers need to make a point of seeking out Indian stories with urban settings.

A few figures, such as Sacajawea and ballerina Maria Tall

Chief, reoccur frequently in basal readers and trade books about Indians. Stories continue to be found that focus on the Indians as the white man's helpers who side with the whites against their own people, sometimes to save the life of one of their children or a white person. An example in a recent fifth-grade reader is the Puerto Rican story of Iviahoca, who gains the freedom of her son by carrying a letter "through enemy lines" to help the Spaniards defeat the Indians.

Traditional folk stories, both Indian and non-Indian, in basals have by and large been transformed. Traditional Indian stories had "realism" represented by Old Man Coyote and other archetypes, but European and Indian folk stories including good and evil characters have mostly been replaced in modern basal reading textbooks with "stuffed animal" fairy tales, with no evil and little conflict in them.

The greatest weakness of the Indian content in current basal reading textbooks is the striking absence of Indian characters in the primary-level stories. The lack of first-grade Indian content in basal readers is especially critical since the early school years not only give students the basics they need for later school achievement but also help to form their attitudes toward school. The greatest strengths are the realistic and well-written contemporary stories in the intermediate-level readers.

The intermediate grade stories would go a long way toward meeting the needs that Gilliland (1983) identified for Indian children who are reluctant readers. However, the two or three stories at any grade level in any given reading series are too few to create sustained interest. Teachers need to search for additional reading material that portrays American Indians in a nonstereotyped manner, especially material from Indian students' particular tribal backgrounds, to supplement the basal reading textbook in order to take full advantage of the students' interest in stories about their own and other tribal cultures.

Basal reading textbooks alone do not provide enough reading material to allow students the practice they need to become fluent readers. According to Frank Smith "The primary function of reading teachers . . . [is] to ensure that children have adequate opportunity to read" (1978, 187). Children learn to read well by reading a lot of books that they find interesting (Krashen 1985;

Smith 1983; U.S. Dept. of Education 1986). Appendix B provides
a short list of recommended books about American Indians.

Conclusion

Emphasis on textbook instruction in American schools produces
passive students who uncritically accept the "canned" knowledge
of the dominant social group. Such students tend to become bored
with school and drop out either physically or mentally. The alternative to the textbook approach to reading and other subject
area instruction is to provide frequent supplementary activities for
Indian students along with textbook lessons or to abandon textbooks altogether and use regular trade books, as is done in the
literature-based Whole Language approach to teaching reading.
The reading and literature section of this book deals with turning
Indian children from passive to active learners by giving them
non-textbook experiences with language, social studies, science,
and mathematics.

7

Getting Teachers and Parents to Work Together

DICK LITTLEBEAR

A positive working relationship between teachers and parents is essential for the proper education of Indian, Alaska Native, and other ethnic minority children. In all communities a definite need exists for teachers to work with parents. In the words of one Cheyenne elder, teachers need to "cross the cattle guard" that separates the school compound from the community and observe and visit with community members.

There are many reasons why teacher-parent interaction is necessary. Most of the teachers who now teach Indian students are non-Indian and are from the dominant society. Most of their teacher training has been monocultural, presenting the American middle-class as the socioeconomic norm. Teachers need to realize that Indian students are outside this norm and are being influenced daily by another dynamic culture. These teachers must be willing to undergo an acculturation process to become familiar with the particular tribal cultures of their students. Even if the teachers are Indian, they may be urban Indians who have little or no knowledge of traditional cultures, systems, and protocol. These teachers will have to undergo an acculturation process similar to that of the teachers from the dominant society.

Teachers who are from a reservation may have lost touch with traditional Indian values or may have unquestioningly accepted the values of the dominant society as superior to those of the Indian. Their schooling and their teacher training may have "bleached" these teachers inwardly and brainwashed them into believing that anything Indians do is inferior, and they teach from that position. These kinds of teachers need extensive reacculturation. Some of them never become reacculturated, and they may have the most difficulty in working with Indian parents, especially if the community in which they teach has a traditional orientation.

In all of Indian country there is a lack of Indian-developed, culturally relevant curriculum materials that are tribally specific. Through interaction with the community, teachers can bring this content into the classroom. Being able to utilize culturally relevant materials will lead to a culturally relevant education as parents and their children come to see their culture as a vital and necessary part of today's world. A culturally relevant education will help promote the abstract and long-range idea of acquiring an education and affirm all the benefits that can be derived from such an education.

Too often today's Indians are judged in relation to historical circumstances that were not of their making, and culturally relevant education can play a significant role in eradicating such judgments. Stereotypes and misconceptions have been the lot of Indians ever since their first contact with Europeans. Many non-Indians today continue to rely on these stereotypes and misconceptions—very often confusing them with truth. These stereotypes and misconceptions categorize Indians in the worst possible manner. Because of these categorizations, some non-Indians seem to think that if Indians do not want to become middle-class Americans, there must be something collectively wrong with them. Such thinking is fallacious, and teachers must be sensitized to this fallacious thinking.

Indian parents have been systematically excluded from participation in the dominant culture's education of Indian youth. The federal government had, or seemed to have had, a policy of genocide toward Indians. When Indians survived this policy, the government tried cultural genocide. In the vanguard of this attempt at cultural genocide was education in the form of mission, boarding, and day schools. This really was not education in the true sense of the word; it was enforced assimilation.

Excluding Indian parents from the education of Indian children has not worked, and, in fact, has made Indian parents very suspicious of modern American education. A century and a half of enforced acculturation practices under the guise of education has had lasting detrimental effects on all Indians. These effects will continue unless Indian parents are involved in the schooling of their children and until teachers start viewing their students as individuals who represent the sum total of experiences, good and bad, wrought by two different cultures and two different attitudes.

Teachers have to be aware of an attitudinal difference between Indians and other minorities, except for blacks and some Hispanics in the Southwest. The difference is that most of the voluntary immigrant minorities come to America wanting to become "Americans." Thus they rapidly acquire the trappings of the dominant society, like the language and the values. Indians differ because they simply want to be what they have always been: Cheyenne, Sioux, Arapaho, and so forth. They prefer a relationship on their own terms with the dominant society rather than total assimilation. This attitude has always been prevalent among Indians, and the Europeans could not change it—even though they tried mightily, by violent and by subtle means, to make all Indians into English-speaking, brown Americans (see chapter 3).

Historically schools have been a means of destroying Indian culture, but education can also be instrumental in preserving Indian cultures. Through culturally relevant education, especially in the earlier grades, Indians can preserve their cultures. There are, however, many obstacles that still have to be overcome. One is Indian suspicion of modern American education. This kind of education is still associated with punishment and deprivation because that is what it meant to the grandparents and parents of today's children, but changes in education can lead to changed attitudes.

By developing and implementing culturally relevant curricula, Indian educators will be helping Indian students to live a better life in a rapidly changing world. By developing strategies to garner a positive working relationship between teachers and parents, they will be helping Indian students succeed in any endeavor.

There are channels now available to promote and produce a positive working relationship between parents and teachers. For instance, the federal government mandates parental involvement in those educational programs it funds. However participation in parent advisory committees (PACs) must be affirmed as an important contribution to the children's education in a direct fashion, otherwise parents will not bother to participate. PACs must be listened to and given some real power to determine the shape of school programs.

Finally, there is no such human as a generic Indian, though there are some general similarities including hair and skin color and life-styles based on geographical location. For instance, there are similarities among Plains Indians. In fact, if there is some notion of a generic Indian, it is modeled on the Plains Indian, associated with the horse, tipi, buffalo, and feather regalia. There are, however, great dissimilarities among all Indians, the Plains Indians included. These dissimilarities include language, world view, economic condition, degree of acculturation to the dominant society, spiritual outlook, religion, myth, and clan structure.

The following recommendations are based on the idea that there is no generic Indian, just as there is no generic white person.

Recommendations for Teachers Working with Indian Parents

1. All teachers need to become aware of themselves as being from a particular culture. Culture is not the exclusive domain of minorities. Teachers from the dominant society should be aware of their own ethnic and cultural origins so they can better understand American Indian cultural differences and how they relate to the students.

2. Teachers need to become aware of tribally specific differences. What this means is that what is acceptable in one tribe may be a taboo in another. For instance in all Plains Indian cultures, eagle feathers are sacred. Yet among the Cheyennes, eagle feathers must not be touched by Cheyenne females. So, something that may seem logical to a teacher, like awarding an eagle feather or a likeness of one to a Cheyenne female for an athletic or academic accomplishment, would violate Cheyenne beliefs. Yet, doing so in a classroom with students from another Plains Indian tribe might be perfectly acceptable.

3. Teachers must learn about their students' tribes including their histories and the aspirations of parents and the local community. Teachers should not just read books (usually written by whites) on Indian cultures but should also actually talk to tribal members.

4. Teachers should not rely on preconceived stereotypes and popular misconceptions of American Indians. For much too long, American Indians have been thought of as similar in appearance, speech, and behavior and as indifferent to what the dominant society has to offer. Remember that there is no generic Indian. A teacher who assumes this is doing a great disservice and a grave injustice to American Indian children.

5. Teachers need to make modern American education more acceptable to Indians. One way that teachers can accomplish this is by asking parents to come in and share their experiences with the students because parents represent those values and habits that will make the curriculum relevant to the students' backgrounds.

6. Teachers should encourage parents to take college courses, to return to college or a postsecondary vocational school, or obtain a high school proficiency certificate.

7. Teachers should be aware of linguistic differences and influences on their students. There is also no generic Indian language except maybe sign language. Each tribe, regardless of the degree of language erosion, is still affected by their native language. The language spoken by the elders still has an influence on children. While many of these children come to school speaking English, their English is nonstandard "survival" or "Indian" English, which is adequate as a social instrument but inadequate for academic comprehension and achievement.

8. Teachers should keep their expectations high. This is true in academics, athletics, and discipline. Starting low and switching to high expectations will lead to a loss of credibility. Do not lower expectations for any reason, but especially not because the students are Indians.

9. Teachers must remember that their students are not yet sophisticated in their own culture, so to expect them to be able to give a lot of information about their culture is unrealistic. Culture is acquired over a lifetime. Students may also have been taught at home that certain information about their beliefs is not to be told to outsiders.

10. Teachers should be very careful of what they say. If a need to speak about a local person arises, teachers should be well acquainted with the person to whom they are talking. This cautionary recommendation is included here because of the extended families, clans, and factions that characterize the social structures of Indian communities. These are closely interwoven, and regular communication among community members is a characteristic of Indian communities. This regular communication can bring much grief to an unsuspecting teacher if he or she is not mindful of the possible connections between people. It is only a slight exaggeration to say that everyone in an Indian community is related either by blood or marriage. A good rule is do not say anything about a person away from him or her that you would not say about that person in his or her hearing.

11. Teachers should be aware of the factors that can enhance the self-perception of Indian students, such as instruction on Indian contribu-

tions to the country, positive Indian values and their relevance to modern society, and the intricacy of Indian kinship systems. Teachers can also teach students about the geography, ecology, history, and government of their reservation.

12. Teachers can encourage leadership skills among their students. Having students work in groups and giving students opportunities to make meaningful decisions about classroom activities can help develop leadership skills.

13. Teachers can introduce preventative strategies and alternatives to alcohol and drug use to their students at an early age.

14. Teachers should be aware of the communication patterns of their Indian students. Sometimes when a teacher asks a question, he or she does not allow enough time for a response and will end up answering the question for the students. Indian students take more time to answer questions not because they are less intelligent, but because they want to digest the question and then formulate a correct response. The response must be correct because Indian cultures require precise communication, not just haphazard utterances.

15. Teachers should not deliberately shame a student. Shaming and censure are social control devices among many tribes. It is done only when needed, and corrective instructions are expected to follow. To shame students in front of their peers will evoke considerable negative responses.

16. Teachers should not have a "savior" complex. The Indian student does not need saving, except possibly from people with savior complexes. The student needs to be shown how his culture, heritage, and Indian ethos are positively related to the values of the dominant society.

17. Teachers should try to grow while they are on Indian reservations. Many teachers who have had a long tenure on an Indian reservation limit the value of the experience by repeating the same lessons over and over again each succeeding year. The children deserve teachers who are willing to keep learning. Classes can be taken at Indian tribal colleges on the local culture or summer courses can be taken at colleges and universities that offer courses in bilingual and Indian education. And, again, teachers should become acquainted with the local elders and community people.

Recommendations for Indian Parents Working with Teachers

1. Parents should know that non-Indian teachers are almost always not sophisticated in a particular tribe's culture and are bound to make some mistakes. Parents must realize that it takes time to become acculturated, especially for people from the dominant culture who

have had no compelling need to familiarize themselves with minority cultures and who may have allowed misconceptions and stereotypes to color their perceptions of other cultures.

2. Parents should volunteer for in-class help if their schedules allow. This not only exposes Indian students to positive role models, but it also will enable parents to appreciate the rigors that teachers undergo daily and how the teachers' education has prepared them for their profession.

3. Parents must go to the school to talk to teachers and administrators about the education of their children. Parents need to go to school especially when there is no crisis. Going to the school should become a regular occurrence, not just to attend a school-sponsored activity. Appointments are useful because of teachers' and administrators' schedules.

4. Parents can reinforce what is taught in school and find out what is being taught by talking to their children as well as visiting the school. If a parent disagrees with what is being taught at school, this disagreement needs to be talked out with the teacher, or if that does not work, with first the principal, then the superintendent, and, as a last resort, the school board.

5. Parents are the first educators of their children and they must instill in them the need to be educated.

6. Parents must reinstill the many positive Indian values that time and social circumstances have distorted. If reinstilling these values is not possible, at least an explanation of why these values have changed should be given. Otherwise, students may ask, for instance, why they should respect an elder who obviously has not earned or does not merit that respect.

7. Parents should be careful about expressing dissatisfaction with the school or with school personnel in the presence of their children who are students. They should go to the school to try to work out their differences with how the school is run. This is because whenever parents talk negatively about the school or its staff, they are validating any negative opinions their children already have about attending school and implicitly encouraging them to be disruptive and ignore what is being taught.

Some Recommended Readings

Biglin, J. E., and Pratt, W. 1973. *Indian Parent Involvement in Education: A Basic Sourcebook.* Las Cruces, NM: ERIC Clearinghouse on Rural Education and Small Schools. (ERIC Document Reproduction Service no. ED 076 273)

Ferguson, Sherry, and Mazin, Lawrence E. 1986. *Parent Power: A Guide to Your Child's Success in School.* Florence, AZ: Pinal County School Office.

Howes, G. R., Weiss, H. G., and Weiss, M. S. 1980. *How to Raise Your Child to be a Winner.* New York: Rawson, Wade.

Sattes, B. D. 1985. Parent Involvement: A Review of the Literature (occasional paper 021). Charleston, WV: Appalachia Educational Laboratory.

III
Language Development

8

Language and Literacy Development

T. L. McCARTY

RACHEL SCHAFFER

The first-grade classroom in the public school on the Tohono O'odham (formerly Papago) Reservation in southern Arizona hums with activity. At one table, several children listen to tape recordings of a favorite book in O'odham. At other tables around the room, pairs of students create stories in English from wordless picture books. If a writer has a question about spelling, the partner can help; invented spellings are encouraged. In another part of the room, three students read from a "big book" with their tutor, a third grader.

The teacher, a fluent speaker of O'odham and English, walks among the groups, stopping to ask or respond to a question, or to listen as students read their completed stories. Another first-grade teacher, temporarily released from her own classroom, observes

Descriptions in this chapter of American Indian classrooms are based on a 1988–89 study by T. L. McCarty and Margarita Calderón sponsored by the Arizona Department of Education, with funding from the Andrew W. Mellon Foundation, Council of Chief State School Officers, and the U.S. Department of Education's Office of Bilingual Education and Minority Language Affairs. A full discussion of the research will be published in the forthcoming proceedings of the 1991 annual conference of the National Association for Bilingual Education. We wish to express our gratitude to the Indian educators and children who participated in the study and whose work is described here: Verna Enos, Ann Francisco, Anna Gray, Daniel Lopez, Elaine Lopez, Ida Norris, Yolanda Two Two, Julee Tyler, Kevin Tyler, and the students at Indian Oasis Primary School; and Margaret Ferrick, Randy Huntley, Doug McIntyre, Theresa McIntyre, Karen Snow, Barbara Stanton, Jeff Williams, and the students at Sanders Unified School District. By their examples, these educators demonstrated the learning possibilities within explorer environments. We also thank Nancy Mendoza, Stephen Krashen, Jim Cummins, Yvonne Freeman, David Freeman, John Martin, Richard Ruiz, and Yetta Goodman, who read and commented on earlier versions of this chapter.

and assists. Later, the two will meet to share their observations and plan subsequent lessons. The school principal is also present, not to evaluate, but to listen, read, and discuss with students and teachers. The walls in and outside the classroom offer colorful displays of students' artistic and written work, in O'odham and English.

Three hundred miles to the north, in a high school language arts class near the Navajo Reservation, students and their teacher sit around a table to read and discuss poems each has written. Over the past two weeks, the class has been reading works of fiction, nonfiction, and poetry dealing with a theme they selected: love. At several other tables, students work with one or two partners to write poems on this theme, sharing their drafts and asking each other questions to clarify meanings. Though the poems are written in English, much of the discussion about them is in Navajo. The teacher, whose first language is English but who has studied Navajo and several European languages, encourages students to use their native language. When students are satisfied with their final versions, they will publish them in a class anthology to add to the classroom library.

These are real classrooms in American Indian communities in the Southwest. While the schools they represent differ markedly in their demographics and institutional arrangements, the classrooms share an essential feature: they are environments rich in oral and written language—places where students learn about language, but more important, where they learn about themselves and the wider world through their own language and English. In the process, a powerful and lifelong message is communicated: that students are full members of a community of language users, with all the attendant rights and benefits of membership. Students in these classrooms, to use Frank Smith's term, are assured of their unqualified membership in the language and literacy "club" (Smith 1988).

These learning achievements cannot be attributed solely to the teachers—the students played critical roles, as did school administrators—but without the teachers, the conditions and possibilities for learning would have been different. Both teachers brought to their classrooms a set of understandings about learning, about language, and about students' and teachers' roles as coparticipants in the learning process. Acting on those understandings, the teachers created instructional contexts in which they and their students could tap a wealth of linguistic and cultural resources to explore new ideas and academic content. Their explorations were driven by students' interests, their natural motivation stemming from those interests, and their active involvement. Each child in these classrooms could make sense of the activities, as they had both personal and social meaning. In engaging in these activities, the children not only exercised and expanded their language and thinking abilities, they affirmed their identities as thinkers, and as speakers, readers, and writers with important ideas to communicate.

In a recent analysis of bilingual education, Freeman and Freeman note that the assumptions educators make can limit or expand the potential for learning in the classroom. "Unfortunately," they add, "many assumptions about bilingual learners have hindered, rather than helped" (1988, 2). This has been the case throughout the history of schooling for American Indian children, as low expectations and the devaluation of students' experiences have reduced education to senseless drills aimed at ameliorating presumed language "handicaps" while ignoring the tremendous competence children bring to the school situation.

In this chapter, we take as our starting point Vygotsky's principle that "any learning a child encounters in school always has a previous history" (Cole et al. 1978, 84). The classrooms and teachers just described show how application of this principle can help Indian students realize and utilize their prior knowledge, and most important, their potential for new learning. In the discussion that follows, we examine more specifically how this can occur in the context of children's language development inside and outside of school.

What Every Child Has

Children are born for language. The human capacity for language is innate, and every child, barring certain physical or mental conditions, uses this native ability to acquire the specifics of the language or languages in her or his community.

Language, then, is a human universal. But most impressive is the universally natural, effortless, and rapid process by which children grasp such a complex symbolic system. In the course of their growth and development, children learn not only the phonemic, morphemic, and syntactic or grammatical regularities of their language community, they also acquire an extensive lexicon, the ability to interpret that lexicon (semantics), and an understanding of how the language is used to accomplish a wide variety of social goals (pragmatics). Moreover, even in environments where print in the form of books is limited, children learn from the print around them—street and building signs, what comes through the mail, and the labels on food packages and household items, for instance—gaining insights into what written language is used for and how it is patterned (Smith 1988; Hudelson 1989). All of this occurs by the time children are four or five, without the benefit of an explicit curriculum, without drill and structured analysis of their language, and without "objective" measures of assessment.

In short, children master the basic structure of their language or languages in natural settings *before* they come to school. While they differ in their control of more abstract aspects of language (just as individuals differ in other types of knowledge or abilities), all children bring to school immense linguistic, social, and intellectual resources. Successful teachers recognize and build upon this foundation. They do this by approximating in the classroom the processes by which children naturally learn and acquire a language. The following section considers those processes and their implications for teaching and learning in American Indian settings.

Language Development Inside and Outside of School

"With the language they've already learned," Ken Goodman writes, "children bring to school their natural tendency to want to make sense of the world. . . . That's why learning language in the real world is easy, and learning language in school should be easy, but is often hard" (1986, 8).

We make language learning hard if we assume that it occurs primarily through direct instruction or the imitation of adult models—an assumption that permeates the skill-and-drill sequences of still popular grammar-based methodologies. The grammar-translation approach, for example, requires students to memorize and recite English words and idioms, verb conjugations, noun forms, and rules governing sentence structure. Similarly, the audiolingual or "hear-say" approach of many English as a Second Language (ESL) programs features scripted drills in which students mimic teacher cues, and students' responses are reinforced behaviorally by praise or correction. Both of these approaches divorce language from its communicative context, breaking it into isolated bits and pieces, and both vastly underestimate—and limit—children's potential.

When we look at how children actually use language, we see a much more creative, child-directed, and interactive process. Consider the following example, from the first-grade class described earlier, of an introduction to a story written by two Tohono O'odham first graders:*

It was SoweN The suN is ʃup
It was snowing. The sun is up.

So was up the hos
Snow was on top of the house.

The key was ʅuN on Gramu Bud
The kitty was laying on Grandma. But

Gamu greM ubot pacacs
Grandma dreamed about pancakes.

. . .

We can learn a great deal from these children's writing. First, we see here invention rather than mimicry; in "SoweN," "greM," and especially "ʃup" and "ʅuN," the students are creating new representations and symbols to express their ideas. Second, the ideas control this process. The surface *form* of children's English is subordinate to the communication of ideas. For the children, it is the ideas—the communications—that are important; the linguistic forms are but the means to express those ideas.

This is exactly how language develops outside the classroom. Seldom do children give primacy to the form of language in the process of acquisition. Instead, their concern is with communicating, and with responding to the communications of others (cf. Cummins 1985). Using a language to communicate is infinitely more interesting and creative than the repetition of drilled sequences stripped of context and intention. (Otherwise, a traveler to a foreign country could memorize a dictionary and a gram-

---

*Text in regular type was transcribed by McCarty exactly as written by the students. Text in italics was recorded by McCarty as the children read what they had written.

mar and get along splendidly—until the instant he or she must respond to an utterance not contained in the book.) As Veit nicely puts it, learning about grammar has about the same effect on the ability to use language "as learning about leg muscles has on the ability to run" (1986, 252).

Instead, children's language acquisition is a subconscious but actively constructive process. Children continuously intuit and try out the rules of the language around them; they acquire language by using language for its purposes at the moment (Smith 1988). Initially, their communications only approximate those of adults. But as they use language and others respond to those uses, children come "to mean and to express more in accordance with the adult system" (Lindfors 1985, 44). Throughout this process, children's interest in understanding and affecting the world around them motivates the progression toward adult grammar, and that progression, especially for young children, is rooted in and facilitated by the social contexts in which language is used.

The evolution of children's language is not haphazard, but follows a natural order or sequence that is in many respects similar across languages and cultures (Dulay, Burt, and Krashen 1982; Lindfors 1987). The sequence includes movement from primarily nonverbal to verbal expressions; from shorter and simpler constructions to longer, more complex ones; from regular to irregular or idiosyncratic cases; and from uses embedded in the immediate "here and now" to ones that are more abstract and context-reduced. Very early in this sequence children typically experience a period of delayed oral practice or silence. Far from a passive stage, this is a time when children are actively taking in and processing language input (Krashen 1982; Postovsky 1982). Eventually they are able to analyze, discuss, and write about language itself (Lindfors 1985; cf. Krashen 1982; Cummins 1989).

Stephen Krashen describes this process for oral language as "i + 1." In both their first and second language, children acquire language by making sense of input (i) that is comprehensible, containing structures that are meaningful but "a bit beyond" (+ 1) their current level of understanding. This natural, subconscious "picking up" of a language accounts for nearly all of a child's linguistic competence (Krashen 1981, 1985; Chamot 1981).

The same type of process underlies the development of literacy, in which oral and written language interact and overlap. The reciprocity of oral and written language is obvious in the writing of the Tohono O'odham first graders, as well as that of the Navajo high schoolers discussed at the beginning of this chapter. By talking about text in light of their experiences, children build relevant background, making input from new text more meaningful. By writing about what they discuss, they see that spoken language can be written, but they discover too, that the functions of written language far exceed the recording of speech (Goodman 1986). Through listening and reading, children add to their storehouse of knowledge, developing more sophisticated and effective cognitive strategies with which to interpret new spoken and written language (cf. Krashen 1984).

There is absolutely no reason, then, to "hold children back" from challenging second language literacy experiences simply because they are still developing their oral English proficiency. ESL learners can write in English even as they acquire it: "they can create their own meanings" (Hudelson 1989, 35; cf. Freeman and Freeman 1988; Moll and Diaz 1987). Further, children become proficient users of written language just as they become effective speakers: by making sense of written language input and using written language to communicate. To develop as readers and writers, children need rich and authentic opportunities to read and write (Hudelson 1989).

As the students in the Tohono O'odham and Navajo classrooms show, this involves more than purely linguistic or cognitive processes. Language acquisition is intrinsically social and collaborative as well. In natural situations outside the classroom, much of this collaboration occurs with caretakers, who use a "simplified register or code to get children to understand" (Krashen 1982, 21). In the first-grade class described here, the caretakers include the teachers, but more important, the children themselves. In cooperation with each other, the children make spoken and written English comprehensible. They are able to do much more together than any child can do alone.

This is the essence of Vygotsky's notion of the zone of proximal development—the difference between what children can do independently and their potential for learning as a result of collaboration with others (Cole et al. 1978). The Tohono O'odham students, especially, demonstrate the power of this concept as they construct oral and written text in their second language about something they have probably only experienced in books—snow. Together, they not only make "snow" and "snowing" comprehensible, they use their combined understandings to create something new.

The Tohono O'odham first graders, like the Navajo poetry writers, make these achievements not only because they are motivated by the task at hand but also because they are motivated by the broader social transactions that make them a group. What they are doing matters to them personally *and* socially. Every communication in the classroom—from the public celebrations of previous work, to the interests of teachers and school administrators, to the inherently rewarding social interactions among the students themselves—encourages them to use their growing sociality to make sense of the world.

The Native Language and English

"What's good for the first-language learner is good for the second," Judith Lindfors reminds us (1989, 43). Lindfors is referring to the very similar processes of development in the first and second language. To her remarks we can add that the best foundation for learning through a second language is the linguistic, cognitive, and social-affective knowledge acquired naturally through the first.

An overwhelming body of research supports this view, showing that subject matter teaching in the primary language, coupled with comprehensible input in English, expedites the acquisition of English and of academic content learned through English (Krashen and Biber 1988; Cummins 1989, 1990; Moll and Diaz 1987; Hakuta 1986; Tikunoff 1984; Crawford 1989; Watahomigie and Yamamoto 1987). This is because the native language and the intellectual capacities developed through it are *resources* that children can use to acquire new linguistic and intellectual content (Krashen and Biber 1988).

Language functions and forms developed in the primary language transfer readily to the second. Just as no teacher of French or Italian at the secondary or college level assumes that students must learn to speak or read all over again to learn French or Italian, there is no basis for assuming that American Indian students learning English as a second language are "starting from scratch." While the surface forms of the languages differ, a *common underlying proficiency* facilitates the transfer of both spoken and written language abilities from one language to another (Cummins 1984, 1985, 1989; Krashen and Biber 1988; Freeman and Freeman 1988). This same principle holds in the acquisition of new intellectual content: the understandings of subject matter developed in the first language reinforce and, indeed, accelerate the acquisition of content in English.

But beyond these cognitive relationships, there are equally important social and affective relationships between use of the native language and how well Indian students do in school. In the hypothetical foreign language class above, there is no question of the integrity of English. The necessity and prestige of English in our society are unparalleled, and English is reinforced by virtually every social institution children encounter, especially schools. Quite the reverse is true of American Indian languages, and schools, in fact, have attempted to eradicate these languages. Enabling Indian children to use their primary language to acquire new subject matter as well as English not only allows them to demonstrate what they know in a language they control, but validates their primary language as a tool for learning about themselves and the wider world. This can only enhance students' sense of self-worth and efficacy, while also enabling children to experience directly the powerful advantages of their bilingualism. In the meantime, of course, they are reinforcing their capacity to learn through English, as well as their English linguistic proficiency.

Some Practical Recommendations: Building Background Knowledge

Teachers can enhance their ability to build on American Indian students' cultural, linguistic, and personal resources by learning more about those resources. One obvious way to do this is to work in partnership with children's parents. This can involve home visits as well as parental visits to the classroom. An even more effective way to acquire this knowledge is for teachers, students, and parents to explore their community together, in a manner not unlike the way children naturally acquire knowledge of their language and community.

For example, collaborative research on such topics as local history, geography, flora, fauna, institutions, and people enable students and teachers to interact with community members about issues of mutual interest and relevance. By interviewing community members, discussing their findings with others, relating those findings to correlative materials in books, and then writing about their experiences and publishing the results, students have opportunities to develop their oral and written language abilities in both the native language and English, and to deepen their understandings of themselves and the local natural and social world while learning "new" academic content. Such study also provides a multitude of opportunities to bring parents and elders directly into the classroom as teachers. All of this enriches the shared experiences of teachers, students, and community members, increases the pool of knowledge to be tapped for future learning, and builds the general climate of support for education.

Doing such collaborative work also shows the teacher's respect for the local people, their language, their lives, and their histories. This presupposes some knowledge of those community resources. Even for teachers who are from the community, and especially for those who are not, this requires assuming the role of the student—learning something of the local language and culture. This effort is not minimal. But the benefits to Indian students and the positive relationships generated with the community amply reward the extra effort such collaborative work entails.

This firsthand knowledge of the local language and culture can be complemented by formal study. Most colleges and universities offer English linguistics courses, and often courses are available on specific tribal languages, either through local colleges and school districts or tribal education offices. Regardless of the teacher's language background, linguistic study of English and of the indigenous languages represented in the classroom is immensely valuable, providing a great deal of information about the languages and their phonemic, grammatical, semantic, and pragmatic structures, as well as knowledge of how languages in general are organized and can be described and analyzed. This develops a sense of language as an integrated, rule-governed system, while also affording insights into the linguistic knowledge American Indian children employ in the process of acquiring English.

For example, languages differ tremendously in terms of which grammatical features are marked morphemically with some type of affix (prefixes or suffixes). English marks nouns as plural or possessive (-*s*, -'*s*); verbs as singular, past tense, perfect, or progressive (-*s*, -*ed*, -*ed* or -*en*, -*ing*); and adjectives as comparative or superlative (-*er*, -*est*). English also contains other affixes that change the meaning of a word (*pre-*, *un-*, -*ive*, or -*ment*, for instance). American Indian languages, in general, handle verbs and nouns quite differently, so the distinctions marked in English are not at all natural or intuitive to Indian students learning English as a second language.

This can be seen in Crow, a Montana Indian language, which has one ending for singular verbs with singular subjects and another for plural verbs (Kates and Matthews 1980). English, on the other hand, marks singular verbs only in the present tense and for third-person verbs, as in *she walks, he sleeps, it looks rainy;* there are no separate singular/plural endings for any other tenses or persons. A teacher of Crow students could therefore expect them to omit the -*s* ending on other person-singular present-tense verbs in an unconscious effort to "regularize" the English forms. Crow also does not mark verbs for tense as English does, and Crow speakers frequently shift tense in writing English or omit the -*ed*, -*en*, or -*ing* endings.

Second language learners do not usually try to impose their first language's distinctions on the second language, adding markers where there are none, but they do omit or overgeneralize markers in the second language for which their first language lacks distinctions. These are areas where teachers can raise their own consciousness, as well as their students', about the structures of the native language and English.

The important point, however, concerns *how this linguistic knowledge is used,* for while linguistic analysis illuminates rules guiding children's language use, their language proficiency develops not through structured analysis of language, but by using language in context for meaningful communication. Linguistic study can supplement this, helping teachers and students better recognize and build upon the linguistic competence children bring to school. Such study also helps develop an objective, nonjudgmental and descriptive attitude toward all language varieties. This is as important for students as it is for teachers, not only in understanding differences in English usage ("standard" versus local or regional varieties), but in discerning and accepting those same variations in the native language as well. Teachers knowledgeable about the standards governing students' use of English and the native language can capitalize on language diversity within the classroom, using that diversity to enrich students' understandings of themselves, their language and culture, and to promote their proficiency in the native language and English.

Teachers can also benefit from comparative sociolinguistic study of language use in Indian communities. The ethnographer Susan Philips, for instance, identifies the structures for verbal participation and learning in the Warm Springs, Oregon, Indian community and contrasts these structures to those in the classroom (Philips 1972, 1983). Whereas learning in the Indian community emphasizes silent observation and supervised participation, Philips likens primary school teacher-student interaction to a "switchboard," with the teacher calling on individual students, forcing them to respond on demand in front of the class. Not surprisingly, the non-Indian teachers in Philips's study interpreted students' reluctance to respond under these conditions as shyness, boredom, or sullenness. And yet, Philips observes, the same students willingly cooperate in small groups where they direct the activities themselves. Hence, she says, "the differences in readiness to participate in interaction are related to the way in which the interaction is organized and controlled" (1972, 379; cf. Philips 1983; Moll and Diaz 1987).

Philips's study points out the vital importance of going beyond narrowly linguistic, structural analyses of English or the local language to a deeper understanding of the sociocultural context in which language is used inside and outside the classroom. This includes what is acceptable or appropriate language use; the contexts for silence and for speech; the patterning of verbal turn-taking, touching, smiling, and eye contact; and expectations for cooperation, competition, leadership, and the teacher's role itself. Teachers who reach out from the classroom into the community and take the emotional risks necessary to become, from time to time, students themselves, can learn from experience these local communicative structures. Nonetheless, published accounts such as Philips's can facilitate those understandings and provide comparative data to interpret these patterns in the classroom.

An Explorer Classroom

For any teacher, one of the most significant and challenging tasks is to create an environment in which each child can use what she or he already knows to learn more and to develop positive feelings about learning. Freeman and Freeman suggest that teachers of bilingual students begin by thinking of their students as "explorers who interact with their environment, their peers, and their teachers as they learn about the world" (1988, 4). In what these writers call an "explorer classroom," instruction "develops the potential of bilingual students rather than limiting it" (1988, 4).

What would an "explorer classroom" for American Indian students look like? First, in an explorer classroom, both students and teachers have acknowledged contributions to make to what is learned. No one comes with nothing; everyone comes to the classroom with personal, social, and cultural-linguistic resources from which others can benefit. Learning is thus collaborative and interactive; the teacher's role, as Jim Cummins points out in chapter one, is not to transmit a predetermined body of knowledge, but to ensure that the learning environment supports students in giving meaning to their experiences and in communicating those meanings to others.

The teacher of Navajo high school students mentioned earlier did this by establishing a classroom climate of choice, authenticity, and trust. Students selected the themes to be explored, analyzing other writers' expressions of those themes in light of their own interpretations and experiences. Because students chose how to approach their work, not all were engaged in the same activity at once. This is very much the pattern of work in the world outside the classroom. In this classroom, action and communication had real-life purposes, and the utility of individual effort extended well beyond the task at hand.

The teacher in an explorer classroom is also a learner, taking many of the same risks students are asked to take. The high school teacher, for example, wrote and shared her own poetry about an intensely personal subject. In doing this, she communicated her acceptance of students and their work, and showed that what they did, she valued enough to do herself. Through their mutual interrelationships, the students and teacher supported each other in the risk-taking that leads to purposeful, creative language use and intellectual activity.

Explorer classrooms, then, are learning communities where those who are more capable at some things help others to succeed (cf. Smith 1988). The Tohono O'odham first-graders were helped

by their teacher and an older child, but also by each other. Their
varying backgrounds and abilities in O'odham and English, and
their teacher's bilingualism, became the foundation for strength-
ening each child's language abilities and thus his or her resources
for acquiring new academic content.

An explorer classroom is communication-based, providing
what language learners need most: sufficient comprehensible input in a socially supportive, low-anxiety environment. The teachers of Navajo and O'odham students, in the way they organized
classroom activities, ensured that students had enough understandable second-language input to make the activities meaningful *and* challenging; as students used English to communicate,
they acquired new English structures and forms. Because their
focus was on communication, students all learned from the activities, regardless of their level of English fluency. The teachers
assisted this by using a wide variety of teaching strategies (including paired reading and writing, cooperative research, and
multimedia learning centers) and by enriching spoken and written
language with pictures, other visual aids, models, and actions.
All of this afforded a great deal of contextual information, enabling students to use cues within the immediate environment and
their prior knowledge to acquire new content and new language
skills.

Explorer classrooms, like these classrooms, ground language
learning in rich, multifaceted academic content. Mohan (1986)
emphasizes the importance of this, particularly in ESL settings,
giving as an example an elementary ESL teacher who used co-
coons, photographs, charts, films, and student-drawn pictures in
a unit on insects (cf. Goodman 1986; Chamot and O'Malley
1986). The teacher did not claim to be an expert on the topic, but
like the two teachers described here, served as a guide for helping
students answer questions on their own. Rather than building
lessons around isolated grammar points, these teachers all concentrated on meaningful and interesting content, taking advantage
of that content and the nature of the activities to foster language
learning. In doing so, they also ensured that language inside the
classroom developed as it does outside of school: hand in hand
with children's intellect and with their growing social skills as
they learn about the world.

Organizing Classroom Explorations

These teachers' practices and the concept of explorer classrooms are not restricted to American Indians; all students and teachers can benefit from the basic approaches described here. Especially noteworthy about these teachers and their classrooms, however, are the specific ways they tapped into and made use of the uniquely Indian resources of their students and communities. The teachers did this by focusing classroom inquiry not on textbooks or basal readers "standardized" for the general population, but on interests and themes generated by the students themselves. Themes explored in the Navajo high school class, for instance, included love, fear, fantasy, success, heroes, and heroines. The Tohono O'odham first graders investigated themes relevant to but extending beyond their desert community: desert plants and animals, shelter, water, local village life, and the concept of community itself. Themes such as these become the connectors between disciplines and content areas, enabling students to explore new content using multiple literatures and research strategies and, most important, their own prior knowledge and experience. All of this creates a natural context for collaboration both within the classroom and among students, teachers, and resource people outside the classroom.

In illustration of these points, consider a thematic unit on cultural change undertaken by a class of Navajo eighth graders. The initial focus of this unit was Scott O'Dell's classic novel *Sing Down the Moon* (1970), which tells the story of Bright Morning, a young Navajo girl growing up at the peak of Navajo-white conflict. Captured by Kit Carson's troops and forced with thousands of Navajos on the Long Walk to Fort Sumner, New Mexico, Bright Morning sees her world of family, friends, and livestock disintegrate. She survives the brutality and deprivation of Fort Sumner, finally returning home. There, her home, fields, and livestock destroyed, Bright Morning begins to rebuild her life.

Because it describes an adolescent's passage into adulthood and her triumph over danger and despair, Bright Morning's story conveys universal themes with which all children can identify. Her experiences have direct relevance to American Indian students who, through her story, can critically examine their own personal and social histories and relate these to broader social and historical events. In this eighth-grade class, students first read the novel in small groups, coming together with the teacher to discuss the text in depth (cf. Short and Pierce 1990). Each group decided upon other readings and projects to extend their literature study. One group, for example, used locally produced texts as well as current newspapers and magazines to compare the causes and consequences of the Navajo conquest with colonial experiences elsewhere in the world and to critically analyze, discuss, and write about existing cases of political and economic subordination. Another group used biographical and autobiographical accounts—including their own, those collected from community members, and the published accounts of Navajo people—to create an anthology of Long Walk experiences (cf. Johnson 1975). Still other students interviewed community members and tribal government representatives about Navajo history, using these sources and locally produced materials to rewrite textbook versions of Indian-white relations. Throughout these projects students studied and created topographical and political maps, made murals on people and events in Navajo and U.S. history, and related Navajo geography and history to the development of the United States. The bilingual publications resulting from students' investigations became a permanent resource for future research in this and other classrooms at the school.

The possibilities are endless for extending such a unit and for integrating it with a diverse range of disciplines and intellectual activities. What is important here is how the potential for learning and language development expanded by grounding those processes in students' language and literacy interests and in their resources—not in what was unfamiliar. Instead of the "repeat-after-me" and "fill-in-the-blank" exercises of grammar-based drills, work in this class revolved around communication for purposes with real meaning to students, and this served as a springboard for probing new ideas in the realms of geography, history, and literature. Instead of depending on a textbook to organize their learning, these students developed their own research strategies to analyze critically and rewrite textbook versions of Indian history and Indian-white relations. By opening investigation to the world outside the classroom, teachers, students, and community members learned together, deepening their understandings of the local language and culture, relating those understandings to the wider world, and sharing in the educational enterprise. This type of study, in short, had all the qualities of an explorer classroom and of natural learning and language development in contexts outside of school.

Creating Positive Change

Explorer classroom environments are the antithesis of what schooling historically has been and continues to be for many American Indian students. The reasons for this stem ultimately from the sociohistorical relationship between indigenous communities and the larger society, and the attendant lack of local and tribal control over education entailed by that relationship (McCarty 1989; Reyhner and Eder 1989; Cummins 1989, 1990; Ogbu 1987; chapter 3 of this volume). Recent tribal initiatives toward local control have altered these disempowering social-structural relationships, yet their long-term consequences have been school failure and the social and educational disenfranchisement of Indian students and their communities.

Reversing historical patterns such as these requires far more than changing pedagogy, and many of the necessary bureaucratic and institutional changes are outside the control of individual educators. Educators are, nonetheless, highly significant participants within the educational system who have the power to change that system. This can begin when teachers and administrators work collaboratively, much as in the classrooms described here, to base pedagogy on the strengths that Indian children bring to school. By becoming cognizant of and utilizing those strengths, educators can transform their own roles within the system and, in so doing, transform the school and life opportunities of their American Indian students.

9

Oral Language Development

EDWINA HOFFMAN

Many Indian students still speak their native language, while many others who no longer use their tribal language do not speak standard English. A growing body of studies document the variation between "Indian English" and standard English, the English that determines success in school (Leap 1978; see also chapter 10). Since these students are taught from the time they enter the educational system using materials based on standard American academic English, there is clearly a disparity between the language many Indian children speak socially and the language they are expected to control in the academic environment. The teaching techniques described in this chapter can be utilized with both students who speak nonstandard varieties of English or who come to school speaking only their tribal language, and they all conform to a greater or lesser degree to the experiential-interactive instructional model recommended by Jim Cummins in chapter 1 of this volume.

Multisensory Approaches to Language Instruction

With very young children as well as older learners, it helps to use a multisensory approach to language teaching. The more "input" channels that are accessed, the more likely it is that children will retain the language information being shared. The different sensory channels provide alternative memory anchors on which children can fix vocabulary and syntax. Multisensory activities require more planning and more collection of materials and realia (real objects) on the part of the teacher than do standard textbook-based instructional approaches, but the motivation and memory advantages of these activities justify the extra effort. Crayons, clay, cooking or building activities, action songs, puppetry, and drama enhance students' total physical and mental involvement in the language-learning process. The current emphasis on James Asher's (1986) "total physical response" (TPR) method is consistent with the multisensory approaches found successful with second-language learners. Children respond naturally to the energy levels required of such active instructional/ learning models. Any adaptations of this approach that incorporate local Indian culture and environment enhance student interest even more.

Teachers need to develop a collection of language games, realia (real world objects), and hands-on learning activities that they can use in their classroom to teach language. Excellent examples of classroom activities can be found in Cohen and Cohen's *Games and Activities for Teaching English as a Second Language* (1982) and Christopher Sion's *Recipes for Tired Teachers* (1985). Teachers can identify other resources and avail themselves of the books that match their students' ages, interest levels, and cultural needs.

In collecting realia or play facsimiles, teachers may want to categorize the objects and store them in colorfully decorated shoe boxes for use during related lessons. It should be recognized that any hands-on activities, whether cooking, clay, or finger painting, have a built-in potential for pandemonium; any organizational strategies that reduce the chaos will enhance learning. Teachers should plan accordingly, keeping in mind that the objects they collect will serve as memory anchors, to which the children can attach the meaning of such words as measuring cup, spoon, stove, or comb. The effectiveness of having realia handy can be illustrated by the example of a teacher trying to explain the word "fuzzy" in comparison to having something at hand for students to handle and pass around as they anchor in their memory the meaning of the word "fuzzy."

Where storage space is an issue, one very successful idea tried on the Navajo Reservation is to develop a picture file. In this case, the teacher collected over a period time relevant pictures related to her secondary-level social studies program. When she had to explain certain events or concepts, she relied on her picture file to enliven the discussion. As in the collection of realia, the compilation of the picture file would be an on-going, never-ending project, with the children possibly contributing by bringing pictures from home. Teachers can identify topics and objects they need pictures of and give extra credit to students who contribute appropriate pictures.

Using Storytelling to Teach English

Children worldwide respond to storytelling. American Indian children are no less enthusiastic in their enjoyment of narrative tales. Storytelling is quite consistent with Indian oral traditions. For centuries Indian elders have woven history, culture, and ethics into compelling tales.

Teachers exposing Indian children to forms of standard English should tell stories or read extensively to the youngsters using picture books with clear, relevant illustrations. These illustrations can serve as referents for new vocabulary and help the teacher to teach words and concepts in context. Teachers who read to their students might limit in the beginning the selection of stories to a few favorite titles that would be read and reread. By keeping the content focus narrow, the teacher creates an atmosphere of familiarity that promotes confidence in the student through repetition. It also shortens the so-called "silent period," when speakers of a new language are reluctant to try an unfamiliar tongue. As children become familiar with the repeated stories and their patterns, they join in by completing lines of the tale or responding to questions related to the text. Teachers can quickly identify favorite stories appropriate to their students' age group. Stories related to the students' tribe, other tribes, or the local community are usually of high interest. If time is short, teachers can tape record the books or stories during the storytelling activity and make the recordings available through a listening center so youngsters can listen to them again and again. By using a bell or traditional tribal instrument such as a drum, the teacher can signal on the recordings when the child should turn the pages.

The students develop through this activity a heightened awareness of the sounds, rhythms, and patterns of English as well as a comfort with picking up books as a means of relaxation or entertainment. Story-reading as opposed to storytelling serves to emphasize the non-Indian's stress on print as a means of preserving information and culture as well as extending the self. Teachers can weave traditional storytelling with story-reading to tap and enhance both cultural skills.

As with the storytelling and story-reading activities, which encourage reading for pleasure, teachers should collect comics for older students to pick up and enjoy during leisure periods (as described in chapter 13 of this volume). Particularly helpful to students who are "reluctant readers" are comics that come with tape cassettes or records. Those with narrative and dialogue that match the pictures allow students to hear the sounds of English while they read along. In teaching with such materials, I often loan students the comics without the recording to encourage interaction with the printed portions of the text. When students are familiar with a story line, a teacher could even white-out the words in the speech balloons and let students develop their own dialogue, which would then involve writing in English. Intermediate and advanced students might enjoy doing this with totally unfamiliar cartoon strips or narrative comic books.

Since many young people do not read much for pleasure, it is important to encourage any meaningful interplay with written English. This builds the students' knowledge of polysyllabic words, which occur more frequently in print than in speech. In analyzing the text in many comic books I was surprised by their sophisticated vocabulary. The syntax is not that complex, but many words are at the fifth-, sixth-, or seventh-grade reading level. Most people develop their command of a polysyllabic, academic vocabulary through reading. Often it takes multiple contextual readings of a given word to "own" it—to incorporate it into the reader's vocabulary. Comics with recordings provide an ideal integration of speech, print, and referent to enhance the acquisition of new words. The recording provides the correct pronunciation, the print a reading opportunity, and the cartoon illustrations a referent for the vocabulary word's meaning. Stephen Krashen, after carefully researching the effects of comic book reading on student's reading skills and habits, concluded that comics at worst have no effect and under the best of circumstances enhance reading skills and the love of reading (Krashen in press). A variation on the use of comics would be to use teen or other magazines in conjunction with language development activities. Scholastic publishes several such magazines for various age levels that focus on topics of interest to contemporary youth. Both old and current issues of *National Geographic* are also popular with students.

Laughing It Up Together

Rhymes, limericks, tongue twisters, and jokes provide opportunities for children to refine their production of difficult or new sounds in a fun way. Sensitive teachers would have already apprised themselves of the new or problematic English sounds for the students through contrastive analysis information available on the child's native language, whether it be a tribal language or an Indian English ("Rez") dialect. By concentrating on familiar sounds in new word positions, the teacher slowly progresses through the activities to entirely new articulatory combinations in all three word positions—initial, final, and medial (for example *sh*are, pu*sh*, then wa*sh*ing). Personal experience indicates that it is easiest to teach a new sound when it occurs in initial position. The second most difficult position is final, followed by medial. Small pocket mirrors for students to compare the positions of their mouths as they produce the sound, or cupping one's ears and pulling them forward as the new sound is being produced, helps in the isolation of the production of these unfamiliar sounds.

In my classes I have students first produce sounds in rhymes. Then we play a game in which the children draw a slip of paper and read the tongue twister written on it to the group. (I store the strips in a small woven Miccosukee Indian basket.) Students are told to work in pairs and memorize the tongue twisters, and then they come back to the larger group and say them correctly. Variations on the tongue twister games are equally enjoyed. They include timed activities in which speed and accuracy of pronunciation count.

Another enjoyable repetition activity involves telling "knock knock" jokes using the same format of drawing a slip of paper to read to the group. The pattern is predictable, except for the punch line ("Knock knock! . . . Who's there? . . . Dewey. . . . Dewey who? . . . Dewey have to listen to all this knocking?"). Intermediate students respond better to the double meaning in the punch lines. Using humor with children helps to lower the anxiety levels often associated with learning a new language or operating in an unfamiliar environment, in this case, school. Lowering the "affective filter" through humor improves the learning atmosphere (Krashen 1983).

Games

Along with the love of humor that characterizes many Indian communities is a distinct enjoyment of all types of games and competition—particularly those involving physical prowess. Where teachers can set up teams to demonstrate mastery of multiplication tables or spelling words through a game (particularly a game involving physical activity), the children will often respond with enthusiasm to an otherwise onerous memorization task.

Hot Potato. A game that helped my students learn third-person singular pronouns for males and females is called Hot Potato. Many Indian languages do not mark third-person singular pronouns with a separate category for males and females. In the southeastern part of the United States, this often means that Indians will interchange "he" and "she," much to the chagrin of both speaker and listener. The game of Hot Potato calls for the students to sit around a smooth-topped, preferably round, table. The object of the game is to quickly slide a bean bag to another student while saying "I pass it to him" or "I pass it to her." The bean bag is considered the "hot potato," so students have to get rid of it quickly. I like to tell the children to release the "hot potato" right away so that it will not "burn" their fingers. The speed of the game requires the students to think quickly of the appropriate pronoun. When a student incorrectly uses a pronoun by passing the bean bag to a girl while saying "I pass it to him," play halts and a point is placed on the chalkboard next to the errant speaker's name. The student with the least points at the end of the game is the winner. To speed up the game, the phrase said while passing the bean bag can be changed to "It's his" or "It's hers." Another variation would be to say "She's a girl" or "He's a boy" as the bean bag is passed. Of course, the object of games like this is learning, not winning, with a side benefit of some fun. Placing too much emphasis on winning will create a high-anxiety environment that will impede learning.

Other games.   There are many high-interest board games and card games involving speaking patterns. Teachers should develop game centers to encourage such play. Some games that elicit spoken English include the card game Go Fish, the board game Sea of Vowels, and any Twenty-Questions-type oral game. The rhymes recited while jumping rope or playing jacks are also fun ways for children to practice the new sounds of English. For older children, board games such as Monopoly and Careers both entertain and provide learning experiences for students.

Music

Students, both young and old, respond to learning English through music. Since in most songs the singer holds the notes on the vowels, songs help the listener hear the distinct quality of the vowels. This is important because vowels are exceptionally difficult to master in English. Many Indian languages contain fewer vowel sounds than the English language. Frequently the native vowel sounds do not have precisely the same quality as the English versions. Even native speakers of English have difficulty learning to read aloud English vowels. Imagine the difficulties for American Indians unfamiliar with even the production of the new sounds!

Through music, teachers can sensitize the students to vowel sounds through the natural hyperaccentuation of holding the notes. I developed a series of dictation activities based on pop music and pop culture for my secondary students. Although the intention was to develop "ear training" activities for the patterns of English, it also helped students to "chunk" the language into meaningful units and was an excellent vehicle for teaching vocabulary within context. Noting the appeal of the music activities for the secondary students, I next used pop posters culled from teen magazines to teach descriptions and to develop language-experience-type reading activities. With the pervasiveness of video cassette recorders (VCRs) in many Indian communities, videos can be used for language learning as well. Teachers may have students view and discuss videotapes or record their own performances.

Active Teaching Strategies for the Content Areas

Content-area instruction is clearly the "meat" of school work. Unlike the high-interest, fun activities discussed previously which lower the affective filter, content-area work is the essence and purpose of school. To enhance the language development of the students, teachers should rely more on the use of visuals, hands-on activities, demonstrations, realia, and conscious repetition in a meaningful context of new vocabulary and syntax. "Active teaching" is a perfect label for such interactive multisensory content instruction.

My version of active teaching involves the following steps:

1. Introduce the subject through a "grabber": A "grabber" is some personally related anecdote or question that pulls the students' experiences into the discussion of the topic. An example would be to start a lesson on dental health by asking, "Has anyone ever had a toothache?" The teacher provides the students with an opportunity to share personal experiences with having a toothache. As children volunteer to describe their experiences, the teacher consciously weaves in the specific vocabulary related to the health unit by repeating information: "So you could feel the hole in your tooth, you could feel the cavity in your tooth." Discussion is the key to the aural/oral introduction of vocabulary.

2. Use visuals to relate information: The prepared teacher has a wall chart or plastic model handy to describe to the students the parts of a tooth and why a toothache hurts.

3. Have students do a drawing (homework or seatwork assignment): The instructor can then ask students to trace or draw a picture identifying the parts of the tooth.

4. Involve students through an experiment or demonstration: The teacher may also want to initiate an experiment to illustrate the result of tooth decay. A tooth dropped in a glass of cola will disappear after several days, much to the amazement of the students.

5. Highlight key information in the text: Prior to making a textbook assignment, the teacher should, using a marker, highlight critical information for slow readers or limited English speakers. The children are free to read all the information if they are proficient readers, but if

they are not good readers, they know where to focus their efforts. The highlighted material signals what is important.

6. Assign a workbook activity: Teachers should screen items, highlight those items within a students linguistic competency, and keep such assignments to a minimum.

7. Evaluate students: Teachers may need to be creative in their evaluation of students. Paper and pencil tests invariably test knowledge of the English language as well as knowledge of the content area being studied. If a student is not yet particularly proficient in academic English, teachers should find creative evaluation strategies, such as projects, dioramas, or oral interviews, to evaluate student understanding.

8. Reteach: If key points have not been mastered, the teacher should reteach using different or modified strategies.

Content-area teachers should at all times stress multisensory approaches and avoid such nonteaching activities as assignments on the chalkboard to "Read pp. 39–45 and do the questions at the end of the chapter." The "explorer classroom" discussed in the previous chapter and activities suggested in the content-areas chapters of this book all enrich the American Indian classroom. For limited-English-proficient students it is important that material be previewed and introduced with as much care and attention to vocabulary and language development as is given to the content-area objectives, because as much academically related language development may be going on as there is mastery of specific content objectives. Vocabulary should be introduced using realia, visuals, or demonstrations. It should be repeated and reinforced contextually, and any evaluation or testing should be designed at the students' level of language competence. In so testing, teachers reduce the interference of limited language proficiency as a factor in the testing of content objectives.

Within the content areas, teachers should organize their classes to encourage cooperative learning. Most traditional Indian societies are characterized by a high degree of cooperation. Children raised in such environments respond enthusiastically to problem-solving through small group activities. Teachers can develop a series of problems or questions for students to resolve. Even projects such as making a diorama involve language and hands-on efforts to perform a task. Initially teachers may have to develop a reward system to keep youngsters on task, but once the students become accustomed to the independent small group activity, they usually prefer it. For teachers, there is an obvious positive effect in having more youngsters use academic English in communicative contexts related to the content. Students practice content vocabulary as they discuss concepts in personally meaningful ways.

Discipline Strategy for Peer Activities

Teachers tempted to use peer-tutoring or other peer-related cooperative activities to enhance classroom management are often concerned about misbehavior and the use of non-English languages during the cooperative activity. Teachers can incorporate a *temporary* reward system in order to condition children to the responsibilities of any new instructional management activities. There will be situations, particularly when students are working with difficult content-area material, where peers might appropriately use their home language to give an explanation. But in paired pattern practice games or problem-solving activities, teachers would probably prefer the use of English and as little tomfoolery as possible. Students can be told that you want them to speak only in English in order to practice their "school English." The key is to set up a nonthreatening reward system that stimulates students to follow the rules.

Several variations of the following ideas are possible. Create an attractive bulletin board where pockets or envelopes represent groups that will be working together. Depending on the children's ages and the bulletin board might depict a large fish tank where the envelopes represent the sharks, the manta rays, the barracudas, the dolphins, and so forth. The board can be designed to show rodeo riders, NFL teams, Indian tribes, rock stars, cartoon characters, popular race cars, or circus animals. Protruding from each envelope are the rewards—play money, smaller fish, make-believe game tickets, pennants, and balloons for example. At the beginning of the activity, the teacher explains that each group has already earned ten balloons, ten pennants—whatever token suits the group. The students are forewarned that if there is misconduct or excessive use of the home language during the activity, they will lose one item—a fish for horse-play or a pennant for using the non-English language. Since the groups already have these coveted objects, group members will work at maintaining the rules in order to keep the objects. Teachers will find it is easier to catch misbehavior than to reward good behavior. The play money, fish, balloons, and so forth that are earned at the end of the activity can be used later to buy privileges (no homework over the weekend, extra time for art or crafts, and so forth) or school supplies such as pencils or erasers.

Teachers not attracted by this strategy are encouraged nevertheless to develop a reward system appropriate for their students. Some teachers use stickers to reward positive behavior; others, a noisy gong—à la "The Gong Show"—to catch naughtiness or broken rules. Depending on a teacher's philosophy on rewards, the activity should be tailored to both teacher and student comfort. For example, I do not favor rewards of candy, but I do like the envelopes/take-away strategy. Suffice to say that temporary introduction of a reward system serves to condition youngsters to the new behavior.

In concluding this discussion on language development for Indian children, I would reiterate the importance of using students' existing learning strategies. The strategies we have suggested tap into some of the shared characteristics of traditional groups, such as cooperative learning and visual and auditory learning styles (see chapter 5 for a more complete discussion of this topic). Whether a teacher's task is to teach English or to add standard English to the child's Indian English dialect, experiential-interactive instructional strategies such as those discussed in this chapter are humane and pedagogically sound means for achieving that goal.

10

American Indian English

WILLIAM L. LEAP

English is the language of instruction in American education, and teachers and teacher aides who want to increase educational opportunities for American Indian students must do all they can to strengthen these students' spoken and written English skills. To meet this goal, language arts instruction must take into account the knowledge of English that Indian students bring into the classroom, as well as their use of that knowledge in classroom settings. Otherwise, their instruction, for reasons discussed in this chapter, will create even more language problems for Indian students.

Understanding what Indian students already know about English is a relatively recent development in American Indian education. Policymakers have been aware for some time that classroom English is a "problem" for many Indian students. Mindful of this concern, some educators constructed lists of particular problem areas for teachers to use in creating lesson plans and setting goals. These areas have included deletion of the past-tense (or "D") marker, confusion of "mass" and "count" nouns, weakening of articulation for stops and spirant sounds when they occur as the last sound in the work, and high frequencies of double and multiple negation. Table 10.1 provides such a list prepared for use on the Northern Ute Reservation in northeastern Utah.

Persons familiar with the teaching of English to speakers of other languages are familiar with this type of list. However, persons familiar with American Indian languages reach different conclusions. The problem areas associated with a particular Indian community's English often show striking parallels to critical features of the community's ancestral or tribal language. For ex-

TABLE 10.1
Sample Characteristics of Indian English
from the Northern Ute Reservation

Syntactic Features

1. Devoiced (or "whispered") vowels in middle and final word position.

2. Devoiced consonants in word final position; *no* evidence of reduction or deletion of consonant pronunciation in that position.

3. Reworking of syllable structures into a C-V-C-V sequence.

4. Tense marked only once per clause (e.g., on the helping verb *or* the main verb but not on both elements).

5. References to unreal, contrary-to-fact conditions by violating the restrictions in item 4 (e.g., tense marking on helping verb and main verb constructions).

6. Right-to-left arrangement within sentence-level constructions (e.g., the pronouns precede rather than follow their antecedents).

Discourse Features

1. Information processed from a written text in terms of the meanings of whole sentences, not single words or phrases.

2. Narrative structured around the elaboration of discrete themes, not through sequences of themes.

3. Subjective, personalized assessment assigned higher value than objective, detached commentary.

4. Opinions linked to explanations for stated position; opinions never offered in isolated statements.

5. Responses consistent with the terms set by the task, though not always restricted to those terms.

ample, when the details of D-deletion are examined in specific community contexts, absence of past-tense marking in Indian English sentences and paragraphs frequently coincide with instances where the community's ancestral language does not use verbal suffixes to indicate past-tense reference or uses contrasts other than present versus past to indicate the tense of verbal action. Similarly, inconsistent subject-verb agreement, explored more carefully on a community-by-community basis, suggests the presence of noun-verb relationships entirely different from those marked by distinctions of singular or plural number. Further research shows that reference contrasts, idiomatic expressions, metaphors, assumptions about cause and effect, and other features influencing the "logical form" of sentences and paragraphs are other areas where community English and ancestral language tradition can coincide.

Researchers find that different Indian communities show different types of parallels between English and ancestral language tradition, suggesting that just as there are many different American Indian languages and language families, there are many different varieties of American Indian English. The features characteristic of the Indian English used in one community setting are not necessarily going to predict the features characteristic of Indian English used in another setting. These discoveries have important historical implications, suggesting that the conditions that created these codes were different. English has a long-standing time depth among the tribes of the southeastern United States, for example, while in the Southwest, English was introduced relatively recently, building on a tradition of community-focused Spanish and ancestral language fluency that older members of these communities still retain.

One factor helping to shape Indian English traditions in many tribal speech communities was the boarding schools. English language development was a central theme in the educational agenda of these schools, and every effort was made to shift Indian student language fluency from ancestral language to English at these schools. Indian students reacted to this requirement in various ways, and the learning of English became a key element in Indian students' resistance to this pressure as well as in their accommodation to it. Boarding school students returned home as speakers and usually writers of English, creating a distinctive shift in the language profile of their home communities. Creation of on-reservation Bureau of Indian Affairs (BIA) and mission day schools and public schools to educate the next generation of Indian students continued this trend as did adults serving in the armed forces during the first and second world wars. In addition, the movement, sometimes voluntary and sometimes forced, from the reservation into the cities and the effect in recent years of television, portable cassette players, and video cassette recorders has furthered the process of language shift.

It is difficult to account for the parallels between community-based English and ancestral language fluencies in any of these settings merely as instances of linguistic interference—that is, a carryover of elements from one linguistic tradition into another, usually explained as a failure on the speaker's part to maintain these languages as separate and distinct linguistic systems. For many Indian communities, there probably was a period when speakers constructed a foundation for English proficiency by integrating newly acquired English skills into the grammars of the languages—Indian or otherwise—that they already spoke. However, because of the shift in community language profiles described above, today's speakers of Indian English varieties are not necessarily proficient in their community's ancestral language or languages. In fact, in an increasing number of instances, Indian English is the only "Indian-related" language spoken in these settings.

Whatever the connection between English and ancestral language fluency, we can understand why community members might want to retain control over a nonstandard, community-based English code, and why they might be reluctant for fluency in standard English to replace such language knowledge. Indian English, in each of its many occurrences, is closely tied to the "package" of historical, political, and psychological experiences that define tribal and community identity in contemporary American society. Fluency in these codes offers speakers a powerful means of representing and renewing these themes in *every* facet of daily experience. The classroom, as we will see in the following section, is no exception to this rule.

The Effects of Classroom Experience

What happens when speakers of Indian English bring their knowledge and skills in these varieties of English into the classroom? Is Indian English an asset to students' educational experiences, or does familiarity with these codes inhibit children's chances for school success?

To answer these questions, let us look briefly at several of the parallels between Indian English proficiency and Indian student academic performance that have emerged from a ten-year (1979–89) study of Indian English varieties used on the Northern Ute Reservation. My work at Northern Ute was sponsored and supervised by the Tribal Department of Education, the Title VII–funded *Wykoopah* bilingual program in the on-reservation public elementary schools, and by the tribally based, community-focused English and Ute language literacy project (Leap 1990, 1991). My work in the public school setting began with the construction of an inventory of significant features of the English variety spoken by Ute students. Table 10.1 shows a modified version of this inventory. To explore the educational significance of Northern Ute English, I conducted a series of detailed classroom and playground observations, seeing how Ute students interacted with other Ute students, non-Indian classmates, teachers, teacher aides, and the mostly non-Indian school staff.

In addition, I interviewed individual Ute students and held discussions with small groups of Ute students. Some of these were free-flowing exchanges; others explored student responses to particular school-related tasks. I also interviewed non-Indian students, which provided invaluable data for contrastive analysis. .

Several of the tasks included in these discussions were reading related. In one case, I selected a chapter from an English language storybook written slightly above the reading level of the student participants. I asked each student to read the passage silently, then to read it out loud. Afterward I asked students to respond to some content-centered questions about the passage they had just read. Here is a section from one of the stories, the question I asked about that section, and the discussions with five Ute fourth graders that this question prompted:

TEXT: Slim had been asleep when Rowdy frightened him—sound asleep. But he did not look as if he were asleep. His eyes were wide open. This did not seem strange to Slim. He had never closed his eyes in his whole life. He couldn't, because snakes have no eyelids. Slim's eyes stayed wide open all the time much like a Teddy Bear's glass eyes. (Harris and Harris 1960, 5)

DISCUSSIONS (*Students are answering the question, "If you looked at Slim Green, could you tell if he was sleeping?"*):

Student 1
    S: He never close his eyes.
    R: How come?
    S: Cause other things might get him.

Student 2
    S: His eyes were wide open.
    R: How come?
    S: Maybe he couldn't sleep.

Student 3
> S: Yeah because I could see his eyes.
> R: What about his eyes?
> S: They are green.

Student 4
> S: Yeah he was wide awake.
> R: How come?
> S: Cause snakes never sleep.

Student 5
> S: Because he looks like, to me it always looks like they are dead when I see snakes.
> R: How come they look like they are dead?
> S: Cause they lay all still.
> R: What about if you looked at his eyes, could you tell if he was sleeping by looking at his eyes?
> S: (*shakes head*)
> R: No? How come?
> S: Because it looks like he is awake and, um, he is, um . . .
> R: He looks like he is awake? Is there something about him that looks like he is awake?
> S: He has his eyes open.
> R: Yeah, and how come he has his eyes open?
> S: Cause he don't got no eyelids.

It is clear, from the transcripts, that these students were willing to answer direct questions about the passage that they had just read. There are no instances in my sample of the stereotyped "silent Indian student," reluctant to engage in academic-related discourse within a formal interview setting. Granted, I began these interviews only after being "in residence" at the school for an extended period of time, so I was in no sense a stranger to the students with whom I was talking. Still, not all familiar non-Indian faces elicit verbal cooperation from non-Indian students, especially in unfamiliar academic settings. Something else was working in my favor here: the Ute English correlate of the procedures governing question-asking in Ute language settings. Briefly described, question-asking is restricted to settings where the speaker is confident in the listener's ability to provide an answer; otherwise, asking a question could embarrass and insult the listener, something that no Ute speaker wishes to do under normal social circumstances. Ute listeners are also constrained by Ute question-asking rules. Being asked a question carries with it the speaker's implicit "vote of confidence" (in the sense just described), but that, in turn, makes a response to the question virtually unavoidable. To do otherwise becomes a violation of the speaker's "faith" in the listener's abilities, and that could embarrass and insult the speaker, something that no Ute listener wishes to do. In terms of the present discussion, by asking the student a question about Slim Green's appearance, I signaled my belief that the student should be able to answer it. The student, being asked the question, was now obligated under Ute cultural rule to respond.

There is an additional Ute language-related obligation that comes into play at this point in the interchange. Ute language tradition places a high value on *individualized* response-making. A good speaker of Ute is expected to leave a personalized signature on any response made. The grammar of the Ute language accommodates this principle in many ways. It allows flexible word order in sentences (while certain sequences may be favored under certain circumstances, subject, object, and verb forms can generally be positioned in any combination), variable placements of tense and aspect markers (for some speakers, tense suffices may occur at any point within the sentence, regardless of the syntactic function of the headword), and multiple combinations of smaller sentences within more inclusive constructions. It encourages transmission of meaning from speaker to listener by means of imagery, inference, and individualized references rather than through precise identification of topic or themes. And it encourages individual speakers of Ute to create their own combinations of sentence form and meaning guided by these constraints, in order to further the personalized quality of their comments.

The interview passages presented above contain ample evidence of personalized commentary, even though English rather than Ute was the channel through which students expressed these goals. Notice that even though all of the responses are grounded, in some way, in the information presented in the reading passage, each of the respondents presents an individual interpretation of story content, all of which depart from the given story line in creative, and often quite unpredictable, ways.

Someone who is not familiar with the rules of Ute English can easily misunderstand this dimension of these students' statements. Examined at face value, they suggest that the students who made them are not able to discuss with accuracy the information they glean from their reading, or are simply unable to understand what they read. However, readers familiar with Ute language rules of discourse and the ways in which speakers of Ute English use those rules when asking and replying to questions will see the connections between the students' replies and a Ute English-based "knowledge of language." These knowledgeable readers will have no problem understanding the students' answers.

Practical Solutions

If fluency in an Indian language–related variety of English can have such effects on the educational experience of American Indian students, even in this one area, then Indian English needs have to be taken into account by *all* areas of the school curriculum. In order to meet this goal educators must be willing to revise considerably their instructional materials, classroom practice, testing procedures, and evaluation activities. Given how frequently Indian students change schools during their academic careers, educators must be willing to coordinate these efforts across grade levels and school district boundaries. These are formidable tasks; and in these times of shrinking budgets and declining revenues, particular in the areas of social services and human resource development, it will not be easy to find ways and means to achieve them.

Fortunately, there are some things that teachers and classroom aides can do to address the English language needs of Indian students, even if changes on a larger scale have yet to occur.

As a first step, all of the school staff need to recognize that the characteristics that separate Indian English from other forms of classroom usage are not indicators of language deficiency but grow out of differences between standard English usage and traditions of English language usage that have considerable time, depth, and cultural significance within the students' home community. Indian students need knowledge of standard English to function effectively within school settings, but they need proficiency in the Indian English of their home community even if they are also fluent speakers of their ancestral language in order to function effectively in the community.

Classroom activities that require Indian students to renounce Indian English–related proficiency before they can develop standard English skills should be avoided. A more appropriate goal for school-based language arts programs is for students to master the requirements of standard English proficiency without sacrificing control over Indian English tradition, as many people within every tribal community have been able to do. Let these persons and their language skills serve as models for language arts instruction in American Indian education. Then keep the following suggestions in mind while preparing lesson plans and carrying out specific language development tasks within your classroom.

1. Be realistic.   There is no language learning activity that, by itself, will transform nonstandard English–speaking students into proficient users of standard English. Instead of looking for global solutions, or "teacher proof" instructional packages that promise to "do it all," try to target instruction toward the students' particular areas of language need, making sure that instruction shows students how to combine new areas of language knowledge with the skills in English communication that they already have acquired.

2. Broaden perspectives on language use.   Do not be held captive by the expectations of standard English discourse. Be aware that the language tradition ancestral to the student's home community structures the flow of communication and the presentation of meaning in terms quite different from those familiar to you. Spend some time watching and listening to Indian students as they talk with each other, then look for similarities in the ways they participate in discussion within more formal teaching and learning settings. Spend some time exploring these themes with parents, community language authorities, tribal educators, and the many resource persons from the students' home community who may work at the school. Some of these persons will be intrigued by the ideas you are exploring and may want to work with you in this area in other ways.

3. Promote diversity.   Assume that every response given in Indian English is in some sense or at some level a meaningful statement. Then work diligently to try to construct the meaning. If the signals are unclear, find ways for the student to recast the response, without making the student feel as if the initial statement was poorly constructed. A useful strategy here is to ask the student or another classmate to provide an alternative way to make the statement. Asking this question frequently encourages students to think about language options and invites them to experiment with constructions of various types. These are important skills for the English-speaking student to possess, whatever the variety of English in use at a given moment.

4. *Encourage eloquence.*   Most Indian English varieties are characterized by brevity, imagery, and frequent invitations for active listener engagement. Many of these features are obscured in the tightly scheduled, businesslike environment of the standard English classroom. Make certain that the students have ample opportunities to express their ideas according to *their* own sense of completed, well-formed commentary.

Student 5's responses to the Slim Green question given previously illustrate the importance of this suggestion. Notice how the flow of the discussion ultimately led this student to arrive at a response that satisfied the expectations of both participants in this exchange. The key element here was the use of questions that kept the discussion within the frame of reference established by the student in his opening comment:

> S: Because he looks like, to me it always looks like they are dead when I see snakes.

Stated more succinctly, the student was talking about "how snakes look to me." The statement that expressed this frame of reference is markedly Ute English in its detail—for example, the subordinate clause relationship to main clause relationship is a mirror image of the pattern commonly found in English grammar. The content of the comment is highly speaker centered and quite text unrelated, for reasons already explained. But neither point should distract your attention from the significance of the message or its effect on the comments that follow. Insisting that the discussion remain focused around the intent of the question disregards the student's willingness to participate in this discussion, provided he can do so, in good Ute fashion, according to his own sense of priority. Encouraging this student to establish his own focus for the discussion and developing his comment fully show respect for the student's knowledge of language and his ability to use that knowledge effectively in such settings—points that, until quite recently, were not always given much emphasis in the classroom.

References and Source Materials

Discussion of many facets of American Indian English can be found in collections edited by Leap (1977), Bartelt, Jasper, and

Hoffer (1982), and St. Clair and Leap (1982, pt. 3). Kwachka (1989), Miller (1977), Penfield-Jasper (1980), and Stout (1979) offer more detailed descriptions of particular Indian English variations. Leap (1978) examines the education implications of these codes in general terms. Philips's (1983) contrast of Warm Springs English with standard non-Indian classroom usage, McLaughlin's (1989, in press) description of oral and written English literacy in Navajo school and community, and a series of papers (Leap 1988, 1989, 1990; Manuel-Dupont 1990) based on recent work at the Northern Ute Reservation examine the significance of Indian English fluencies within particular educational settings.

IV

Reading and Literature

11

Teaching Reading Responsively

JON REYHNER

Too often American Indian students are taught from textbooks designed for use by suburban middle-class white children (as discussed in chapter 6). Basal reading textbooks in particular are not appropriate for Indian students, and teachers responsive to their Indian students' needs will seek out culturally appropriate curriculum, especially reading material. Luckily, teachers wishing to supplement or replace basal reading textbooks with Whole Language and literature approaches have a wide variety of American Indian books they can use.

Hap Gilliland (1980) lists, with evaluations, 1,650 children's books about Indians. He found that American Indian children with reading problems are more likely to relate to stories about Indians set in the present than in the past (1982). Indian students, to have equal educational opportunities, need to be given "books, materials, and methods developed for use in the Indian society" or relevant to the students' background and culture in order to reinforce positive self-concept, motivate reading, and develop reading comprehension skills (Gilliland 1983, 1–2). More recently, McEachern and Luther (1989) in a Canadian study found that Indian students comprehended culturally relevant stories better than culturally irrelevant ones.

Dealing with Stereotyping in Literature

Basal reading textbooks, since they are frequently updated and receive careful editorial screening, do not contain the more objectionable minority-group stereotypes. However, teachers who go to their school libraries to find books about American Indians often find older books, some considered classics, that contain the most objectionable kinds of stereotypes. For example, in *The Adventures of Tom Sawyer,* the villain is "Injun Joe"—a "murderin half-breed" who tortures women (Twain [1876] 1958, 87, 148). In Laura Ingalls Wilder's *Little House on the Prairie,* first published in 1935, "two naked, wild [Indian] men" who are "tall, thin, fierce-looking" with eyes that "were black and still and glittering, like snake's eyes" visit the Ingalls homestead (1971, 134–39). The fact that these men just visit and do no harm does not take away from the negative description of them. Walter D. Edmond's 1941 award-winning book *The Matchlock Gun* has attacking Indians that "hardly looked like men . . . trotting, stooped over . . . like dogs" (39). At the end of the book a "crippled" Indian is killed, an event that does not merit the author's discussion (50). In Betsy Byars's *Trouble River,* an Indian with "oily skin" who moves "with the silent ease of an animal" visits a homestead and a young boy and his grandmother are forced to flee (1969, 33, 35).

Mary Byler (1973) found stereotyping, depersonalization, ridicule, derision, and inauthenticity in children's books with Indian characters. Many books for young children portray non-Indian children or animals dressing up and playing Indian. The Council on Interracial Books for Children describes some of the problems associated with this activity:

"Playing Indian" is a common play activity for children—in the United States as well as other countries. . . . Undoubtedly most, if not all, of us have seen children hopping up and down, patting a hand against their mouths and yelling "woo-woo-wooo," or raising one hand shoulder high and saying "how" or "ugh." The perpetuation of these and similar white-created "Indian" behaviors reflects the influence of peer socialization, schooling and movies. They mock Native cultural practices and demean Native people as subhumans, incapable of verbal communication. (1981, 12).

Stereotyped characters cannot be avoided in stories because stereotypes represent a very visible portion of reality. The danger to students is not the stereotypes themselves, but the possibility that students will come to believe that the stereotypes accurately represent a whole group. Teachers can avoid this danger by making students aware of stereotyping and giving students a variety of literature to read.

Students who read books or view movies with stereotyped characters such as those described above need to have an explanation of Indian cultures, of frontier settlers' attitudes toward Indians, and of how Indians felt toward settlers who moved in on Indian lands, sometimes in defiance of treaties with the U.S. government and with no attempt to buy the land. For example, in the Caldecott Medal–winning book *They Were Strong and Good,* the pioneer grandmother did not like Indians because

They would stalk into the kitchen without knocking and sit on the floor. Then they would rub their stomachs and point to their mouths to show that they were hungry. They would not leave until my mother's mother gave them something to eat. (Lawson 1940)

An explanation of Indian customs would help students put such descriptions in perspective. For example, teaching about Indian expectations of mutual hospitality would explain the reason for their wanting food from strangers. A lesson on sign language as a method of communication with people who speak another language could also help. American tourists in Europe can be seen every day using "primitive" sign language. Books by authors who lived on the frontier and who had extensive contacts with Indians (such as Mari Sandoz's *These Were the Sioux,* 1961) or, better yet, books written by Indians (such as Charles Eastman's *Indian Boyhood,* [1902] 1971) can do much to correct negative descriptions by authors who had only passing contact with Indians.

Ethnocentrism in Stories

Negative stereotypes are a symptom of a larger problem of ethnocentricism. There is a natural tendency for each culture to perceive itself as superior to all other cultures. This tendency to see other cultures as inferior, called ethnocentrism, has led to much inhuman treatment of minorities, such as the American Indians, by dominant cultures. Ethnocentrism comes naturally to children who are brought up to believe that the way of life of their parents' culture is the only way to live, as many children are. Villains and fools in the stories the children hear are often portrayed as coming from another culture. When these children grow up and interact with persons from other cultures, they may think those persons' behavior is not just different but wrong. Since the children think that they know the proper way to live and that these persons are acting wrong, they naturally feel superior to the ignorant outsiders. Ethnocentrism lies at the heart of the problem of Indian education. Attempts at communication between the white and Indian cultures, rather than being communication between equals, have tended to be a matter of the dominant white society trying to use the Indians or, at best, trying to assimilate them. The original ideal of Indian education was to "civilize" and assimilate the Indians into the dominant culture that the emigrants from Europe imported to America. Behind these efforts was power—military, political, and economic power—which is controlled by the dominant culture.

Indian children are no different from children from the dominant culture. They have a right, like all children, to be educated in schools that reinforce the culture of their homes. The curriculum of the school should utilize as much as possible local (tribal) stories and history to teach reading, language arts, and social studies. As Indian students get older they need to be introduced to the wider non-Indian world in such a way that does not make their own world seem automatically inferior or superior.

Ethnocentrism has become resurgent as immigration of non-whites has increased into the United States. In 1985, more people immigrated legally to the United States than to all other nations in the world combined, and the number of illegal immigrants is even larger. White non-Hispanic Americans will in a few years be minorities in California and Texas (Bouvier and Gardner 1986). The fear of becoming a minority has led to the formation of groups wishing to enforce assimilation on all U.S. minorities. "English only" organizations, which advocate adopting English as the official language of the United States, jeopardize the use of culturally appropriate curriculum for minority group children and the early education of non-English-speaking American children. Similarly, the "cultural literacy" movement, which received a lot of media attention in connection with the recent book *Cultural Literacy: What Every American Needs to Know* (Hirsch 1987), jeopardizes the teaching of non-European and non-Judeo-Christian heritages in our schools.

The results of the Kamehameha Early Education Program (Project KEEP) indicate the importance of understanding and using minority cultures in schools. Project KEEP was set up to find ways to improve the educational attainment of native Hawaiian children. Even though native Hawaiian children come to school speaking only English, they have done poorly in school. Initially, a phonics-oriented program was tried, but it failed to bring students to the level of the non-native students. After an ethnographic study of the students' homes, a culturally compatible curriculum was designed that emphasized reading comprehension, with the result that the average student reading score rose from the twenty-seventh percentile to above the fiftieth (Jordan 1984).

In the new curriculum, classroom organization was changed from large group to small group instruction, which emphasized active student participation in learning, including peer tutoring and a monitoring of student progress through criterion-referenced tests. Teachers worked with small groups of students in reading lessons that began by relating the reading material to the students' prior experiences. The reading lessons then focused on comprehension of the material read and were followed up with activities that related the material back to the students' lives. Students not receiving direct instruction from the teacher worked in small groups at learning centers (Jordan 1984; Tharp 1982).

Building on the Strengths of Indian Students

Rather than recognizing the cultural and linguistic strengths of children from ethnic and racial minorities, schools and school textbooks often ignore students' home culture and language while considering the students underprivileged, culturally deprived, or educationally at-risk. The native language or dialect and values the children have learned at home are considered handicaps to be overcome as quickly as possible rather than positive assets on which to build. American Indian students, often taught at home to be independent and cooperative, are often expected at school to be dependent on the teacher and to compete with other students. Many Indian students, instead of receiving initial instruction in their native language, are submersed in English and are expected, in the words of William Bennett, secretary of education, "to speak, read, and write English as soon as possible" (1986, 62).

There is also a tendency for teachers to assume that their minority students with reading problems can be successfully diagnosed using English language tests and treated in a prescriptive fashion through a Special Education or Chapter I–type remedial reading program. In those programs the reading process is segmented into a series of discrete, "basic" skills that are taught in a very mechanical way (Cummins 1984; Savage 1987).

Treating poor reading skills as a student-centered problem is based on a victim-blaming mentality that focuses a teacher's efforts on testing the student and on remediation rather than on finding meaningful reading materials and culturally appropriate ways to teach and motivate students. Scripted, mechanical reading programs lack intrinsically motivating elements to encourage students to succeed.

Native language literacy is avoided because the average non-Indian teacher is not able to speak a tribal language. Students cannot read in a language they cannot speak, so reading programs for non-English-speaking student groups should start with reading in the language of their home for the best prospect of success. Meanwhile, the students can participate in an oral language development program to become fluent in English. Bilingual stories such as those developed by the Hays Bilingual Program in Montana are an example of the local materials that can be used to develop both native language and English literacy simultaneously (Allen 1986).

The Responsive Teacher

The problem of teachers whose students do not respond to the standard curriculum is not new. Teachers responsive to the needs of their students have always sought ways to better suit their teaching to the needs of their students. Sylvia Ashton-Warner's experience teaching the indigenous people of New Zealand, the Maori, as described in her book *Teacher* (1963), is just one example of a teacher adapting to meet the needs of minority students.

Ashton-Warner, teaching in a New Zealand infant (kindergarten) school, called her responsive approach to language experience teaching "organic reading." While she used her approach to teach English to her students, it is equally suitable for use in teaching reading in tribal languages. Drawing children's beginning reading material from their own experiential background, as she did, ensures that students have the prior experiences necessary for reading comprehension.

Ashton-Warner emphasized the power of words, an idea that is familiar to Indian cultures:

First words must have intense meaning for a child. They must be a part of his being.

How much hangs on the love of reading, the instinctive inclination to hold a book! . . . Pleasant words won't do. Respectable words won't do. They must be words organically tied up, organically born from the dynamic life itself. They must be words that are already part of the child's being. (1963, 33)

For children to give maximum attention, they must already have a deep emotional tie with the words they first learn to read. Using words written on the chalkboard that were suggested by her students, Ashton-Warner built up what she called a "key vocabulary." These words were put on cards for the children to identify. The words then were combined to form sentence-length captions for drawings done by the students. Then children wrote their own simple storybooks, which were then used to teach reading. She also encouraged autobiographical (journal) writing. Daily journal writing is well worth encouraging throughout school and as a life-long activity, leading students to practice writing and to examine their own lives.

It was important to Ashton-Warner that the students' words and writing were not criticized. She believed in using rather than suppressing students' energy, letting them work together, and having them read to each other.

Responsive teachers such as Ashton-Warner work with students rather than just make students work. Their role is that of guides and facilitators rather than just authoritative sources of knowledge or unreflective disseminators of textbook material. They view their work as going beyond the classroom when necessary to encourage literacy in the home and community. Family literacy supports school literacy. Programs such as Reading is FUNdamental (RIF), which provide free books for children to take home, encourage reading in the home. On the Navajo Reservation in Chinle, Arizona, parents have contracted with responsive teachers to listen to their children read at home.

Students who are extrinsically motivated to learn at school (usually by their parents) and who know the language and culture of the teacher and the textbook can survive academically in the classroom of a nonresponsive teacher. Nonresponsive teachers assume that they know what children need to learn and are not troubled by their students' feelings or prior knowledge about course content.

Responsive teachers are especially important with students of a cultural or language minority since these teachers are willing to shape the curriculum to meet those students' needs. They are more likely to adapt curriculum based on discussions with students, to focus lessons on topics meaningful to the students, and to allow students to practice language and thinking skills in real interactive situations. In group discussions and by allowing student talk in group work, responsive teachers allow students to use language and to develop their competencies in communication.

Scripted curriculum materials such as Direct Instruction Teaching Arithmetic and Reading (DISTAR) and the teaching guides for many popular basal reading series tell the teacher what questions to ask and provide the "right" responses expected of the students. These scripted teaching guides inhibit real dialogue between teacher and student—the kind of dialogue that was extremely effective in the Kamehameha Early Education Program. Reliance on these scripted materials also implicitly limits the teacher's discussion of how a story's words, characters, and situations are similar to or different from those of the children's native language, culture, and experiences.

The not so subtle message to the student of nonresponsive teachers is that the school's curriculum is more important than the students and that the culture of the school is more important than that of the home. The students are being educated to live in the dominant culture even though, in reality, they often live as adults in an environment closer to their native culture than the dominant culture. Also, the students are ill prepared by the nonresponsive teacher to participate in a democratic society as they learn in school to listen to the directions of authority figures and to memorize information without expressing their personal opinions or reflecting on what they are learning.

A Heritage Reading Program for Indian Students

Responsive teachers work to produce a curriculum suited to the needs of their students. Arthur Gates indicated almost thirty years ago that basal readers should be only a "small fraction" of the total reading program (1962, 445). More recently Peter Winograd has written that "basal readers are least effective when they are used as the total reading program and children spend all of their allocated instructional time in the basals program, reading selections and completing various exercises" (1989, 1). Goodman et al. (1988) thoroughly investigated the publisher's claims about basal readers and gave a brief overview of the promising alternatives to basal readers being practiced in the United States and abroad.

It is up to the teacher to introduce students to literature beyond the bits and pieces that appear in basal readers. Children from the dominant culture can often learn to read well in spite of the school because their parents recognize the need for providing reading material in the home and encourage their children to utilize public and school libraries. For Indian students, whose parents may be less familiar with books and libraries, the teachers' role in providing interesting literature for their students is especially critical if the students are to learn to read fluently and succeed in school.

Indian students need a "heritage reading program." Students from minority cultures should first be introduced to their own cultural heritage and then the Western European heritage on which much of the U.S. governmental system was built. A global, multicultural curriculum should be built on the foundation of the students' family and national (dominant) cultural knowledge.

Teachers at the classroom level are in a position to get to know their students' backgrounds and to encourage their school librarians, administrators, and boards to acquire supplemental literature appropriate to the students' backgrounds. Under our economic system such literature will only be produced in large quantities if a market is created through such requests.

Teachers can model learning to their students by becoming familiar, through ethnographic literature and home visits, with their students' home cultures. Then they can adapt their teaching methods through trial and error to see what kinds and forms of classroom activities motivate their students to become literate. Teachers need to learn as much as they can about the particular community in which they work. Taking an interest in their students' lives in itself can make a difference in students' academic performance (Kleinfeld 1979a). When reading material about the community is not available, students can produce their own reading material through the language experience approach to reading (Allen and Allen 1982). To give more meaning to the various exercises that students do in school, the Whole Language approach (Goodman 1986; and chapter 12 of this volume) can utilize culturally appropriate stories to integrate the various subjects taught in school into a more comprehensible whole.

Reading textbooks need to be supplemented through classroom libraries. These libraries should have paperback books and other reading materials at various skill levels and on different topics (fiction and nonfiction) so that students can select books and magazines that interest them. Minority group students need stories that relate to their lives as well as stories through which they can learn about the outside world. Stephen Krashen examined ten studies that compared students using sustained silent reading (SSR) as part or all of their reading programs with students not receiving SSR. He found that students who practice and refine their reading skills using self-selected, free reading in SSR programs did as well or better on tests of reading comprehension than students receiving no SSR in their reading program in eight out of the ten studies, including one study in which SSR was the exclusive language arts program (Krashen 1985).

Conclusion

Schools need to have a variety of reading material from which students, parents, and teachers can select. From this reading material a teacher can structure lessons as described in the following chapters on reading comprehension and Whole Language, and the student can through exploration find out the variety of information and entertainment that is available through reading.

Colin Scott (1908, 212–13) wrote over eighty years ago, "If the schools do no more for reading than to teach people to read, it may be said paradoxically that they are not even teaching them to read." Students who find in school that reading is boring and uninteresting learn to avoid reading, and so never get the practice needed to become fluent readers.

If Indian students are to become productive tribal members, informed citizens, and problem solvers of the future, they need to start reading with meaningful, realistic literature about which they can think and hold discussions. Reading textbooks can, at best, only provide an appetizer to encourage students to explore classroom, school, and community libraries as well as book-stores. If meaningful and interesting stories are too difficult for beginning readers to read, then teachers need to read them aloud to students.

The modern Whole Language approach to reading—with its emphasis on letting students choose from a variety of literature and integrating reading with the teaching of social studies, science, and other subjects—has proven particularly effective with Indian students. King (1990) presents a Bureau of Indian Affairs school's ten years of experience with Whole Language, noting that not buying basal reading textbooks frees up money for buying children's books. A special report by the BIA describes how "whole language maximizes the learning experience of each student-participant by building upon the student's knowledge gained outside the classroom" at the Chuska and Dilcon Boarding Schools (1988b, 45).

The following chapter provides practical suggestions for implementing Whole Language teaching strategies. Chapter 13 focuses on teaching strategies to enhance students' reading comprehension. Chapter 14 provides an overview of literature written by American Indians, while appendix B gives sources for obtaining children's books by and about Indians and a short list of recommended stories about Indians.

12

The Whole Language Approach

SANDRA FOX

The philosophy behind the Whole Language approach to teaching language arts is to make language instruction meaningful to children by giving them an active role in the learning process and by integrating the various aspects of language (listening, speaking, reading, and writing) instruction. The Whole Language approach is based on (1) implementing language instruction using content from students' own experiences, (2) not artificially separating the different aspects of language use, and (3) actively involving students by giving them choices about what they will listen to, speak about, read, and write.

Whole Language instruction involves a variety of language uses. Students write on many different subjects and have a chance to write every day. They use familiar language from both their home and "kid" cultures in their classwork. They receive reading strategy instruction on pronunciation, comprehension, critical thinking, and so forth. They are read to every day and have other chances to develop listening skills. They read silently for enjoyment. They share with other students information about the books they have read and stories they have written, and they are given frequent opportunity to develop their oral language skills in real situations.

Whole Language programs include units incorporating reading, listening, speaking, and writing. Various components of a Whole Language program are described below, followed by a sample unit.

Listening

Listening is an important language arts skill. It is estimated that people spend 45 percent of their daily language-use time in some form of listening activity. Listening is especially important for Indian students who need to expand their vocabularies to gain command of words for use in speaking, reading, and writing.

In a Whole Language program students practice listening when they are read to daily, when they hear other students contribute to language experience stories and bring familiar words for word lists, and when they share literature. Primary students need an environment rich in oral literature: songs, singing games, poetry, storytelling, and oral play. They need many opportunities to listen to stories, songs, and poems.

In intermediate and upper grades, the same kinds of listening practice need to take place; in addition, students need to practice listening to understand and learn, listening for pleasure, and listening critically. It is essential that listening not be neglected. For Indian students, especially, more time must be devoted to it.

Speaking

Speaking, like listening, is not given enough emphasis in most classrooms. One of three major recommendations for improving language skills of Indian students is to provide more oral language practice for them. Indian students must spend more time mastering spoken language before they are expected to read and write. In early grades the practice of having children bring things to school to share with the rest of the class in "show and tell" is an excellent way to provide students with oral language experience. More sophisticated forms of show and tell can be used in the upper grades with students telling about their experiences in and out of school. Positive comments rather than direct questions will often get students to talk more about their experiences.

In a Whole Language program, speaking (oral language practice) comes into play when students discuss an experience they have had, which then provides the teacher with the content for a story based on that experience. This type of story is called a "language experience" story. For young students, the teacher writes the story down on a chalkboard or chart paper, or the students can write using their own inventive spellings. Speaking is practiced when students bring familiar language to the classroom to suggest words or phrases for lists—for example, of sports terms, names of toothpastes, or words with the same meaning such as "awesome," "humongous," and other synonyms for "large." When students share literature they have enjoyed (or hated) by telling a story or reading aloud a poem or from a book (or telling why not to read a certain book), they are practicing oral language.

Other opportunities for practical oral language include reciting poetry and individual or choral readings. Students should regularly participate in skits or plays, give short oral reports, speak into tape recorders, share experiences, and be involved in discussion. Any activities through which students have an opportunity to converse with each other provide excellent oral language practice. Teachers should stress the utility of speaking effectively and try to make the situations meaningful and real. For example, a class could practice a play and present it to students in a lower grade or to parents. The setting should be as natural as possible, and the focus should be on the activity and not on the language itself. Much of the source for oral language practice can come from the many stories that Indians have always told. Students can tell traditional stories, make original speeches, or recite the speeches of other Indians (for examples of Indian oratory see Virginia Armstrong's *I Have Spoken,* 1971). Students can also turn legends into plays.

In schools with bilingual programs, the inclusion of speaking activities is even more important. Only when students speak and get reinforcement for speaking do they learn to use a language. The classroom environment created for language use should include concrete objects and situations as much as possible. Conversational proficiency in a second language should be promoted by immersion at the classroom level, where students are encouraged to speak without translation in the language they are learning.

Writing

Students should also write every day. Students can keep their written work in file folders or large envelopes. Revising and editing are essential parts of the writing process. Peer editing allows students to get other students' opinions about their own writing in a nonthreatening atmosphere, and students can work jointly to improve written works. Two kinds of writing need to be practiced in schools: independent writing and controlled writing.

Independent Writing

With independent writing, students are encouraged to put their thoughts and ideas on paper. Writing is viewed as the ability to write one's own ideas and present them for others to read. It should be stressed that one's own ideas are important. Ideas can be expressed through factual (expository or nonfiction) writing or through imaginative (fictional) writing.

Independent writing should be stressed from a child's first day at school. Children want to write, as shown by their crayon marks and scribbles on paper and walls. They need to write in kindergarten because from the beginning, they must believe they can write. They should be allowed to scribble, draw pictures, or write alphabet letters, if they know them. Then they can be asked to tell what they have written, and they should be praised for what they have done.

Young writers in kindergarten and first grade can also draw or paint pictures to put their ideas on paper. Each artist can tell about his or her picture, and the teacher can extract two or three sentences that will describe the picture or tell the story. By the next day, the teacher can have attached a story strip to the bottom of each child's picture with the two- or three-sentence descriptions on it. The students share the pictures again and read the "stories" that go with them. Later on, students can write their own stories to go with their pictures. Children can also transcribe stories.

Independent writing requires selection of topics. Selecting topics is difficult for children at first, so teachers may have to provide topics from which students can choose. Gradually, as they gain confidence, students should be encouraged to select their own topics.

The writing process.   Teachers should model writing for their students. After the teacher chooses a topic or, better yet, the class helps choose a topic, the teacher models how he or she thinks about and organizes writing. The teacher should think out loud and actually write short essays on the chalkboard, making corrections and reorganizing ideas while doing so. When teachers write language experience stories for young students, they also model writing. If students come to a word they want to use but cannot spell, they are encouraged to circle words they know they need help on, to use inventive spelling, or to ask the teacher or a writing partner for help later. Grade-appropriate dictionaries should also be available for students to check without having to first ask the teacher for permission.

Students need to make corrections and edit their independent writing. Editing should start out simply, with all students turned into editors after being writers. They can edit individually or in pairs. At first, they should simply read the work to see if it makes sense. Later, they can check for correct paragraph indentation, capitalization, punctuation, and spelling. Older students might have a checklist of things to look for.

The teacher can help students edit by modeling the process using some papers put on an overlay as examples of how to edit. Copies can be made of a paper (typed or written, with the name omitted) for all to see as a teacher points out things to be changed, or sentences from many papers can be extracted as examples. Teachers should be careful to choose papers written by students who are better writers so as not to discourage the creativity of those less confident about their writing.

As a regular practice, students should be encouraged to illustrate written works. This reinforces the ideas used in the writing as well as the skills practiced. Students can also write captions for cartoons and create their own comic books. Teacher and students should look for real situations where students can use writing, such as writing letters to local newspaper editors, pen pals, tribal councils, and so forth.

Some of the students' writing should be "published." Students' work can be displayed on bulletin boards and school hallways or compiled and put in book form to be read by others. Students can also write individual books or contribute to classroom or school anthologies. Classroom and school newspapers can also provide useful outlets for students' written work. The teacher can be the "senior editor" in these cases and review "drafts" with the students before final copies are made. Final drafts do not have to be perfect. The amount of perfection expected depends on students' ages and abilities.

Projects for older students can use the "Foxfire" concept of gathering and writing down information about the local community for inclusion in a book (Kazemek 1985; Rigg 1985) and the writing of "life stories," as described by Allen in her book *Writing to Create Ourselves* (1982). Both the Foxfire and life story approaches draw on material that is immediate and familiar to students. Students can also write articles on any topic for local and school newspapers.

Poetry adds spice to the writing program. For early writers, rhyming words, after the first one, can be left out of poetry so that students can fill in the blanks. Later, students can write their own poetry. They get to feel and use a lot of language when they write poetry. Students should not think that all poems have to have rhyme.

In summary, classrooms should have many opportunities for independent writing daily. Students can keep journals and write in them every day. In early grades, a teacher can suggest topics. Journal notes are not corrected or edited, but the teacher may respond to them by writing comments in the journal and modeling correct spelling and grammar in the process. Older students, who should keep journals more like diaries and write what is on their minds, may not want teachers to review their journals. Classrooms can also have message boxes where students can answer and send messages to the teacher. Throughout, the real world utility, purposes, and applications of independent writing should be stressed.

Controlled Writing

In *controlled writing* the teacher controls the topic and form. This is useful for beginning writers and for older students who need to improve their writing. One form of controlled writing is to have students copy written works (this works best when students copy language experience stories that they helped compose and that the teacher has transcribed on chart paper, chalk board, or overlay). In early grades, students can copy short poems, songs, language experience stories, and other short works. It is best if these works are already familiar to the child.

A second form of controlled writing is having students write word lists from their experiences and surroundings (not from their spelling book!). For example, students can write names of things in a picture or in their classroom, school building, school yard, town, or home. The students suggest the items for the lists and then write them down. They may have to ask for the names of some things. These can be written by the teacher and their spellings discussed one at a time, or students can make their own lists based on the topic and exchange them for spelling correction by their peers. The teacher should be on hand to explain and confirm spellings. After a word list is complete and correct, more advanced students can write paragraphs utilizing the words about a current topic of interest or about their classroom, school yard, living room, and so forth. Students can do specialized word lists, such as things on a Christmas tree or things having to do with other holidays or special days. They also can do rhyming words after the first word is given. They then write poetry with the rhyming words. Word lists can be done by groups of students or used by tutors or teacher aides with individual students.

A third form of controlled writing is the dictation of sentences for students to write. Length and number of sentences depend on the level of the students. Sentences can include students' spelling or vocabulary words, or they can be from an experience the class or a student has had. After each sentence is written by the students, the teacher should write it correctly on the chalkboard for students to compare with theirs. This provides immediate feedback on their success at writing, spelling, punctuation, and capitalization. The teacher or tutor directs students to check to make sure they have capitalized, put a period, and so forth, one aspect at a time, emphasizing things with which students are having difficulty.

More advanced students may have short paragraphs dictated to them. No hints are given, such as "end of sentence," only the words are dictated. Students then have to check to see if they have divided the paragraph into sentences correctly, if they have properly indented the first line, and if they have correct spelling, capitalization, and punctuation. Short papers can be dictated to see if students can divide ideas into paragraphs as well to check on other skills.

A fourth form of controlled writing is to convert questions into statements. The instructor should explain or review the difference between questions and statements. Students are then directed to write a paragraph of statements in which they answer questions such as, What is your name? What school do you attend? What grade are you in? What is your teacher's name? How many students are in your class? Is your school work easy or hard? (Outlandish questions can add some interest to this exercise.) The length of sentence and the paragraph will depend, of course, upon the level of the student or group. Questions can also be given individually, and students' statements checked after each is written. Questions can be on the same topic or on unrelated topics.

A fifth form of controlled writing is to have students write a set number of sentences each week from spelling or vocabulary words. The teacher can count the number of errors and put it at the top of the page. Students should work toward having fewer and fewer errors. They become confident when they see they are eliminating errors. Students at higher grade levels will have more sentences to write. However, there should be few enough so the teacher can look them over quickly, maybe even correct them with the students as they are handed in. Otherwise, the instructor should arrange a time to conference with the students about their errors. A simple record of types of errors being made should be kept for each student. Students soon discover that many of the errors they make are from carelessness. Controlled writing should be done as long as needed; the content should depend on the types of errors made by students.

Organizing a Whole Language Program

The practical examples in this chapter are just a sample of the many Whole Language activities in which students can be involved. There are many others. However, most teachers are used to structured programs outlined in textbooks. There seems to be too many things to do in the Whole Language approach and no set way to do them. To provide some structure to Whole Language one could use a thematic approach. If a topic, book, or special happening is of interest to students, the teacher should organize a Whole Language unit based on it with related Whole Language activities.

For example, the teacher might choose the theme "horses" for American Indian students at about the fourth-grade level. Student activities could include the following:

Oral language practice: Have students tell about a horse they know. They can describe the horse and tell a story about it.

Reading to students: Read a book about horses such as Paul Goble's *The Sacred Dog* to students.

Reading strategies: Have students brainstorm a sheet of horse-related words for meaning analysis and word attack instruction. Have students do a concept mapping of the story.

Language experience story: Have students summarize *The Sacred Dog* for the teacher to write on the chalk board or chart paper.

Students reading to themselves (Sustained Silent Reading, or SSR): Have students read stories about horses.

Sharing literature: Have some students tell about their favorite horse stories.

Using familiar language: Have students tell the names or types of horses they know. Have the class discuss the listed words' meanings, spellings, and so forth.

Writing every day: Have students write papers based on horse themes. Papers can be edited. Students should write in their journals every day. They may do some controlled writing also.

The various activities of the Whole Language approach do not have to be in any particular order. Concepts from other academic areas, such as math or science, should be included if they relate to the topic. The Whole Language classroom should be full of stimuli for reading, writing, speaking, and listening. Some Whole Language classrooms have reading, writing, speaking, and listening centers. In fact, the whole school should be a literacy environment. Students can write and illustrate stories on butcher paper and display them on hallway walls.

The Whole Language approach is a much more exciting way to teach than just following textbooks and using worksheets, and its procedures also can be used in content areas, such as science and social studies. The teacher would plan reading, writing, speaking, and listening activities on the topic being studied. The Whole Language approach can also be used with Indian languages as well as English. Students can use simple word-processing programs on computers to write, spell check, edit, and publish their stories.

More examples of classroom Whole Language activities can be found in Allen and Allen (1982), Graves (1983), Grobe (n.d.),

Stauffer (1980), Goodman (1986), and Routman (1988). Regie Routman's book, *Transitions From Literature to Literacy*, is especially to be recommended for both the practical suggestions it gives for teachers and the author's personal insights regarding how she became converted to the Whole Language approach to teaching language arts.

13

Improving Reading Comprehension

DANIEL L. PEARCE

Outside of school, people read either to understand or to enjoy. In the schools, the purpose of reading instruction is to help students become capable readers and help produce students who want to read. Both reading to learn and reading for enjoyment are aspects of comprehension. In my experience, teachers of Indian students spend too little time teaching them how to comprehend what they read. Consequently, this chapter focuses just on reading comprehension.

Unfortunately, it is not possible to give a simple way to improve students' comprehension. This is because reading comprehension is not a single skill. Some of the factors that affect comprehension include the reader's prior knowledge about the topic, motivation, language facility (similarity between the reader's language and the author's language), and familiarity with how to read different kinds of print materials.

While it would take more than a chapter to answer fully all questions of how to improve the reading comprehension of American Indian students, this chapter presents background information on reading comprehension, some instructional guidelines, and some classroom examples of ways teachers of Indian children can help improve their students' comprehension.

Background

Different authors (Cooper 1986; McNeil 1987; Pearson 1985) have noted that the meaning of "reading" and of "reading comprehension" has changed over the last twenty-five years. One of the reasons for this change is interdisciplinary investigation into reading.

Beginning in the 1960s, researchers from a variety of areas, such as psychology, reading education, sociology, and linguistics, started looking at reading and comprehension. As a result of this attention, the reading act has come to be perceived as inseparable from comprehension. Comprehension is not just the result of decoding; the two are intertwined, with comprehension facilitating decoding. Comprehension, in turn, has come to be seen as the reader's process of creating meaning through active interaction with the ideas in the text.

In the early 1960s, reading was viewed by some educators as a product of decoding (Fries 1962). While appealing, this notion is both simplistic and inaccurate. Students can appear to be reading when they are only pronouncing the words. A hundred years ago, when Indian students were taught by teachers who did not speak the students' native language, teachers noticed that the Indian students tended to "parrot" words without comprehension (Standing Bear 1928). Reading means comprehension, and reading comprehension involves more than successful decoding or fluent oral reading.

As a result of investigations into reading comprehension, a distinction has been made about what comprehension means. When most people speak of reading comprehension they are really referring to two different aspects, process and product. The distinction between process and product is the difference between the act of comprehension (process) and the end result (product).

Up until the late 1970s, comprehension was frequently viewed as the ability to recall information from a passage in either differing degrees of abstractness (such as understanding word meanings, recognizing explicit facts, and drawing inferences; Davis 1968) or by different levels of thought (such as literal, inferential, evaluation, and application; Barrett 1972). These efforts approached comprehension in terms of the product. While ability to recall information is an important aspect of comprehension, it is just the end result and tells us little about how a reader arrived at answers.

In comprehending a passage or arriving at a product, a reader's mind does not just record the information in the passage and then give it back. The human mind doesn't work that way. A reader is not a passive recipient of knowledge. Instead a reader constructs meaning by taking ideas from the page and relating them to ideas already in his or her mind (schemata). The text serves as a sort of "blueprint" that guides the reader in building a mental model of what is meant through supplying clues to what the author intended (or what the reader thinks the author intended). During this "building" a reader fills in points and makes inferences; after all, no text can explicitly give all of the information, underlying concepts, and relationships necessary to understand what the author is talking about. Consequently, comprehension requires a reader to play a very active role in constructing meaning. The act of constructing meaning is referred to as the comprehension process.

Comprehension, then, is the result of factors interacting within the mind while a reader goes through the processes necessary to arrive at a product. Good comprehension (having an acceptable answer or product) is dependent on several factors: having the necessary background information; being able to relate that background information to what is being read; being familiar enough with the text's structure so that meaningful predictions can be made about what is likely to occur next (this makes it easier to form new understandings); being able to vary strategies used during reading; and "metacognition"—being able to monitor one's own comprehension through knowing when something is not making sense and switching to another strategy.

The act of comprehension, or the process by which a reader constructs meaning through interacting with the text, is not inherently different for Indians than it is for other readers. Regardless of race, color, or creed, good comprehenders approach reading as a meaningful activity and interact with the ideas in the text in an active manner. What is different for Indian children is the kinds of background knowledge they bring to the reading task, their command of the language structures the texts use, and their experience with being active readers. The purpose of reading comprehension instruction for Indian children is to help them do those things good readers do when comprehending. This means helping them become active readers on their own.

Instructional Guidelines

The reading comprehension of Indian children, or for that matter any child, can be improved through balanced instruction within the school program. Before presenting some classroom examples, seven aspects necessary for effective comprehension instruction are presented.

Independent reading of trade books. Children need to relate to reading as more than decoding words, reading out loud, or answering questions after reading a selection. Children must have an opportunity to read for pleasure, see teachers and others reading, talk about and share what they have read, and achieve some success in reading. Whether used as a supplement to a core reading program or as the core of the program (literature-based reading), from the primary grades through high school, students must have a variety of books in their rooms and be given an opportunity to read them. (For some suggested books to which Indian children can relate, see appendix B.)

There are various ways to promote reading within a class. Both sustained silent reading programs and "self-selection" programs have been effective with second language and limited-English students (Krashen 1985). For several practical ways to use children's literature to enrich a reading program see Cullinan (1987) and Routman (1988). Efta (1984) presents a good overview of one teacher's silent reading program.

Children must have an opportunity not only to read the books that they select but also to share and discuss those books. By sharing and discussing I do not mean a formal written or oral book report. I mean a chance to talk to another person or small group of people about what has been read. One way of encouraging sharing is periodic individual conferences between the student and the teacher in which they talk about books read. While not specifically aimed at Indian children, Nancie Atwell's award-winning book *In the Middle* (1987) about her efforts teaching seventh- and eighth-grade students has several excellent suggestions regarding both individual conferences and book sharings—ideas that can be applied at any grade level. Cooperative reading (and sharing) of a story is another excellent technique for Indian students (Gilliland 1988; Hirst and Slavik 1990). Other suggestions are to have students make a commercial to convince others to read a story or keep a "book kite" listing books read independently.

Another way to encourage wide reading is to integrate trade books into the study of other subjects. Identify a subject to be studied (in any content area), identify some trade or children's books on that topic, and have the students read selected individual books and share what they have found. My experience is that trade books in content subjects are infrequently used in classrooms with large numbers of Indian students. A videotape showing how trade books can be used in a social studies class is available through Jan V Productions (Ammons 1987).

Background knowledge. Students must be "prepared" to read a selection. In several places the importance of background knowledge has been mentioned as a prerequisite for comprehension. Prior knowledge is important to helping a student come up with an "acceptable" comprehension product. The more a person knows about the subject of a text, the easier that text will be to read. Whether one is talking about reading a basal selection or a chapter in a history book, in order for comprehension to occur, students must have some knowledge about the topic they are going to read about. Not only must the students have some knowledge about this topic, they must also be able to identify the right memories (schema) and be able to relate what is being read to what they know.

While Indian students have background knowledge, it may not be adequate for understanding a selection. A reality in today's schools is that textbooks are the major source of instructional reading material and textbooks are aimed at middle-class white audiences. Textbook authors make assumptions about what is known, and these assumptions, which *may* be valid for some students, are not likely to be valid for students who are not from the mainstream. Indian students may not have had the kinds of experiences necessary to understand the concepts presented in a selection, so it is important to introduce key concepts through prereading activities.

Various prereading activities have proven successful with American Indian students. Successful techniques include brainstorming (Vacca and Vacca 1989); categorization of major concepts from a selection before reading that selection (Moore, Readence, and Rickelman 1988); and identification by the teacher of a major concept within the story or passage to be read, followed by introduction of the topic to the students and their discussion of it (Alverman, Dillon, and O'Brien 1987).

Exposure to different active reading strategies. Children need help in becoming active readers. Helping students improve their comprehension involves more than practice in answering questions about what has been read. While no two people will read a passage exactly the same way (after all, no two minds are identical), active reading involves some common traits. These include previewing difficult material before reading; using cues within the text while reading to make predictions about what is likely to occur next (and reading to confirm those predictions); and switching the rate of reading to fit the material and the task.

In order for students to become active readers, they need to be exposed to and have an opportunity to practice different strategies. This is achieved through a combination of teacher modeling (the teacher demonstrating different strategies for the students) and students practicing using those strategies with both print and nonprint materials, such as films.

Teachers will discover that the strategies needed to help a student read actively will vary depending on the difficulty of the text and the sophistication of the reader. Ideas and strategies that have been used successfully with Indian children include the following: the Directed Reading Thinking Activity (Stauffer 1976), Re-Quest or Reciprocal Questioning (Manzo 1969), and the Guided Reading Procedure (Manzo 1975). For additional ideas on ways to develop active readers see Cooper (1986) and McNeil (1987).

Integrate reading with language arts.   Reading must not be taught as an isolated subject. Comprehension development is tied to the other language arts. Through talking about and writing about what they read, students develop background knowledge, gain a deeper understanding of material read, and begin to become active readers.

Having students write about what they read is an effective way of improving students' reading comprehension. Writing does not mean formal report writing but, rather, putting ideas down on paper while reading a story (journals and personal notes) or after reading a story (such as a letter to one of the characters in a story). These kinds of activities can help students actively work with the ideas in a story or in a selection they are studying. However, in order for these kinds of writing activities to be useful, students must be willing to put their ideas down on paper. American Indian students will not be as likely to express themselves if a teacher goes through and grades each writing activity for aspects of form (spelling, grammar, and complete sentences). In his review of Indian students and writing Sawyer (1988) makes the point that these students may have particular problems writing English and that teachers need to encourage students to write through deemphasizing form and changing the format of writing assignments. For ideas on how reading and writing can be integrated, see Atwell (1989, 1990), Dionisio (1983), and Gambrell (1985).

Vocabulary instruction.   Children need help enlarging their vocabularies. Vocabulary knowledge plays an important role in comprehension (Anderson and Freebody 1981). This is especially true with Indian children because of their limited backgrounds—limited in the sense that they frequently have not been exposed to certain concepts and words, and because of the bilingual nature of many of these students.

Vocabulary instruction includes efforts to develop both oral and reading vocabulary. Reading vocabulary instruction means exposure to and practice in using new, specialized vocabulary as well as "old" words in different ways. It does not mean memorizing definitions, doing numerous worksheets, and taking periodic vocabulary quizzes. Students need to identify and practice using words in different settings and formats. For some examples of useful vocabulary activities and ideas on how to develop a student's vocabulary see Johnson and Pearson (1984) and Nagy (1988).

Questions.   Answering questions on what has been read is a time-honored practice within schools. It is also a practice that will continue because of the nature of schooling. Questions are not in and of themselves bad. They are a way for teachers to assess students' comprehension; however, in order for questions to be of assistance in increasing comprehension ability (the process of comprehension) they must clarify and not just assess the recall of information within the text. As Herber and Nelson (1975) have noted, a student's answer to a recall (or product) question is either right or wrong, and practice answering questions will not necessarily result in an increase in a student's ability to arrive at an answer independently. That is because questions on reading material usually focus on information within the text and the answers to those questions are products of comprehension.

In order for questions to be of any value for comprehension instruction, they must do more than assess students' abilities to recall detail, identify main ideas, or draw conclusions. This is one reason most commercial "comprehension" kits actually do little to improve students' reading comprehension. Teacher questions, in addition to clarifying information, should also focus on the process of comprehension. Further, such questions may help students develop metacognition (an awareness of their own reading). Process-oriented questions may be used with either stories or content material. These are some examples of process questions for a story:

Which parts of the story do you like best?

Which parts of the book or story are the hardest ones to understand? Why are they harder?

Which parts are the easiest to understand? Why are they easier?

The following are adaptations of process-oriented questions developed by Sandra Rietz of Eastern Montana College over a passage from a biology textbook. These questions can be adapted for use with any reading selection.

If you had to organize the ideas in this selection to study them for a test, which idea would you have to understand *first*—before you could understand any of the others?

In which order would you study the ideas?

Which new words were hard to understand?

If you were to break the passage up into a few *most important* ideas, what would these be?

What parts of the passage did you have to read over? Did you have to read any part of the passage more than twice? What part(s)?

How did you prepare or set up for reading this passage? What else could you have done?

These and similar questions help students become aware of *how* to comprehend text through helping the students monitor their own reading. These questions also can give teachers an opportunity to model comprehension techniques by answering a question themselves and demonstrating what they did during the reading of a passage. In my experience this is very effective with Indian children. For additional information on using questions to improve students' comprehension, see Pearson (1982) and Richardson and Morgan (1990).

Content-area reading.   Children need comprehension instruction during reading class and in their other subjects. Simply put, in order for comprehension to develop, teachers must expose students to reading in the content areas. Children need exposure to different text styles, author styles, and language patterns. All text is not the same. In order for students to be able to comprehend different material, they must have an opportunity to practice different instructional strategies.

The importance of content-area reading for comprehension development cannot be overstressed. In my work in reservation schools I have observed a common phenomenon. A teacher presents a good basal reading lesson in which he or she develops the students' background knowledge and then involves the students in an active reading of the story. Then, this same teacher will have the students read a content assignment independently with little or no instructional assistance. Students need to use active reading techniques in their content textbooks in order to comprehend what they read. For some examples of content-area reading see Richardson and Morgan (1990) and Vacca and Vacca (1989).

Examples

Prereading.   The importance of prereading activities was mentioned earlier in the section on background knowledge. One instance of using prereading activities to build background and motivate students involved a fifth-grade teacher whose students were Arapaho. The children were going to read a selection on Greek myths (a subject most of the students were not really knowledgeable about or interested in). The day before beginning reading, the teacher introduced the topic of myths in a general way and Arapaho myths were brought up. The teacher had the students ask parents, friends, and anyone they wanted about any stories they might know that explained things (especially Arapaho stories). Each student had to come in with at least one story or myth.

The next day, the class had a discussion in which the students' examples were introduced. The teacher then asked the class whether any of the students had ever heard certain common terms, all of which were derived from Greek myths, such as the tale Atlas or of Mercury. These terms were introduced and the students brainstormed what they thought each of the common terms might mean. Then, terms from the stories were introduced and related to the terms the students knew.

By doing these activities the teacher helped her students relate to the reading topic in a general way, introduced key words and concepts, and also created a natural "hook" for the children's curiosity ("Let's read this and see if your ideas are right and what else you can learn").

Integrating writing with reading. One fourth-grade teacher whose students were predominantly Crows incorporated oral language and writing into a basal reading lesson through a form of substitution. Substitution involves students replacing the characters, places, or events in a story with their own.

An overhead transparency of two paragraphs from a story was shown to the class. They were told to read it to themselves. Then the teacher told the class that it was possible to invent a new story by changing some things in the story. She then read the two paragraphs out loud, changing the sex of every character.

Following her reading of the "new" story, the class was asked what other things could be changed. The students' suggestions (animals, places, etc.) were written on the board. Students by this time were anxious to read their own version aloud. Each student "read" his or her version to a partner (this helped more students be involved than if only a few volunteers read theirs).

The next step involved using a story from the basal reader. The students were reminded of what they had done and were referred to the list on the board. The students were told to substitute anything they wanted for what was in the first two paragraphs of the basal story (just like they had done before) and write out their new story.

The students' retellings varied in creativity and in how much they changed the story. After writing, the students were given a chance to read each others' stories. Not only did the children enjoy creating a new story, they also enjoyed sharing their stories with each other.

This activity allowed the students to become actively involved in manipulating the events and characters in the story; they were involved in being active readers. Furthermore, substitution can be easily adopted for use in other content areas. For instance, a music teacher working with Crow students identified a song her students knew, "Jingle Bells," and wrote it on the board. The students substituted words appropriate for Valentine's Day. The students' songs were put up in the hallway where other students read them.

Practicing with films.   In the previous section on exposure to different reading strategies, the suggestion was made to let students practice using strategies with nonprint materials, such as films. One sixth-grade teacher of Northern Cheyennes did just that. She had a videotape of a movie about Chief Joseph, *I Will Fight No More Forever* (Congress Video Group 1985), and used some "active participation" techniques with her students while they were watching the movie.

As the class watched the movie, the teacher stopped the videotape periodically. During the first pause, the class was asked to tell what had happened up to that point in time. An important character in the film was selected by the teacher and the students were asked to come up with a list of everything they could remember or guess about this person. This list was written on the board. The class was asked to choose which things in the list they thought would be most important in the story and why. The class was then asked to guess what would happen in the movie. These predictions were also written on the board and later confirmed or rejected.

A variation of the above was repeated every time the videotape was stopped. Students made predictions about what would occur based on clues from the film and their own knowledge of Chief Joseph. At the end of the movie the teacher held a short class discussion on how the students had used what they were watching to predict what would happen.

Afterward, with a reading assignment, the class was reminded of what they had done while watching the movie and told that they were going to do the same thing while reading. The advantage of using nonprint materials is that children can be introduced to and practice using strategies with materials that are easier for them to process.

Using ReQuest.   ReQuest (Manzo 1969) is a form of reciprocal questioning that helps students ask questions about reading material. This strategy involves students and teachers taking turns asking each other questions about the material.

A fifth-grade teacher of Northern Cheyennes used this technique successfully in her social studies class. A passage in the textbook dealt with the geography and people in Peru. The teacher introduced the lesson with an announcement that today the students were going to have an opportunity to "be the teacher" by asking her questions about what was in the book.

The students and the teacher read the first paragraph silently. Then the teacher closed her book and asked for questions about what had been read. She tried to answer all questions honestly. After the questions stopped, the teacher asked the students questions about the first paragraph. This helped assure that important facts were brought to the students' attention.

This process was repeated with the next paragraph. When the teacher was asked a question that could not be specifically answered just by the information in the text, she told the class what she thought the answer might be and how she had reached her conclusion: "I have to guess since the book does not tell me that. My guess is this because the book does tell me the following things."

Periodically, the teacher would ask the students a higher-level question, which was not explicitly answered in the text, and ask for an explanation of the answer (as the teacher had modeled for the students). The entire lesson seemed almost a game. The students enjoyed it, practiced being active readers, had active reading modeled for them, and remembered the content in the chapter.

In follow-up lessons, once the students became more proficient at asking questions, some modifications were tried. For example, they had a contest between the teacher and the students in which a point was offered for every question that could not be answered. Two rules were established: questions had to be about the chapter, and "petty" questions (e.g., What is the fifth word in the paragraph?) were not allowed. Another time students competed against each other. Teams were formed by the teacher and students had a short period of time to read a passage. (Would you believe that some students read more than the assigned passage?) Then the students' teams played each other.

If ReQuest, as presented above, seems like a game to you, it is. However, it is a game that involves the students in the reading material through offering instructional assistance. Not only does this instructional assistance aid in the development of comprehension, it also helps the students remember what is in the book.

ReQuest also works well with students who need extra help in learning to read, such as Chapter I and Special Education students. One Chapter I teacher who used ReQuest with her elementary students (Crow, Cheyenne) found that it worked very well in ways she had not expected and in different subject areas. Science and mathematics were among the subjects for which it was most effective.

Content reading and writing in mathematics. A junior high school teacher, whose students were mostly Crows, used a series of content reading and writing techniques to help students learn mathematics. The students were seventh- and eighth-graders operating two or more years below grade level in reading and in mathematics. The students were involved in reading and writing activities as part of their mathematics instruction.

One set of techniques involved vocabulary activities. In and of itself, mathematics vocabulary affected the students' abilities to read and understand mathematics. The first set of activities involved the students creating and writing their own definitions for mathematics vocabulary. But instead of just telling the students to write, the teacher first had the students talk about the words. The teacher wrote a word on the board (such as "fraction"), the students brainstormed about that word, responses were mapped on the board, a key word was introduced (i.e., "denominator"), the students discussed it, and then students wrote their own definitions of "denominator." An adaptation was when the students were paired up and told to produce a definition for a word, write that definition down (if both agreed with the definition), and share their definition with the others.

Both of these vocabulary techniques were well received by the students. Even more important, the teacher saw an improvement in mathematics vocabulary (ability to read mathematics) and in the way the students responded to the study of mathematics words.

Another set of activities involved having the students read story problems using active reading techniques. One effective technique was an adaptation of the Directed Reading Thinking Activity (Stauffer 1976). The students first brainstormed about the problem ("What operations could it use?" "What will it be about?"), the problem was introduced on an overhead transparency line by line, the students confirmed and/or rejected their

choices and made new predictions, and when the story was entirely read the students talked about what hints were in the problem. A second effective active reading technique was ReQuest
(see the previous classroom example.)

The final set of content reading techniques involved the students in writing their own original story problems. The first few
times the teacher tried to have her students write problems, the
problems were short and frequently unsolvable. However, as the
school year progressed, the teacher had the students continue
writing problems and the students enjoyed it. She allowed students to group together to produce problems, let them talk about
what is in a problem, and allowed them an opportunity to share
and revise problems.

If you will think back to the various parts of this chapter, you
will recognize that this teacher was utilizing most of the basic
principles covered in this chapter. She was helping her students
learn to be active readers. Over the past ten years, I have seen
many teachers of Indian students use the ideas presented in this
chapter. I am convinced that with exposure and practice any student can become an active reader.

14

Teaching American Indian Literature

JAMES R. SAUCERMAN

Numerous studies of education in the 1980s have made similar sweeping recommendations for improving American education. For example, the 1986 report of the Carnegie Forum Task Force on Teaching as a Profession called for the "rebuilding" of America's educational system beyond literacy. Among the recommendations are that teachers must be able to think for themselves and must "be people whose knowledge is wide-ranging and whose understanding is deep" (45). To develop such teachers, the Task Force recommended,

a rigorous undergraduate curriculum that embraces a common core of history, government, science, literature, and the arts. That core should develop the essential skills of comprehension, computation, writing, speaking, and clear thinking. It should deepen appreciation of our history and culture, foster an understanding of the theory and appreciation of science and technology, develop aesthetic sensibilities, and inspire creative impulses. (50)

Knowledge of American Indian literature should be a part of this curriculum for teachers. The teacher of junior or senior high school students in Indian communities must know the American Indian literary heritage and forms of expression and be as sensitive as possible to the subtleties of images, themes, and aesthetics of that heritage. In addition, he or she must be alert to the development of a positive self-image in each student, to which the literature can often contribute. This knowledge will allow a teacher to select material and modes of presentation appropriate to the region, tribe, and community without limiting intellectual inquisitiveness. For example, sensitivity to the importance of one's name in developing self-esteem helps the teacher avoid the blunder committed by the teacher in Phil George's short poem "Name Giveaway," (1975), who insists on calling her young student by the foreign name "Phil George," refusing to recognize his real name, Two Swans Ascending From Still Waters.

While American Indian literature—much of it oral, of course—has existed since American Indians have existed, not until the early 1970s did it finally break free of history and anthropology. No matter how well intentioned historians and anthropologists have been as individuals, or how inescapably important history and anthropology are to understanding the literature, recognition of Indian literature as more than a curiosity and historical record has been a long time coming. Today, American Indian literature has arrived and should be given its rightful place in the understanding and enjoyment of the American experience.

This chapter does not provide specific lesson plans or course designs. Those are left to teachers, who can draw on their own backgrounds and experiences and on other published materials, such as Paula Gunn Allen's extensive works (1983, 1989). Appendices B and D provide a number of sources for information on American Indian literature; also to be noted is Rough Rock Demonstration School's Navajo Curriculum Center, which publishes a two-volume *Teaching Guide for Indian Literature* (Campbell 1983). It rests with teachers to know enough to select appropriate literary texts for their students. With that understanding, the purpose of this chapter is threefold:

1. to provide background on the nature of American Indian literature that can guide the initial direction a teacher might take;

2. to identify some Indian works that have become (or are becoming) classics, which are essential in any review of the literature regardless of what other specific selections may be included in a particular teacher's reading assignments; and

3. to identify useful secondary source materials that can help teachers to understand the nature of American Indian literature and to select reading appropriate to individual classes or situations.

As does all good literature, the best American Indian literature strikes at the heart of essential truths and how they are derived from our relationships to the spiritual presence, the landscape, and each other. At the same time, each work is highly personal.

Although many literary works carry universal meaning and have universal appeal and values, no one poem or song or novel speaks for all American Indians. Literature is the expression of the universal artist engaging the world around him or her, as heard in the voices of W. B. Yeats, William Faulkner, Yasunari Kawabata, Ovid, Joy Harjo, N. Scott Momaday, Simon Ortiz, or Leslie Marmon Silko. The personal nature comes from a characteristically intense participation of the individual with the wholeness of the surroundings, or the fragmenting failure to find that wholeness. Just as Yeats speaks from his experiences in Ireland, Faulkner from the American South, and Sarah Orne Jewett from Maine— so does each American Indian voice speak from its own world in America and from the unique position of being native to the land, even while sometimes separated from it by the dominant, white, modern American society.

The voice evokes the presence of "What Moves-moves" (in Lakota: Taku Skanskan), described by Kenneth Lincoln in the Introduction to *Native American Renaissance* (1-2). In spite of the rich, varied texture of Indian literature, this "conception of the human voice invoking power" (1983, 2) is not only pan-Indian, as Lincoln would have it, it is pan-human. To lead students into the universality and the uniqueness of American Indian literature, a teacher must recognize the essential truths localized in the particulars of existence, whether given in biography or in a highly fanciful poem or story.

I cite works from the more traditional canon of literature merely to reinforce the idea that American Indian literature is literary art in its own right and shares a certain thematic and aesthetic presence with those other, more familiar works in the long-established literary canon. It is time that we recognize the literary art of past and present Indian writers rather than shining on them only the floodlight of anthropology, or of "historical/sociological place." Even though the cultural matrix intensely informs such works as Leslie Silko's *Ceremony* (1977), Momaday's *House Made of Dawn* (1968), or Joy Harjo's *She Had Some Horses* (1983), let us also shine the light of imaginative literature on these works that we may better appreciate their value as literary art and thus enrich our lives, just as we might by listening to good Western classical music or looking at French or Flemish paintings.

Ralph Waldo Emerson writes in "Circles," "Our life is an apprenticeship to the truth that around every circle another can be drawn, that there is no end in nature, but every end is a beginning" (1981, 263). That idea is exemplified in much American Indian writing. Emerson furthermore adds,

The life of man is a self-evolving circle, which, from a ring imperceptibly small, rushes on all sides outwards to new and larger circles, and that without end. The extent to which this generation of circles, wheel without wheel, will go, depends on the force of truth of the individual soul. (1981, 264–65)

American Indian literature, too, records the individual soul's inward search of itself, and the rushes of that soul outward through many circles to the further reaches of our encircled existence where it shares a commonality with the world at large. Looking at it in this way can help increase a young person's self-esteem, help each student know that he or she is somebody—as in Emerson Blackhorse Mitchell's story "I Do Have a Name!" (1967). Within the most expansive circle are smaller circles of communal tribal experiences. American Indian literature lives, as does the literature of many cultures, at each extension of awareness, from the personal, self-evolving circles outward to the larger, more inclusive circles, gaining strength from both the universal values and from its own more particularly shared tribal values. It is important that young students recognize those personal and shared values residing in the individual literary pieces selected for study. It is especially important for young American Indian students who are in great danger of alienation from the rest of American culture, or who are caught between or may reject both the Indian and the dominant cultural aspects of American experience. The figure of the circle within circles is appropriate because American Indian literature does not lie outside the established world literature, but like each cultural circle or entity around the world has its unique being within the larger circle, a part of it rather than apart from it.

If we were to teach a course in so-called world literature (which often means literature of the Western world—perhaps from ancient Greece to modern Europe), all of us would recognize and accept the impossibility of adequate, thoroughly complete studies of all literatures within that domain. Recognizing that impossibility, we would accept the selectivity of the course; so must we not demand of any one class an in-depth study of all Indian literatures of all nations and all time. The governing principle must be the same as that accepted for a course in literature of the Western world, along with the same freedom to choose pieces most appropriate to the objectives of the class. Above all, in spite of a commonality among Indian literatures, we must not pretend that all are alike in the very particulars that give the literature life.

One commendable feature of Nathaniel Hawthorne's works (*The Scarlet Letter,* for instance) is that Hawthorne does not keep the past out of the present or the present out of the past. We should not, then, find alien the same trait in American Indian literature— whether we find an ancient song of wholeness or a contemporary song of struggle within a fragmenting modern world. Abel's struggle in *House Made of Dawn* provides a classic example. Abel's fractured life is made whole through his return to the values of natural rituals, especially the restorative Navajo Night Chant, and the healing power of words. Momaday's conscious use of ancient rituals is an obvious connection with the past, but we must not think the past exists in present literature only in direct borrowings, whether in Momaday, Silko, Thoreau, or Hawthorne. The importance of the accumulation of past literature as it informs the present dare not be lost. As the teacher of Hawthorne must be aware of America's Puritan and revolutionary past, so the teacher of American Indian literature must constantly be aware of two worlds: the ancient tribal world and today's modern world. Many conflicts depicted in Indian literature and the resolutions of those conflicts are generated by tensions between those two worlds: in Phil George's short poem, Charles Eastman's autobiographical accounts, N. Scott Momaday's *House Made of Dawn,* Leslie Silko's *Ceremony,* John Mathews's *Sundown* ([1934] 1979), Mourning Dove's *Co-ge-we-a* ([1927] 1981), and the dynamic poetry of Simon Ortiz, Joy Harjo, and Wendy Rose.

One of the best tools for unlocking the ancient tribal values and the new, re-created aesthetic participation is Owen Barfield's book *Saving the Appearances* (1965). Although he does not discuss American Indian literature specifically, Barfield offers a concept and a vocabulary to help us better understand the literature. The core of Barfield's argument lies in two closely related concepts. First, the difference between the tribal outlook toward nature and the "modern technological" outlook is more than merely a difference in thinking about phenomena (which he labels alpha thinking); it is also a difference in *figuration,* the process by which the mind constructs phenomena from sense experience.

As modern readers of ancient myths and tales, "we are in contact with a different kind of thinking and a different kind of perceiving altogether" (Barfield 1965, 29) because we experience not with our impartial senses alone but with other things, such as "mental habits, memory, imagination, feeling, and will" (20). Furthermore, "the striking difference between tribal figuration and ours [modern Euro-American] is that the primitive involves 'participation,' that is, an awareness, which we can no longer have, of an extra-sensory link between the percipient and the representation" (34). The relationship between the early tribal poet and the outer world is not the same as the relationship that our mechanomorphic consciousness might assume. Early people participated in a world that, for them, was not "outer" at all.

Because phenomena are collective representations, they change from one era to another, from one culture to another. This is Barfield's second major concept: "evolution of consciousness." Barfield argues that, just as there has been biological evolution, so has there been an evolution of consciousness that causes us to differ in our figuration of phenomena. That evolution has caused particles to become separate, unrepresented objects existing independently of our participation. This path toward nonparticipation, toward isolation, in the Euro-American world leads from the emergence of Greek reflective thought and the direct and purposeful rejection of participation in ancient Israel, to the modern scientific revolution, which made a *fait accompli* of the detachment of the outer and inner worlds. Without denying either tribal or modern scientific phenomena, awareness of the history of this evolution of consciousness can help us imaginatively to recreate another kind of participation, a symbol-creating activity akin to the nineteenth-century Romantic imagination that had Goethe as a patriarch and Samuel Taylor Coleridge and Ralph Waldo Emerson among its disciples.

All this is to say that teachers trained in the literature of Western Europe should not find the participatory mode of apprehension so strange as surface details might suggest. A little care can attune the thoughtful teacher to the participatory nature of much American Indian literature. American Indian literature often makes use of the remembered original participation and the re-created final participation, a quality which it shares with great literatures worldwide. Failure of the reader (or teacher) to recognize this participation creates a separation that can limit understanding of contemporary writers who aesthetically restore participation. What does a junior high or senior high school student care about the Barfieldian analysis of phenomena reviewed above? Not much. The literature must speak for itself if the student is to respond. However, teachers must know and care if they are to focus historical and critical light on individual selections so that students may read the literature with greater understanding and enjoyment. Students must also come to see the literature as works of art, worthy of admiration and enjoyment quite beyond, but not in opposition to, the social level of values. This comes naturally to American Indian children, if we are to believe Arthur More's article on "Native Indian Learning Styles" in the August 1989 special issue of the *Journal of American Indian Education*. Among the specific implications of the cognitive processes, he writes, "many Native Indian students frequently and effectively use coding with imagery to remember and understand words" (24). For that reason, he goes on to say, "use of metaphors, images or symbols is more effective than dictionary-style definitions or synonyms in helping many Native Indian students learn difficult concepts" (24). None of this is news to someone, student *or* teacher, attuned to the modes of response to literary art; it merely confirms the value of such attention to literature, which overlaps all engagement with literature. It is just that American Indian students, because of the acculturation that has shaped their learning processes, may have the edge in meaningfully engaging the literature. This ability can be used by the teacher to help compensate for other reading achievement problems created by the words themselves.

A standard anthology would be the best source for early myths and folktales to be read in either junior or senior high, although the reading level would have to be carefully monitored. Selecting poetry creates more of a problem even though the number of excellent poems appearing in anthologies is a positive development of the last decade. The problem arises when poems a teacher wishes to use in class are not in a single anthology. This problem is indigenous to literature texts generally, for one typically finds that an English or American literature anthology does not include all of the poems by John Donne or Emily Dickinson that a teacher might wish to include in a course. The same principle applies to short stories. For instance, the collaborative story "Chee's Daughter," by Juanita Platero and Siyowin Miller (1973), appears in some anthologies but not all the standard ones, yet it is a very good story to help form a core reading list for junior or senior high school students. The best solution seems to be to select a useful anthology and then supplement it as necessary.

The best assistance in selecting reading materials comes from the bibliographies compiled by Anna Stensland (1979), Paula Gunn Allen (1983), Andrew Wiget (1985), and Colonese and Owen (1985). *American Indian Women: Telling Their Lives,* edited by Gretchen Bataille and Kathleen Sands (1987), also contains an extensive bibliography. Most of these bibliographies list a core of autobiographies and novels appropriate to junior and senior high school students. Stensland clearly identifies and suggests the appropriate level of the literary work, as do LaVonne Ruoff and Karl Kroeber (1983).

In addition to what may be found in anthologies, a brief core reading list of biography and autobiography would include Charles Eastman's *Indian Boyhood* ([1902] 1971), Emerson Blackhorse Mitchell's *Miracle Hill* (1967), and John Neihardt's recounting of Black Elk's life in *Black Elk Speaks* ([1932] 1961). Recent years have seen a surge in autobiographical and biographical publications that should both inform and stimulate students' interest. Swann and Krupat have edited *I Tell You Now: Autobiographical Essays by Native American Writers* (1989), and David Brumble has written *American Indian Autobiography* (1981). Bataille and Sands's *American Indian Women: Telling Their Lives* (1987) is another example, as is Allen's *Spider Woman's Granddaughters* (1989).

A core of novels (including romances) would include D'Arcy McNickle's *Runner in the Sun* (1954; especially suitable for junior high) and *The Surrounded* ([1936] 1978) and Janet Hale's *The Owl's Song* (1974). Stensland also lists Momaday's *House Made of Dawn* (1968) for inclusion in high school classes. That work and Leslie Silko's *Ceremony* (1977) are outstanding novels by

American Indians; however, both are very difficult reading for
students and demand the teacher's careful assistance with concepts and stylistic features. James Welch's *Fools Crow* (1986) is
an outstanding and more recent addition to the canon and, as Jon
Reyhner suggests in his review, deals "in a more clear and positive way with the Indian self-concept" than does *House Made of
Dawn* (Reyhner 1989, 60).

To our good fortune, recent years have brought wider publication opportunities for American Indian writers and publication of
a number of books and articles extremely useful to teachers of
American Indian literature. Diane Long Hoeveler's 1988 article in
English Journal, "Text and Context: Teaching Native American
Literature," is but one example. The resurrection of *MELUS* after
a short hiatus will also help. Likewise, American Indians are
finding opportunities within the "established" canon—more inclusions in standard American literature survey texts and in such
books as Norton's *New Worlds of Literature* (which includes
in equal measure the works of European Americans, Hispanic
Americans, American Indians, African Americans, and Asian
Americans). All of the inclusions in this volume are modern or
contemporary. Linda Hogan, Wendy Rose, Leslie Silko, Paula
Gunn Allen, Louise Erdrich, and Ray Young Bear are included,
although Joy Harjo, Duane Niatum, Roberta Hill Whiteman, and
James Welch are not.

Paula Gunn Allen's *Studies in American Indian Literature*
(1983) includes a list of over twenty periodicals that typically
publish works by American Indians and scholarship about American Indian literature. (Some of the more accessible journals are
listed in appendix D of this volume.) Allen also lists special issues
of periodicals devoted to one or more aspects of Indian writing.

The following bibliographies list major anthologies of American Indian writing and books about American Indian literature
that contain material useful for general studies or particular advice. These are of necessity highly selective lists, of course, and
one should also consult bibliographies appearing in journals.

The teacher of American Indian literature must face several
questions: What makes a circle within the grander circle distinc-
tively American Indian? What basic assumptions are enclosed
within that circle, whether unique to American Indian literature

or universally shared? What shared values and modalities give power to particular forms?

Selected Bibliographies

Bataille, Gretchen M., and Sands, Kathleen Mullen, eds. 1987. *American Indian Women: Telling Their Lives.* Lincoln: University of Nebraska Press. This collection contains an especially useful annotated bibliography (fifty pages) of writing by and about American Indian women.

Colonese, Tom, and Owen, Louis. 1985. *American Indian Novelists: An Annotated Bibliography.* New York: Garland. The Preface to this bibliography states, "This selected bibliography is intended as an aid to students of the American Indian novel and as a guide to the rapidly expanding volume of critical material dealing with Indian novelists" (ix). For each novelist there is a biographical paragraph, one-paragraph synopses of that author's novels, a brief list of other works by that author, and one-paragraph responses of other scholars of American Indian literature, such as Charles Larson, Anna Stensland, Simon Ortiz, Paula Gunn Allen, and Kenneth Lincoln. Entries range from two pages for Dallas Chief Eagle, to five pages for D'Arcy McNickle, to nearly twenty pages for N. Scott Momaday.

Ruoff, A. LaVonne Brown, and Kroeber, Karl. 1983. *American Indian Literature in the United States: A Basic Bibliography for Teachers.* New York: Association for Study of American Indian Literatures. As the subtitle indicates, this volume is especially helpful in locating materials appropriate for classroom use and, therefore, in course planning.

Stensland, Anna Lee. 1979. *Literature by and About the American Indian: An Annotated Bibliography.* 2nd ed. Urbana, IL: National Council of Teachers of English. This has for some time been the major volume published by NCTE. It has served teachers extremely well since its first edition in 1973, and especially since the present, even more useful, second edition. Its great advantage is suggested by the title, for the volume contains fully annotated bibliographies under the following headings: "Myth, Legend, Oratory, and Poetry," "Fiction," "Drama," "Biography and Autobiography," "History," "Traditional Life and Culture," "Modern Life and Problems," and "Music, Arts and Crafts." In this second edition, the entries in each category are grouped under elementary, junior and senior high school, and adult headings. Stensland's bibliography contains capsule biographies of American Indian authors and sections on "Guides to Curriculum Planning" and "A Basic Library of Indian Literature." One shortcoming of this otherwise outstanding bibliography is also among its strengths: the significant presence of non-Indian writers. However, the standard classic works of such writers as

Charles Eastman, Scott Momaday, James Welch, and Leslie Silko (among others) are clearly present. It remains, for its purpose, a benchmark volume unrivaled to date.

Selected Critical Studies

Allen, Paula Gunn. 1983. *Studies in American Indian Literature: Critical Essays and Course Designs*. New York: Modern Language Association. This volume follows Stensland's original work by a decade as the next major study of its type, but it is aimed primarily at college-level courses; therefore, teachers should not expect direct application to junior and senior high school, even though much of the information included is relevant. However, the forty-page "Works Cited" section of outstanding essays by such scholars as Allen herself, Elaine Jahner, Gretchen Bataille, LaVonne Ruoff, Linda Hogan, and Patricia Smith offers substance valuable to any teacher of American Indian literature regardless of level. The chapter titles are "Oral Literature, Personal Narrative, Autobiography, and Intermedial Literature"; "American Indian Women's Literature"; "Modern and Contemporary American Indian Literature"; and "The Indian in American Literature." A useful "Resources" section contains a bibliographical essay titled "A Guide to Anthologies, Texts, and Research," a selected list of periodicals that publish American Indian literary works and scholarly articles about the literature, a further list of periodicals that have devoted special issues to Indian literature, and a selected list of presses that often publish Indian works. The book is an extensive, essential volume for any library. However, it is good only up to shortly before its publication date and should be used with the other more current resources.

Bruchac, Joseph. 1988. *Survival This Way: Interviews with American Indian Poets*. Tucson: University of Arizona Press. One of Bruchac's central points is that American Indian literary artists are not merely those legendary people long dead if not forgotten, but that there exists a healthy contemporary American Indian literature today. This volume includes interviews with some of those contemporary poets (Paula Gunn Allen through Ray Young Bear).

Chapman, Abraham, ed. 1975. *Literature of the American Indians: Views and Interpretations: A Gathering of Indian Memories, Symbolic Contexts, and Literary Criticism*. New York: New American Library. This volume has served teachers well since its publication, partly because of the range of material suggested by its long subtitle. That range is further demonstrated by inclusion in the set of twenty-six selections such figures as John Stands in Timber, N. Scott Momaday, Vine Deloria, Jr., Franz Boas, Mary Austin, and William Bevis. Paula Gunn Allen's excellent essay "The Sacred Hoop: A Contemporary Indian Perspective on American Indian Literature" stands out from among other very good essays in the volume, as does Momaday's "The Man Made of Words" and Bevis's fine essay on the problems of translating poetry from one culture to another.

Harris, Marie, and Aguero, Kathleen, eds. 1987. *A Gift of Tongues: Critical Challenges in Contemporary American Poetry.* Athens: University of Georgia Press. The principal asset of this volume is the range of coverage and the often insightful comments by the variety of scholars included. It includes, for example, an essay by Paula Gunn Allen on alienation, one by Joseph Bruchac on the survival of contemporary American Indian poetry, and a very good essay by John Crawford titled "Notes Toward a New Multicultural Criticism: Three Works by Women of Color," one of whom is Joy Harjo. The volume also includes a bibliography of publishers, journals, and anthologies dealing particularly with feminist, gay, black, Hispanic American, and Asian American as well as American Indian writings.

Lincoln, Kenneth. 1983. *Native American Renaissance.* Berkeley: University of California Press. The introduction, "Sending a Voice," sets the reader on the track of Lincoln's theme. The volume's nine chapters cover the expected range from "Ancestral Voices in Oral Traditions" to "The Now Day Indi'ns." It also includes a useful selective bibliography of primary American Indian works and scholarly studies of the literature. Lincoln has been faulted for being too selective, for omitting essential scholarship, and for his poetic writing style; nonetheless, this book is informative and rewarding to read, an outstanding addition to a personal or school library.

Scholer, Bo, ed. 1984. *Coyote Was Here: Essays on Contemporary Native American Literary and Political Mobilization.* Aarhus, Denmark: Seklos, Department of English, University of Aarhus. In addition to an essay by Scholer, this collection includes outstanding essays by leading writers in the field, such as Wendy Rose, Paula Gunn Allen, Simon Ortiz, Kenneth Lincoln, and Joseph Bruchac.

Wiget, Andrew. 1985. *Native American Literature.* Boston: G. K. Hall, Twayne Publishers. This contribution to the familiar Twayne's United States Authors Series is an extremely useful general study. Although the book is fairly well balanced, Wiget does pay more attention to contemporary American Indian poetry than have some other scholars; therefore, this particular contribution helps fill in one of several gaps in American Indian studies. This volume, too, contains a useful selected bibliography.

Selected Anthologies

Allen, Paula Gunn, ed. 1989. *Spider Woman's Granddaughters: Traditional Tales and Contemporary Writing by Native American Women.*

Boston: Beacon. This extremely interesting and stimulating volume is divided into three parts: "The Warriors," "The Casualties," and "The Resistance." True to its subtitle, it includes "traditional" tales such as "The Warrior Maiden" (Oneida), Pretty Shield's nineteenth-century tale of "A Woman's Fight," and contemporary accounts such as Linda Hogan's "Making Do." The third part provides a good example of the volume's balance of traditional and contemporary material, as it includes a wide variety of Yellow Woman tales—from the Cochiti Pueblo traditional tales to Leslie Silko's "Yellow Woman."

Momaday, Natachee Scott, ed. 1976. *American Indian Authors*. Boston: Houghton, Mifflin. This small (151 pages), out-of-print volume is made excellent by the selections included. Although contemporary materials should be used to supplement it, this book would serve very well as a high school text. It includes not only the inescapable figures (Charles Eastman, Emerson Mitchell, N. Scott Momaday, James Welch, and Vine Deloria, Jr.) but also selections not often reprinted, such as Thomas Whitecloud's fine Phi Beta Kappa–award essay "Blue Winds Dancing."

Rosen, Kenneth, ed. 1975. *The Man to Send Rainclouds: Contemporary Stories by American Indians*. New York: Random House. Stories by Leslie Silko and Simon Ortiz dominate this collection because of both their quality and the number included. This collection, while a good one, could be supplemented for classroom use by more contemporary stories and a wider selection of writers.

Rosen, Kenneth, ed. 1980. *Voices of the Rainbow: Contemporary Poetry by American Indians*. New York: Viking, Seaver Books. This volume is also somewhat dated; however, it remains a more successful text than Rosen's collection of short stories because of the number of poets included and the range and excellence of the selections from the twenty-one poets represented.

Swann, Brian, and Krupat, Arnold, eds. 1989. *I Tell You Now: Autobiographies and Essays by Native American Writers*. Lincoln: University of Nebraska Press. The eighteen writers included in this volume offer brief autobiographical sketches of their lives and discuss their separate developing engagements with the word. The sketches, therefore, provide insight into the sensibilities of American Indian literary artists.

Velie, Alan R., ed. 1974, rev. ed. 1991. *American Indian Literature: An Anthology*. Norman: University of Oklahoma Press. One fascinating part of this anthology is the "Songs" section, which includes a version of the Delaware "Walam Olum" in pictograph, Delaware text (Anglicized), and English. Chippewa songs are included, complete with musical notation.

Turner, Frederick W., ed. 1973. *The Portable North American Indian Reader*. New York: Viking. One of the formidable Viking Portable series, this volume includes a limited but very useful range of writing under the headings "Myths and Tales," "Poetry and Oratory," "Culture Contact," and "Image and Anti-Image." The "Myths and Tales" section seems strongest, although effective individual selections appear in each section.

V
Teaching in the Content Areas

..

15

Social Studies

MARLENE F. LaCOUNTE

Social studies is a difficult-to-define content area recognized by most educators as exceptionally important. What should children learn in social studies and how should social studies be taught are key questions asked by educators nationwide, including those working with American Indian children. However, teachers of American Indian children ask these questions from a somewhat different viewpoint, as teachers of students who are culturally different from the students for whom most published curricular materials are written.

A number of educators frame responses to these questions by examining the content of the disciplines being taught. In social studies, the disciplines of history, geography, political science, and economics as well as psychology, sociology, anthropology, and sometimes philosophy are scrutinized for significant and appropriate content. Regardless of who the learner may be, those educators believe the nature of the content dictates what is taught and the teaching methodology.

Many other educators assert that the key to effective teaching is to focus on the needs of individual learners in their unique educational setting. From this developmental perspective disciplinary content should be used as needed to meet the unique intellectual, physical, social, emotional, spiritual, and cultural needs of the learner. According to this perspective, the way to teach social studies effectively to American Indian children is to focus on their unique personal and cultural needs, covering content as it emerges.

Focusing on disciplinary content without regard to the needs of individuals is ineffective. Likewise, focusing on learners' needs without considering disciplinary content and structure may leave children with dangerous gaps in their knowledge of the world. The key question for this chapter, then, is how can the unique needs of American Indian children be met while teaching essential social studies content?

What Is Social Studies?

Social studies is both content and methodology, how something is taught and what is taught. This integration is so complete that how something is taught may become what is taught. Children learn inductively by observation and participation; therefore, if the ideals of democracy are taught to children using autocratic methods, children may learn that democracy is autocracy.

The content of social studies and children's knowledge interests go hand in hand. Children of all ethnic and cultural backgrounds have the same overriding knowledge interests: to understand and function effectively in their physical and social worlds. This relationship between self and the physical and social worlds defines the content of social studies.

Theory Bases for Social Studies Instruction

The fact that differences within, as well as between, cultures are great is important to remember when planning how to teach social studies to American Indian children. The personal, physical, and social worlds of many American Indian children differ in fact and focus from the worlds of children of other cultural or ethnic heritages, however the major social studies concepts (such as government, religion, time, and values) that students need to learn are the same from culture to culture. In addition, within a specific cultural setting, the situations that require individuals and groups to function effectively are varied, but the range of what humans deem effective functioning is similar from culture to culture.

The works of several individuals provide informational and theoretical bases from which social studies content and instruction for American Indian children may be approached. The work of Barr, Barth, and Shermis (1977) provides a basic description of methodological frameworks used for teaching social studies. The curriculum development works of Benjamin Bloom, Jerome

Bruner, and Paulo Freire are applied within that framework. Jurgen Habermas's theory of knowledge constitutive interests can be used to evaluate the content relevance and methodological effectiveness of each tradition when teaching American Indian students.

Three Traditions in Social Studies

Barr et al. (1977) define social studies as "an integration of experience and knowledge concerning human relations for the purpose of citizenship education" (69). The delineated "objectives required to achieve effective citizenship" were knowledge, information processing skills, values and beliefs, and social participation. What one believes constitutes an "effective citizen" and how one believes individuals reach that status vary with personal and professional philosophies (69).

According to Barr et al., three major traditions persist in social studies teaching: citizenship transmission, social science, and reflective inquiry. Each tradition reflects a philosophical belief about what knowledge is important for all citizens to possess and why and how people learn. Those who subscribe to the *citizenship transmission* approach believe that learning is an external, outside-in process. They believe people learn because they are told to, therefore an external force, such as the teacher, is expected to decide what, when, and how content is presented. The student's role in this tradition is to accept the judgment of the controller of the knowledge. Textbooks, lectures, and other prescribed materials generally constitute the sources of the content that is to be committed to memory by students for their use as needed in later life. Benjamin Bloom's (1981) mastery learning strategy is often used as a direct instruction process in this tradition. The teacher develops specific behavioral objectives and teaching activities through which students develop concrete products that can be evaluated to ascertain student attainment of objectives. Standardized tests of academic achievement are viewed as viable indicators of the amount of knowledge students possess.

Adherents to the *social science* approach claim the content of each social science discipline prescribes what is to be learned and the process by which it is taught. Each social science discipline is composed of basic concepts and subconcepts that constitute the significant knowledge in the field. That knowledge is best learned, proponents believe, by teaching students the processes of inquiry used by social scientists to discover the knowledge in the first place. Thus each student becomes a miniature social scientist, simulating the discovery of a particular concept. In this methodology a student learning history would "discover" multiple causation by analyzing several primary source documents about the events leading up to the Battle of the Little Big Horn, while one learning government would discover different types of leadership by studying the actions of selected leaders.

In the social science approach, as in citizenship transmission, a source external to the student prescribes why and how something should be learned, but the conceptual nature of the "what" could allow the teacher and student to negotiate the specific factual content. Understanding Jerome Bruner's (1960) analysis of the structure of the social science disciplines and conceptualization of the spiral curriculum is essential for structuring social studies content in this tradition. Teachers are assured of systematically teaching essential content of the social sciences when they focus on major concepts underlying each of the social science disciplines and revisit those major concepts as children progress through school.

An advantage of using Bruner's work to structure social studies curricula is that the specific factual content used to introduce and and build upon concepts may vary with the needs and interests of individual children or groups of children. Children may be introduced to essential social science concepts by studying them within the context of their own culture and time. As the children mature and their contexts expand, the same concepts may be revisited as they are encountered in outside cultures or the past or future.

The National Council for the Social Studies booklet *Teaching About Native Americans* (Harvey, Harjo, and Jackson 1990) superbly illustrates the versatility of the conceptual approach. The authors visualize their process as a vending machine. One row of buttons on the machine contains concept clusters, a second row of buttons contains specific Native American cultural groups, while a third row lists time periods. The teacher, informed by the students and/or community, decides which "buttons to push," then develops and teaches the information accordingly. Teacher comfort and success with this approach depend on the teacher's knowledge of the various social science disciplines, the availability of specific resources within the educational setting, the teacher's ability to custom-make curriculum, and the amount of power over curriculum matters accorded to teachers in the educational system. These issues will be examined later in this chapter.

In the tradition of *reflective inquiry* the learner is viewed as the knowledge informant. Learning is seen as an inside-out process, with the learner discovering knowledge on a "need-to-know" basis. The social science disciplines are not the source of content decisions, but individual and social problems experienced by learners are. Problem discovery and problem-solving provide the focus for methodological decisions. Often a social studies curriculum purporting to use a reflective inquiry approach is nothing more than a pseudo-problem-solving process in which the teacher "manufactures" problems for students to solve. The purpose of reflective inquiry is lost if this is the case. Paulo Freire's *Pedagogy of the Oppressed* (1970) provides the essential theoretical framework for curriculum development in a true reflective inquiry model. Freire's method is one of critical inquiry into situations that cause students to be less free than they could be. Curriculum development in the critical inquiry method has the following steps: the teacher communicates with the student about issues of concern; the teacher ascertains how, where, and why students perceive a lack of control over their own lives; and the teacher and student negotiate learning tasks that have the purpose of empowering the students while at the same time helping to reduce injustice in the larger society.

Teachers who use this method for teaching social studies often begin with current problems that concern students. Individuals or small groups of students investigate specific aspects of the problems that are of high interest to them. Students propose solutions for problems and test those solutions in a broader community, for example, the school outside of the classroom, the neighborhood, city, and so forth.

A Broader Philosophical Perspective

What the purpose of learning social studies is and where control over knowledge acquisition should reside are two key issues distinguishing one social studies teaching tradition from the other. According to the German philosopher Jurgen Habermas (1971), control, understanding, and freedom constitute the three reasons humans are driven to acquire knowledge. The acquisition of specific knowledge may allow individuals to gain control over others or assist them in understanding their personal or social environment; knowledge acquisition may also free individuals from controlling forces. An individual may want to know how to tie a knot so she can tie up other people, simply to understand more fully how it is done, or so she can tie a rope onto a branch and thus get down from the tree in which she is trapped.

Individuals in positions of power, such as parents, teachers, or political leaders, may use their positions to control what students are allowed to know, to assist students in understanding the world around them, or to help liberate students from those forces that limit their personal and social power. All three perspectives have proponents in the literature and reality of social studies teaching, as evidenced by the three methodologies previously described.

Figure 15.1 is a visual illustration of the connection between the locus of control over knowledge acquisition and the three traditions in teaching social studies. When placed on this locus of control spectrum, citizenship transmission represents purely a philosophy of external control. Forces apart from the student determine what the content of social studies should be and how students will learn that content. An example of this approach would be when the commissioner of Indian affairs in the nineteenth century instructed Bureau of Indian Affairs teachers to inculcate pa-

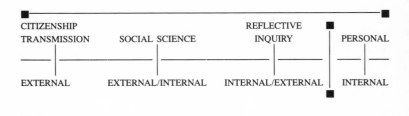

FIGURE 15.1 Locus of Control over Knowledge Acquisition in the Social Studies Traditions

triotism in Indian students and teach them that the United States government had the Indians' best interests at heart.

Although content is prescribed in the social science method, adherents to that approach are primarily concerned that students understand the concepts and processes of the social science disciplines to the extent that they can make sense of the world around them. Therefore, although the teacher prescribes in broad terms the concepts students will study and the discipline prescribes how it will be studied, it is practical to begin with the world the students know and move toward the unknown as the student is ready to do so. The locus of control begins in the external realm and moves toward the internal as the teacher tries to help students understand the concepts and processes.

In the reflective inquiry method the personal knowledge needs of students provide the initial focus; the teacher's role is to help students see their personal needs in the larger context of society, therefore what begins as a personal, internal need becomes entwined with the collective needs of the external society. While the locus of control moves in the social science method from external to internal, the movement in reflective inquiry is from internal to external. The ultimate knowledge goal is to free citizens from the influences that control them so that they can become active, involved citizens who strive to free others. This method is similar to that of the "explorer classroom" described in chapter 8.

Knowledge Interests of American Indian Students

The social studies curriculum should help American Indian students understand and function effectively in the personal, social, and cultural worlds in which they live. Those worlds include not only that of self, family, community, and tribe, but the broader world of being Indian in a predominantly Euro-American majority culture. Indian students have the added challenge of overcoming the realities and consequences of ethnocentrism, prejudice, and political control in order to become effectively functioning citizens.

Social studies curriculum must begin with realities in students lives and with their concerns and then help them understand the relationship between those realities and concerns and the larger world. The outcome of the curriculum is the extent to which students as individuals, citizens, and group members have power to affect both their own personal world and the larger world in which they live. Teachers need to understand those worlds so they can help students move from where they are developmentally and culturally to a functional level of understanding, where they can use basic social science concepts to solve real life problems.

One of the educational realities American Indian students face is that intelligence and knowledge value are judged by non-Indian cultural standards. Howard Gardner provides an important perspective on intelligence within various cultures. Gardner defines intelligence as "the ability to solve problems or fashion products which are of consequence in a particular cultural setting" (Walters and Gardiner 1984, 4). He contends that there are seven types of intelligence: linguistic, mathematical/logical, musical, bodily/ kinesthetic, interpersonal, intrapersonal, and spatial. All humans, unrelated to culture or gender, are born with a greater or lesser capacity in each of the seven intelligences. Each intelligence has a process and language used for solving problems in that realm.

An individual's ability to solve problems in each "language" of intelligence depends on that individual's innate capacity as well as his or her training in and practice with that intelligence. For example, the Euro-American male subculture places high value on mathematical/logical intelligence; consequently, individuals in that subculture are apt to strive for training in that intelligence and jobs that utilize it, such as electrical engineering.

According to Gardner's theory, one intelligence is not of more intrinsic value than another, but cultural groups do place differential value on the products of those intelligences. The reality is that American education is controlled by a Euro-American male perspective. The two major focuses on general intelligence tests and tests of academic achievement are mathematical/logical and linguistic intelligence as displayed by written language. In contrast, Davidson (1989) found the traditional educational focuses of American Indian cultures were insightful knowledge (being able to understand things and people) and interrelational knowledge (being aware of how various events fit together). Insightful knowledge could be likened to the interpersonal and intrapersonal intelligences described by Gardner. Interrelational knowledge seems to focus on synthesis and induction, the opposite of analysis and deduction, which characterize mathematical/logical intelligence. Harvey et al. (1990), in an adaptation of the work of Stone and DeNevi, characterized the "Indian way of life" as being present-oriented, lacking in time consciousness, giving, respectful of age, cooperative, and harmonious with nature—all characteristics consistent with Davidson's assertions. This contrast between the types of knowledge valued and institutionalized by the majority culture and those valued in Indian cultures is an additional challenge to the task of helping Indian students understand and function effectively in the multiple worlds in which they live.

From Theory to Practice

There are many curricular constraints placed on teachers and school districts today by powerful individuals and agencies. Most of those constraints are well meant. Those imposing the constraints use terms such as "quality control" and "accountability" as justification. The standards used to judge quality and accountability, however, generally reflect the values and learning preferences of the power majority, hence the effect is to diminish the learning of minority and nonconventional students by institutionalizing the content and ways of knowing preferred by those in power (Rietz-Weems, LaCounte, and Streeter 1990).

Yet, the situation is not hopeless. What follows is an attempt to consolidate theories and information about teaching social studies and the multiple worlds in which Native American students live into a practical process for critical curriculum development. The process is intended to operate (though not most effectively) within curricular constraints often imposed in American schools. The following assumptions permeate the process:

Learning is most effective when it emanates from an internal locus of control (comes from within the student).

Certain basic concepts, attitudes, skills, and processes constitute essential learning in the social studies.

The desirable educational goal for individuals is to understand their personal and social worlds and *to understand to what extent they can effect change in those worlds.*

Curriculum is most effectively developed by professionally competent teachers who are closest to the students.

Objectives should evolve during the learning process with direction from the teacher.

Teachers need to understand conceptual knowledge and processes of the social sciences, have well-developed skills in interpersonal communication, be able to assess and diagnose student needs in terms of knowledge and affect, and have skill in effectively creating and organizing curriculum.

Developing Critical Social Studies Curriculum

Step 1. Begin by "observing" and "listening" to the concerns expressed by students.   Opportunities to observe and hear concerns should be set up in the classroom by selecting pictures, literature, current events, or activities that initiate and stimulate student conversations about personal and societal concerns (see Sample A).

Sample A:

Observation/Listening Occasion:
   Set up and have students participate in the cross-cultural simulation, "RaFa, RaFa" (BaFa, BaFa for older students). (Simile II; Box 910, Del Mar, CA 92014)

Teacher Observations:
   What happened during the activity?
   How did students behave during the activity?
   Did interactions between students change in any way?
   What was the emotional atmosphere during the activity?

Student/Teacher Discussion:
   Probe for student thoughts and feelings during the game.
   Ask if this game is like anything they have experienced in real life.
   Discuss students' real life experiences.

Step 2. Analyze students' concerns in light of basic social science concepts and generalizations so they can be placed into a larger context.   In this step, the teacher reflects on the information gleaned from the observation and listening activity. In addition, the teacher assesses student responses based on major social studies concepts, skills, and values. After consideration of curricular mandates, the teacher decides on a unit of study that satisfies the mandates as well as the needs of students and the needs of the social studies disciplines (see Sample B).

Sample B:

The teacher notes that the students have had a number of experiences in which prejudice has been displayed toward them. They discuss the concepts of fairness and stereotyping. The teacher looks at the list of concepts, picks out several from assorted disciplines as possible focuses: minority, equality, diversity, change, rights, and prejudice. The teacher knows that state guidelines mandate a unit on the 1960s so begins to plan how to incorporate the concepts into that theme.

The social science concepts found in Figure 15.2 were selected and adapted from lists prepared by several well-known social studies educators (Banks and Clegg 1977; Ellis 1981) and from the professional teaching experiences of the author. The lists are intended to be instructive, not complete. Many subconcepts are presumed to be included under major concept headings—for example, government includes democracy, autocracy, oligarchy, and so forth.

Step 3. Plan curriculum which helps students understand and use the new knowledge to affect those issues that concern them. Figure 15.3 is an initial planning sheet for teachers. It is not a complete unit plan. As is apparent when examining the sheet, the teacher would be systematically developing the concepts presented during class sessions before and after the activities listed. The planning sheet is designed as a means for teachers to assess over the course of a unit their use of current theoretical knowledge about what and how students learn. It includes information about levels of cognition (Bloom), conceptual focus (Bruner), and type of intelligence (Gardner). The specific objectives and activities take into consideration the unique individual and cultural needs of students as well as curricular mandates.

HISTORY	**POLITICAL SCIENCE**	**GEOGRAPHY**
time	power	location
chronology	leadership	place
change	government	interdependence
cause/effect	state	demography
nationalism	equality	resources
prehistory	liberty	habitat
revolution	authority	urban/rural
fact/opinion	justice	migration
civilization	propaganda	transportation
technology	law	ecology
conflict	citizenship	climate

SOCIOLOGY	**PSYCHOLOGY**	**ANTHROPOLOGY**
group	self-esteem	culture
family	self-concept	artifact
role	normal/abnormal	tradition
status	motivation	custom
institution	attitude	ceremony
norm	frustration	settlement
folkways/mores	emotion	tool
minority	learning	acculturation
sanctions	communication	gender roles
cooperation	behavior	race
stratification	maturation	ethnocentrism

ECONOMICS	**PHILOSOPHY**
scarcity	logic
good/service	value
production	religion
money	belief
trade	ethics
labor	inquiry
job	aesthetic
cost	reality
poverty	truth
capital	morality
property	rationality

FIGURE 15.2 Checklist of Selected Social Science Concepts

UNIT TOPIC: The 1960s—Grade 8, American History

Cognitive Level	(Concept) Possible Activity	Intelligence
KNOWLEDGE	(MINORITY) TSW look at a chart of demographic data from the 1960 census and make a bar graph of the population of each group.	Mathematical /Logical-graph
COMPREHENSION	(DIVERSITY) TSW make a poster which demonstrates the differing views and life styles of people during the sixties.	Spatial-Poster
APPLICATION	(EQUALITY) TSW role play events of the sixties which portray evidence of equal and unequal treatment of people in various groups.	Interpersonal-Role Play
ANALYSIS	(RIGHTS) After studying the Civil Rights Act of 1964, TSW create and videotape a mime simulating an incident which could have brought about one of the regulations.	Bodily/ Kinesthetic-Mime
SYNTHESIS	(PREJUDICE) TSW read news articles about prejudicial happenings in the sixties and today and write an editorial on "Prejudice Yesterday and Today"	Linguistic-Written Editorial
EVALUATION	(CHANGE) After viewing a film on civil disobedience, TSW brainstorm ways changes occur and choose action projects which they believe will change prejudice.	Dependent on Project Chosen

FIGURE 15.3 Critical Learning Planning Sheet

Source: Adapted from the "First Sheet," developed by Engin-Uity, Inc.
Note: TSW = "The student will"

Summary

In the long run, if social studies is to be a meaningful subject for American Indian students, institutions that educate teachers must set high standards for the amount and substance of cross-cultural knowledge and sensitivities as well as the social science conceptual knowledge required of teacher trainees. The training of preservice teachers needs to change dramatically. Interpersonal understanding and communications skills need to be of primary importance, as does the capability of preservice teachers to develop customized curriculum.

At the same time school districts and state agencies that control the availability of resources and teachers' and school districts' authority to decide curricular matters must change from an attitude of control to one of empowerment. Methods of assessing the effectiveness of schooling must be altered to consider the unique needs of Indian children and their communities.

Appendixes C and D list some specific books and resources about American Indians that the social studies teacher would find useful, including biographies of important American Indian historical figures, books on the contributions of Indians to modern civilization, and books on specific historical events important to Indians.

16

Science

CARLOS J. OVANDO

In 1976 the American Association for the Advancement of Science (AAAS) prepared a document titled "Recommendations for the Improvement of Science and Mathematics for American Indians." Among the recommendations are (1) that in high school, science classes should be taught utilizing an ethnoscientific approach; (2) that bilingual instruction should be used where non-English language loyalty is fairly intense; and (3) that a vigorous effort should be made to recruit American Indian students for programs in science and technology (Green and Brown 1976). These recommendations raise three important issues in the improvement of science instruction for Indians. First, reflecting the AAAS's ethnoscience recommendation, how can an effective balance be achieved between the traditional, home learning experiences of the students and the formal science curriculum? Second, regarding the use of bilingual instruction, what should be the role of the home language or of English language development in science curriculum? Third, relating to the recommendation for more vigorous recruiting, what is the place of science teaching within the whole school curriculum for American Indians?

The Relationship Between
Home and School Culture

The ways in which we come to learn about science include the following processes: "investigating, discovering, experimenting, observing, defining, comparing, relating, inferring, classifying, [and] communicating" (Holt 1977). Regardless of the level of scientific sophistication, humans all over the world, as they interact

223

with their environment, have had to use these same processes to develop technology that enables them to survive. As Cajete observes,

> Expressions of the science thought process are abundant in historical-traditional Native American cultures. They have ranged from the simple practical technologies developed to survive in a given environment to highly complex and elaborate technologies developed by the "high" civilizations of Mexico, Central, and South America. These expressions of the science thought process have all taken distinctive cultural forms which reflect primarily the way a particular group of Native Americans has adapted to a particular place and environment. The science thought process has been reflected in Native American agriculture, medical practices, astronomy, art, ecological practices, hunting, and gathering. (1986, 4)

Activities, then, that can be applied to formal science education in school are already an integral aspect of American Indian cultures, as they are of all cultures. Therefore, all children bring with them to school a base for scientific knowledge, skills, and experiences. And this base can be related to the school's curriculum. For example, Indian children may have had firsthand experience with issues such as soil erosion, conservation, the use of pesticides, and consumption of traditional versus mainstream non-Indian food. These experiences can be applied to such formal fields of science as ecology, ethology (the study of animal behavior), genetics, geology, and nutrition.

Of course, as Cole and Scribner point out, "how people perceive the environment, how they classify it, how they think about it" varies across cultures (1974, 5). Ethnoscience, as mentioned in the AAAS recommendations, is one field of study that attempts to delineate within a particular culture its patterns of perception, classification, and thought. Working within the context of American Indian cultures, Cajete defines ethnoscience as, "the methods, thought processes, mind sets, values, concepts, and experiences by which Native American groups understand, reflect, and obtain empirical knowledge about the natural world" (1986, 1). Thus, the way in which Indians gain empirical knowledge about their environment may differ subtly or dramatically from the way in which white Americans of the dominant English-speaking culture interpret the environment. If, for example, a lesson dealing with frogs is presented to both Indian and non-Indian students, the subjective reaction (positive and negative!) to touching the frog will be derived not only from the students' individual personalities but from the students' cultural backgrounds as well.

Beyond the rather specific issue of frogs, when dealing with scientific processes a student from a traditional Indian background might be more inclined to see the problem from a holistic point of view while a student from a mainstream white American background might be more interested in breaking down the subject into its smallest components. For example, Maruyama and Harkins, as cited in Cajete (1986), state that Western classification systems tend to be more hierarchical and quantitative, while American Indian systems tend to be more mutualistic and qualitative. Also, Western systems tend to see cause-and-effect relationships as unidirectional, linear phenomena, whereas the Indian thought patterns tend to allow for many possible directions in cause and effect. As Cajete explains, a given "cause and effect cannot be isolated from other causes and effects with which they share a holistic relationship within a system" (1986, 6).

Differing scientific world views, however, do not have to mean mutually exclusive approaches to formal science lessons. In the school science setting both Indian and non-Indian students and teachers can contribute and learn something from each other. If the relationship between the traditional Indian home culture and the Westernized school culture is a two-way street, the quality and practicality of the scientific learning experience can be enhanced. This two-way street means that curriculum and methods reflect the patterns and experiences of the home cultures and, at the same time, introduce the local community to practices or concepts from the formal school curriculum that may have relevance to solving problems in the local environment. On this point, Scribner and Cole make the following observation:

> Changes in textbooks, curricula, and teaching techniques are all needed and important, but they cannot be counted on to bridge the gulf between school and practical life by themselves. A two-way movement is necessary here. The first, which is already under way in some experimental schools, is to move everyday life into the school so that subject matter and activities deal with some of the same aspects of social and physical reality that the pupils confront outside of school.
>
> The second has been little attempted. The techniques of the modern

school need to be introduced into the context of recognized practical problems. Education must be stripped from the schoolroom and made instrumental in traditional settings. (1973, 558)

In other words, interchanges are made between the home culture and the school culture. Guthridge, in an article titled "Eskimos Solve the Future" (1986), points out how he uses the students' own cultural frame of reference to solve future problems. Guthridge has trained teams of students from Gambell, Alaska, to compete in the Future Problem Solving Program. These teams have often won state and national awards. Many of the assigned problems—such as global warming or the use of laser technology—require student research in scientific fields. Guthridge points out that

In Future Problem Solving at Gambell we have learned to apply Eskimo training to the modern school setting. Students find, record, and memorize possible problems and solutions that might be applicable to the assigned subject matter, and then—slowly—figure out what the material means. (1986, 71)

The steps involved in the Future Problem Solving model were originally designed with a Western mind-set and, thus, required a great deal of verbal interaction among the students. Guthridge, however, accepted the students' use of their own communication style and pace until it felt comfortable and necessary to move toward more verbal articulation of ideas. He credits the Gambell students' spectacular success in coming up with highly imaginative solutions to future problems to this flexibility in approach. Students use learning strategies that have served their hunting ancestors well for millennia, but at the same time they acquire skill in using Western problem-solving techniques that they might someday apply to local issues. Regarding the Western world view versus the native world view, Guthridge tells his students that "the human brain is nothing more—and nothing less—than an efficient computer. Why not give it two types of software?" (1986, 72). The activity-oriented classroom that Guthridge describes is very similar to the explorer classroom described in chapter 8.

As discussed above, American Indian students bring to the classroom skills and experiences that can be used as springboards into the scientific process; materials and teaching techniques designed to tap these resources can improve students' mastery of science concepts. However, it does not follow that all science texts must be rewritten to reflect the students' home background. Science lessons need to start with the students' prior knowledge, experiences, and motivation; but teachers must understand and work from this basis—it cannot be done through textbooks alone. As a case in point, Kleinfeld (1979a) has noted in her study of St. Mary's (a successful Alaskan boarding school) that although there was no special curriculum for native students, what seemed to matter most in the school's effectiveness was the close relationship between the students and staff. Character development was of central concern. What we may learn from St. Mary's, then, is that a science curriculum that has been carefully adapted to reflect culturally compatible classroom practices and home experiences may not be effective unless the teachers are deeply committed to their students' academic and personal growth.

The Role of the Native Language and English

Going back to the AAAS recommendations for American Indians' science education, the second important issue is the role of the home language and the role of English language development. According to Title VII guidelines, the dual purpose of bilingual education is to teach English to non-English-background students and to provide effective knowledge transmission. In other words, bilingual instruction is federally mandated not only to provide English language skills for students with limited English proficiency but also to make sure that they progress academically in the content areas.

In an effort to address the pressing linguistic and content area needs in math, social studies, and science of limited-English-proficient students, Chamot and O'Malley (1986) have designed a model called the Cognitive Academic Language Learning Approach (CALLA). This model provides for the development of English through activities in math, social studies, and science. Of course, in American Indian bilingual programs the goal is usually not to provide a transition into mainstream American culture but rather to maintain and develop biculturalism. Nonetheless, the CALLA model has validity as a method for teaching English. In this model, instead of studying English as a second language in the formal sense of the word—as a separate subject—the students use English through science lessons to develop English linguistic skills as well as to gain an understanding of scientific content and processes. According to Chamot and O'Malley, the CALLA approach can be used effectively both with limited-English-proficient students and English-dominant students who come from a minority language background. They point out that an

example of the connection between the science curriculum and language experience is that students must use language actively to reason through an observation from its inception to a conclusion. The process of analyzing a problem, describing, classifying, and other skills that are fundamental to science curricula are an integral part of language development. (1986, 27)

Chamot and O'Malley suggest that science lessons can come not only from mainstream science texts but also from culturally relevant materials and the students' experiences. The following books are examples of Indian resources for science education: *Navajo Farming* (Bingham and Bingham 1979), *Between Sacred Mountains: Navajo Stories and Lessons from the Land* (Bingham and Bingham 1984), *Keepers of the Earth: Native American Stories and Environmental Activities for Children* (Caduto and Bruchac 1988), *Ethnobotany of the Hualapai* (Watahomigie, Powskey, and Bender 1982), and *Waksi: Wich Hualapai Cattle Ranching* (Watahomigie et al. 1983). CALLA science lessons can be based on discovering the scientific properties of familiar things from the students' home backgrounds. Teachers using the CALLA approach, in addition to planning an activity-based science lesson, can address such things as the vocabulary needed for the lesson (for example, the colloquial meaning of "dense" versus its scientific meaning), the types of language structures involved (for example, "more than" and "less than"), and the types of study skills (for example, reference books, diagrams, and tables). In preparing a science lesson, it is important not to water down the content while simplifying the language to the required degree. To maintain the appropriate level of difficulty in content, it may be highly desirable to preview and review the lesson in the students' home language.

Thus in order to maximize the success of a CALLA approach to science, teachers need be well versed not only in science content, process, and activities but also in English as a Second Language (ESL) and bilingual teaching principles and methods. In the American Indian context, which often involves small schools in remote, rural locations, team-teaching and the use of non-school human resources may be important in maximizing the success of a CALLA approach. For example, a local staff member with ESL training might work with a visiting geologist from the university to prepare some lessons.

The promise of this type of hands-on discovery method when used with limited-English-proficient students is buttressed by emerging research evidence. For example, Chamot and O'Malley (1986) cite research suggesting that learning English through science can be effective and fun. Besides being enjoyable, students with limited English proficiency who study science through activity-based lessons simultaneously make strong progress in English language skills.

Despite the usefulness of a partnership between science and ESL, there are also local Indian contexts in which initial science training in the students' home language may be possible and desirable. For instance, in the Choctaw bilingual program in Mississippi, students receive the majority of their classroom instruction, including science, in Choctaw. Doebler and Mardis (1981) found that the Choctaw students in the bilingual program (the experimental group) did substantially better in posttests in social studies and science than did the Choctaw students submersed in English-only classrooms (the control group). As seen in the Choctaw example,

science achievement of non-English background speakers can be enhanced by instruction in the native language continuing for several years after they have mastered basic English-language skills, because students are still more adept at processing abstract cognitive operations through their home language. . . . If sufficient instruction or tutoring cannot be provided in the home language due to the lack of human material resources or to the presence of multiple languages within one classroom, activities designed to use concrete, visual, and context-embedded learning formats will increase the ability of the language-minority student to master required skills and concepts. (Ovando and Collier 1985, 205)

Another example of the successful use of native language science instruction is the program for Navajos at Rock Point Community School in Arizona (Reyhner 1990). At Rock Point, science is taught both in Navajo and English using the experience-oriented commercial program *Science: A Process Approach*.

There are many factors at the local level that will determine
when and to what degree science instruction will be in the student's native language or in English, but three basic guidelines
may be useful:

1. New math and science skills, facts, or concepts are most effectively
   learned in the student's native language.

2. When second-language instruction is incorporated into a math or science lesson, identification of specific language objectives to match
   the targeted math or science objectives will give students more opportunities to practice particular vocabulary sets or sentence structures.

3. The more context-embedded the presentation is (for example, observation of a thermometer's response to hot and cold), the more likely
   that limited-English-proficiency students can master the content even
   if presented in English. The more context-reduced a lesson is (for example, explaining the meaning of gravity), the more important it becomes to provide instruction in the native language. (Ovando and
   Collier 1985, 213–14)

Getting Students Interested in Science

The place of science within the whole school curriculum is our
third important issue. The AAAS recommended that American
Indian students be actively recruited into the fields of science and
technology. This is an important goal, but in order to accomplish
it students need to be exposed to science in a positive and meaningful way early in their elementary schooling experience. Otherwise, it may be too late to attract students by the time they are in
high school. Fortunately, young children seem to approach their
natural environment as a marvelous series of question marks.
They spend hours observing with genuine enthusiasm the world
around them. They seem to be captivated by all forms of life—
bees, antelope, other children, horses, deer, butterflies, trout, and
so forth. They are fascinated by such natural phenomena as electrical storms, snow, wind, and rain. They love to observe what
happens when they throw rocks in the water. Human-made items
like airplanes seem magical to them; so do other human inventions—hot-air balloons, bicycles, computers, radios, vacuum
cleaners, watches, tape recorders, and so on. In other words, children's natural desires to make sense out of their environment
(with all its beauty, complexity, and mystery) can be nurtured formally in the elementary grades so that the spark is not gone by the

time these children are in high school. And the reason for doing this is not just so that we can have a higher number of American Indian scientists later on, but also so that all Indian adults of the future will understand how science affects all of their lives.

Unfortunately, as De Avila (1985) points out, many of the programs that target language-minority students such as Indians suffer from the compensatory education stigma. Because students in compensatory education programs have low test scores in the "basics," reading and mathematics, almost all attention is focused on improving achievement in these areas. Other subjects, such as science, tend to be addressed incidentally and haphazardly after the other work of the school day is done. The implicit assumption seems to be that learning takes place in a linear fashion, that students cannot learn about science until they have achieved mastery of a certain level of literacy. De Avila, however, argues that a discovery-based, activity-oriented science program is an ideal vehicle for the simultaneous, parallel development of thinking skills, literacy skills, oral language skills, and science content.

One way to address De Avila's concerns regarding the way in which many language-minority students in compensatory programs are denied the opportunity to develop scientific discovery skills is to consider the approach known as content-area reading. Pearce, for example, in his chapter on teaching reading comprehension in this volume (chapter 13), provides a number of suggestions for content-based literacy for Indians. Herber (1978), one of the leaders in content-area reading, views science and other subjects as powerful and exciting vehicles for literacy development. According to Herber, teachers should first see reading not as a subject unto itself but as a vehicle for getting from point A (lack of knowledge about a certain subject) to point B (where the source of interest is located). That is, literacy should be taught as a means to an end, thus the current movement for "applied literacy." Reading skills anchored in some meaningful purpose will have greater power over students than reading skills taught in isolation, with no relationship to other subjects. Thus, for example, a teacher who is aware that a student is interested in how the Rocky Mountains came about may wish to select articles or selections from a text that will focus the student on the processes by which nature has produced such mountain ranges. In this particular case, the end, which is discovering how such a mountain range was formed, becomes the driving force for wanting to read the passages. Through the geological reading assignment, in parallel fashion, the teacher can provide instruction in such reading skills as cause and effect and sequence of events.

Much of the difficulty associated with extracting information from science texts has to do with the highly complex nature of the vocabulary, the organization of the text, the language structure, literacy skills, and the study required for mastery of the concepts. Without effective guidance it is easy for students to fall behind, become frustrated, and eventually give up. This may become especially true for students from language-minority backgrounds; vocabulary and sentence structure, for example, are clearly language issues. What Herber says about instruction in general can easily be translated to a situation where the teacher is working with language-minority students, such as Indian students:

> The subjective observation that the student "can't read the textbook" is based on the incorrect notion that they should be able to read that material independently. Assignments are given; students do poorly in their attempts to read the material; the teacher is disappointed; the students are frustrated. (1978, 17)

In the above situation, teaching is not really going on. It does not take any imagination or training for a teacher to tell the students to read a certain section of the book and answer questions at the end of the chapter. The art of teaching comes in providing students with the skills needed to build a bridge between what they already know and what they still need to learn. In Herber's approach, reading for comprehension requires the active engagement of the science teacher with the students so that

before the teacher gives a specific reading assignment he or she discusses with the students the objectives to be attained from the reading;

the teacher and the students discuss prior material or experiences that set the context for the new material to be learned; and

the teacher carefully examines the vocabulary that students need to understand in order to make sense of the reading material (1978, 38).

Bilingual teachers working with limited-English-proficient students in some science assignments may need to review and emphasize beforehand the crucial vocabulary associated with the text. One prereading vocabulary activity is to provide students with a list of terms that will be encountered and have the students write down what they think the words mean. This will relate what they already know to what they are going to learn. Then, using a dictionary, group work, and the teacher's explanations, the students can write down what the words actually mean in the particular lesson. In addition, the teacher may need to help the students identify in the text where the authors are simply giving information, where they are explaining causes and effects, or where they are classifying. The use of the passive tense in science texts may need some explanation, to clarify who or what is doing what to whom or what.

Herber's approach to teaching reading while teaching a subject such as science involves much oral preparation and a variety of prereading activities with the students. He suggests that in these prereading activities prediction can serve to engage the student in the reading process. If students make predictions about what will happen in a given science experiment or study, they are more likely to want to read and to comprehend the assignment in order to see if their predictions were accurate or not. Their predictions function as an investment in what they are about to read or observe.

Both the CALLA approach and Herber's content-area reading can serve to integrate two subjects into one (for example, science and ESL or science and reading). The integration of subject matter may be a method that is culturally compatible with some American Indian traditions. Cajete comments that

There is no word in any traditional Native American language which can be translated to mean "science" as it is viewed in modern Western society. Rather, the thought process of "science," which includes rational observation of natural phenomena, classification, problem solving, the use of symbol systems, and applications of technical knowledge, was integrated with all other aspects of Native American cultural organizations. (1986, 4)

It follows naturally that, in incorporating Indians' traditional background into the formal science curriculum, a variety of areas of study or experiences can be interrelated. As will be seen in the following section on resources, for example, study of traditional myths, legends, and stories about the stars can be integrated with lessons on modern astronomy.

Sample Resources and Ideas for
Teaching Science

In this section, resources in four areas pertaining to the improvement of science teaching for American Indian students will be described:

1. ideas for the use of the local environment;
2. ideas for the use of local history and traditional stories;
3. sample science lesson plans; and
4. organizations and programs for teachers and students.

The following lists, of course, are not comprehensive, but they provide a sampling of materials available. Some materials may be useful as they are, while others may offer ideas for ways in which science teachers at the local level can develop their own materials or lessons.

Ideas for the Use of the Local Environment

The following materials exemplify some exciting ways to use local resources to teach science within the cultural and environmental context of Indian students.

Ethnobotany of the Hualapai (Watahomigie, Powskey, and Bender 1982) is a locally produced bilingual monograph that describes plants in both scientific and common terminology and notes the way in which they fit into the Hualapai culture of Northwestern Arizona.

Nauriat Niginaqtuat: Plants that We Eat (Jones 1983) is another locally produced monograph that was commissioned "to help preserve Inupiaq food wisdom, and to encourage the use of local foods," with a focus on the improvement of nutrition by young Eskimos in the Kotzebue area of Alaska.

Dena'ina K'et'una: Tanaina Plantlore (Kari 1977) is another excellent publication that examines the close relationship between plant life and the Dena'ina (or Tanaina) Indians of Alaska.

Village Science: A Resource Handbook for Rural Alaskan Teachers (Dick 1980) is a highly imaginative and outstanding example of how an area school district has developed a series of secondary-level science lessons using such commonly available things in their region as boats, chain saws, snow machines, wood stoves, guns, vapor barriers, and hand tools. These items are then linked to such science concepts as friction, surface area, inertia, action and reaction, centrifugal force, and center of gravity. Each unit consists of text with illustrations, suggested activities, and student response sheets.

Antler and Fang (Education Development Center 1970) is a small publication that is part of the social science curriculum *Man: A Course of Study.* The booklet explores the interrelationship among caribou, man, and wolf:

Man must kill caribou to live, but man does not have sharp teeth and strong jaws. He does not have great endurance. He cannot run faster than ten miles an hour. He does not follow the caribou through its yearly migrations. How does man find the caribou? How does he get close to it? How does he kill it? What does he do with the dead animal? (22)

Pitengnaqsaraq: Yup'ik Eskimo Subsistence Board Game (Lower Kuskokwim School District Bilingual/Bicultural Department 1983) introduces Yup'ik students to the critical function that the weather and seasons play in subsistence economies dependent on fishing, trapping, hunting, and gathering for their survival. The game provides a natural lesson in ecosystems.

Sometimes an idea for the science curriculum may come from an unlikely source. For example, Hale, a linguist, suggests that

The study of language should form a part of curriculum. Linguistic science has the advantage over other sciences that the data relevant to it are immediately accessible, even to the youngest of students, and it requires a minimum of material and equipment. (1980, 3)

In other words, according to Hale, science teachers can readily utilize the "linguistic knowledge which students possess as a subject matter of science" (3). For example, he suggests that by engaging the students in an analysis of the structure of their own home language, they will "begin to formulate the laws which govern the observable behavior of linguist form. Observing data and making generalizations about it is an important activity at this stage" (7). As an illustration of this point, students in a Papago context may start by using such possessive patterns as "my dog," "my house," "my horse," "my mother," and so forth to try to discover the rules by which the possessive construction takes or does not take the suffix -*ga*.

Teachers of science working with American Indian students need not limit themselves to examining resources labeled, so to speak, "for Indian students." Since there is a dearth of good materials that address the needs of language-minority students, teachers need to look for ideas that will fit our contexts wherever we can find them. The following are examples of general resources that can be useful to science teachers working with language-minority students, including Indian students:

The Scavengers Scientific Supply Company (P.O. Box 211328, Auke Bay, AK 99801) offers a profusion of science education supplies. The catalog offers animal skulls (for example, ermine/weasel, marten, mink, muskrat, red fox, and beaver), fur kits, plant specimens, and slides as well as posters of invertebrates, fish, mammals, birds, geology, plants, and on ecology.

A Guide to Nature in Winter (Stokes 1976) is a general reference publication that is very useful when taking field trips during the winter months to examine such things as animal tracks in the snow and to look for birds, which are then quite conspicuous. As the author notes,

Winter is a particularly good time in which to do this, for with leaves gone birds are more easily seen, and many join together in flocks, making them even more conspicuous. Now is the time to take birds you may have dismissed all summer as "just a Mockingbird" or "only another Chicadee" and relate them on a deeper level of interest. (185)

Man in Nature: America Before the Days of the Whiteman (Sauer 1975) is a reprint of an older book that integrates an American Indian perspective in looking at how man interlates with the natural world. Secondary students have used this book as a textbook.

Ideas for the Use of Local History and Traditional Stories

In the previous section, the use of students' physical environment for the development of science lessons and activities was explored. In this section, the ways in which Indian stories, community lore, and local life histories can be integrated with the study of science will be examined.

Ulgunigmiut: People of Wainwright (North Slope Borough School District 1981) is a student-produced local history of the Eskimo community of Wainwright, Alaska. The monograph itself does not pertain to any specific field of science. However, it serves to illustrate how students working on such a local history project could also be guided to use aspects of their historical research to branch out into scientific studies. In the case of the Wainright book, for example, the salient topic of whaling could be taken to begin study of the physiology and behavior of whales.

The Yukon-Koyukuk School District (1981a, 1981b) has produced a series of autobiographies, or life stories, of Indians of interior Alaska. These autobiographies consist of written transcriptions of contemporary Athapaskans telling orally about their life experiences, and the books are designed as culturally relevant materials for upper elementary students. Again, there is no direct science content in the life histories, but they demonstrate how science lessons could be fused with locally meaningful material. To look at just a few possibilities, the topic of fishing could be incorporated with a study of fish life cycles and food chains; the topic of gold mining could be related to local geology; or the topic of fishing could lead to a study of microorganisms as they relate to food preservation.

Star Stories (Skinner 1986) is a delightful publication that presents beliefs and concepts regarding the cosmos drawn from a variety of American Indian cultures and incorporates these ways of thought into astronomy lessons.

Famine Winter (Reyhner 1984c) was originally an oral account told in the last quarter of the nineteenth century about a Blackfeet family's trip northward in search of a polar bear. The brief account, interesting in its own right as a form of literature and history, could also serve as a starting point for such science topics as ecological regions (plains, forest, tundra), bird migrations, seasons and effect of latitude on seasonal changes.

Sample Science Lesson Plans

The following resources provide detailed examples or collections of science lessons that can be tailored to the needs of Indian students. The first two monographs cited focus on the development of English skills through the concurrent acquisition of science content and processes. The other two references are to materials that incorporate traditional Indian themes into science lessons.

Learning English Through Science (Sutman, Allen, and Shoemaker 1986) includes, in addition to a variety of instructional strategies, narrative descriptions of three sample science lessons in which the strategies are applied. Two of the lessons are at the high school physics level while the third one, on machines, could be suitable for kindergarten or early primary.

A Cognitive Academic Language Learning Approach: An ESL Content-based Curriculum (Chamot and O'Malley 1986) also has three sample lessons in its chapter on science. The lessons state language objectives, science objectives, and learning strategies. They also describe the preparation for the lessons, the presentation, practice activities, evaluation, and follow-up activities. The first lesson, for example, which draws easily on local resources, is on the interaction between rocks and water.

Introduce Science to Students Using the Environment (Richau 1981) contains eighteen lessons for elementary students. A few of the topics included are soils, land and population, miniclimates, the web of life, and ecosystems. All of the lessons are based on locally available outdoor field experiences and include instructions for planned observation. Many of the lessons begin with a "nonscientific" quote from an Indian story or poem that is related to the topic, and these introductions give deeper meaning to the lesson.

Science Lessons for Native Americans (Otto and Eagle Staff 1980) is a collection of lessons, ranging from kindergarten to the adult level. The lessons are adapted to Indian cultural traditions and each one includes a statement on implications of the lesson for Indians. For example, a lesson on necessary conditions for seed germination and development ends with the question of why Indians planted their crops on river bottoms instead of hilltops or buttes.

Organizations and Programs for Teachers and Students

The following are some resources that provide a support structure for information networks and science education opportunities.

American Indian Science and Engineering Society (1630 Thirtieth Street, Suite 301, Boulder, CO 80301) promotes the entrance of American Indians into careers involving the sciences. It publishes *Winds of Change,* a quarterly magazine for Indians involved with science and technology. The publication is designed to provide information on professions in science and to encourage Indian youth to choose science-related careers. It includes portraits of Indian scientists, articles on tribal use of technology for resource development, news on corporations involved with Indian issues, descriptions of schools that are providing good opportunities for Indian students, and information on scholarships.

The Minority Access to Research Careers (MARC) program, sponsored by the National Institutes of Health (Bethesda, MD 20892; phone 301-496-7941), is a highly generous scholarship program to prepare minority students for entrance into graduate programs in the biomedical sciences. Admission to the program is based on strong academic performance.

Conclusions

Working in the field of bilingual education, Lambert (1984) has developed the concept of subtractive versus additive bilingualism. Subtractive bilingualism is described as the students' lack of development in their home languages as they develop their second-language skills. Additive bilingualism is described as continuing cognitive development in the home language while also mastering the second language. Lambert argues that in the case of subtractive bilingualism the lack of development in the child's home language will also lead to deficiencies in the child's mastery of the second language. Additive bilingualism, however, provides the best potential for full development of the child's first *and* second languages. In this chapter we have discussed three main issues:

1. the need for a two-way interchange between the traditional American Indian learning environment and the school's formal science curriculum;

2. the potential for the use of science lessons as excellent vehicles for the development of English language skills in some situations, while other situations call for instruction in the home language; and

3. the desirability of elevating and integrating science study into the web of the overall school curriculum, using science and its connection with the home culture as a means of helping to also teach the "basics."

All of the above points, as well as the material resources that we discussed, reflect in common a need to break down unnecessary barriers between traditional Indian cultures and the Western science framework; between the content area of science and the other school subjects. These things are additive processes. Just as additive bilingualism enriches both the child's first and second language, additive science education can enrich the Indian student's traditional heritage at the same time that it prepares the student for mastery of scholastic science content and processes. An additive science education can do this within a context of more holistic understanding and meaning.

17

Mathematics

DAVID M. DAVISON

American Indian students often experience difficulties in learning mathematics that may have little to do with difficulties in processing mathematical ideas. The typical approach to teaching mathematics in American classrooms is not appropriate for students who are not from the dominant American culture, primarily speak a language or dialect other than standard English, and have preferred differences in cognitive processing from mainstream American students.

Issues in teaching mathematics to American Indian students center on the students' language-processing and cultural orientation. I have addressed elsewhere (Davison 1990) the problems faced by these students in terms of limited English proficiency, cultural influence, and learning style. The extent to which each of these factors, individually or collectively, influences the mathematics achievement of Indian students remains an issue for continuing investigation. What cannot be questioned is that the mathematics achievement of Indian students as a group is below that of white students in the United States. The purpose of this chapter is not to attempt to explain why this is so, but rather to suggest ways of dealing with the problem.

Davison and Schindler (1988) identified three areas in which native students have difficulty in learning mathematics: language, culture, and learning modality. It is too simplistic to attribute the minority students' difficulties in learning mathematics to any one factor alone. For example, minority students perform very poorly on standardized tests from the third or fourth grade on, while in the early years their performance is closer to average (Leap 1988; De Avila 1988).

Standardized group tests, by their very nature, place great importance on language skill, especially reading. A student who is an inadequate reader and has poor mastery of English language vocabulary is at a serious disadvantage. Thus it is clear that a language deficit will automatically lead to a mathematics deficit. Limited-English-proficiency (LEP) students from the majority culture are pressured to succeed by compensating for these deficiencies. Minority students typically do not receive such pressure because influences outside the school are unable to address the problem. Furthermore, minority students are often not motivated by test taking. They find the questions irrelevant to their interests and, apparently, do not respond to them seriously. This problem signals the need for questions that students would be willing to treat seriously. Finally, minority students sometimes perform poorly on tests because they do not understand mathematical processes. Such understanding usually comes through the use of manipulatives and visuals. In short, in competing with mainstream students on standardized tests, minority students are often disadvantaged through an interplay of English language deficiency, cultural dissonance between home and school, and inappropriate and excessively abstract instruction.

Influence of Language and Culture on Mathematics Learning

The influence of language and culture on a bilingual student's learning of mathematics has been investigated by a number of researchers. Leap et al. (1982) observed that American Indian students' errors in mathematics problem solving were attributable to the use of American Indian language mathematics-based problem-solving strategies rather than inaccurate mastery of Western mathematics skills. A review of studies of mathematics learning among a variety of non-Western cultures indicated that indigenous peoples are often unable to solve mathematics problems that are not perceived as culturally relevant (Saxe 1982). As an example the abstract addition of thirty-seven and fourteen is meaningless to some non-Westerners. It would be more meaningful to restructure the problem as the addition of fourteen horses to thirty-seven horses in an American Indian community where horses are important.

Other reports (Davison and Schindler 1986; Schindler and Davison 1985) discuss the potential impact of the study of Crow and English language mathematics concepts and vocabulary. It should be noted that the spoken fluency rate of the Crow language is high among the adult Crow Reservation population, and nearly 80 percent of Crow Indian children typically are fluent speakers of the Crow language (Read 1978). Davison and Schindler explored the relationship between the acquisition of mathematics concepts in the English language and in the Crow language and documented the existence and use of mathematics vocabulary in the Crow language by surveying Crow Indian adults and children from several communities on the reservation. Although all of the students interviewed were classified as bilingual, the effect of years of schooling Crow Indian children in English appears to be loss of much of the Crow language technical vocabulary. For example, only one of the children interviewed could count beyond twenty in the Crow language. Based on the interview data, it appeared that Crow mathematical terms and operations were typically not used to help teach mathematics to these students.

From the survey, Schindler and Davison (1985) found that dominant-Crow-language speakers viewed Crow as the language of the home and English as the language of the school. Such a dichotomy makes it very difficult for educators to fulfil the objectives of bilingual education and to reduce cultural discontinuity between home and school. One intent of bilingual education is the use of the students' mastery of the native language to assist in acquiring mastery of the English language. This happens, for example, through the use of both languages in introducing elementary math concepts. However, in the beginning grades, mastery of mathematical concepts in the Crow language would have to be developed more in the school before they could be used to facilitate the learning of the same concepts in English. The problem was made worse by the students seeing little or no use for the textbook-dominated mathematics they learned in school.

The problem of English language fluency has already been identified. When English is not spoken in the home, or when an Indian English dialect (see Leap, chapter 10 of this volume) is spoken, classroom English is not reinforced outside the school. In mathematics this means that English language mathematics vocabulary may not be used outside the classroom. In addition, confusion occurs when certain terms such as *factor* and *product* have specialized meanings in the mathematics classroom different from their regular English language meanings. Garbe (1985), in his work with the Navajo Indians, suggested that the students were not getting enough instruction in technical mathematics vocabulary. He recommended that vocabulary to be mastered be clearly identified and that student performance in vocabulary be passed on to the teacher of the next grade. Teachers should use students' past experiences with mathematical terms to help give the terms meaning in a mathematical context. The introduction of a new term should be carefully orchestrated through repetition in context and through saying it aloud and spelling it. Chamot and O'Malley (1986) suggest strategies for more effective mathematics problem-solving instruction through the Cognitive Academic Language Learning Approach (CALLA) to teaching mathematics to LEP students (see also chapter 16). Teachers need to build language supports to help students understand the language in word problems and to begin to use English as a vehicle for thought. In addition, steps involved in solving word problems must be made explicit. It is critical that these language factors be addressed by having students hear, speak, and write much more English language mathematics through appropriately guided instruction.

The application of native culture situations to the mathematics classroom represents one way of helping native students to see the relevance of mathematics in their culture and to use this connection as a means of teaching more mathematics. Aichele and Downing (1985) present one project that is doing this in Oklahoma. However, I find that many native students know little about their traditional culture since schools have historically been used to suppress traditional cultures and to assimilate Indians into the dominant culture. Thus the initial premise that cultural background can be used to facilitate the teaching of mathematics is suspect, but I have found that the interaction of native culture and mathematics ideas can be mutually reinforcing. For example, Rosalie Bearcrane, then bilingual teacher at Crow Agency School, taught a sixth-grade class about the Crow Indian Reservation. She divided the map of the reservation into six equal rectangles and assigned each portion to a group within the class. Each group had to enlarge its portion of the map by a scale of 3:1 and then had to make a plaster relief model of the enlargement. The finished products were combined to form a table-sized relief map of the reservation. This task was motivating for the students, and taught them more about their native heritage while they learned more mathematics. In other situations, such culturally relevant phenomena as hand games, arrow throws, and bead weaving have been used as bases for stimulating classroom mathematics.

The examples discussed above illustrate what may be termed an ethnomathematics approach to the curriculum. D'Ambrosio (1985) defines *ethnomathematics* as the mathematics needed by a particular subgroup of the population, be it an occupational group or a cultural group. Ethnomathematics includes curricular relevance but is much more than building a curriculum around the local interests and culture of the learners. Ethnomathematics must be understood in terms not only of the traditional native culture, but also of the culture's emerging identity, one that lives side by side with the mainstream culture. In this sense, an ethnomathematics approach to the curriculum will draw on traditional culture while focusing attention on the mathematics these students need in an integrated society. A curriculum perceived as irrelevant by native students cannot fulfill that objective. Whether the illustrations are traditional or modern, they must engage the students' attention and interest if the students are to be helped in understanding the important mathematical ideas.

Attention to the students' language mastery and perceived relevance of mathematics addresses just one dimension of the students' difficulties with mathematics learning. We also need to consider the effect on the students of the method of presentation of the mathematics.

Relevance of Learning Style

Typical mathematics learning materials are prepared on the assumption that all students learn mathematics in the same way. An examination of such resource materials indicates that the dominant mode of mathematics presentation is abstract. However, evidence from research and observation indicates that native students usually do not respond to a verbal, abstract style of mathematics learning and prefer familiar tactile and visual stimuli. Wauters et al. (1989), for example, found that Alaska students strongly prefer visual and tactile modes of learning.

Rhodes (1990), in an investigation of the learning styles of Navajo and Hopi students, found dissonance between the students' learning styles and their teachers' teaching styles. The "watch me and do as I do" procedures used in traditional schooling appear to be less appropriate than a process of "watch me and try it when you feel comfortable with it." Rhodes asserts, "Once the teachers become more sensitive to the learning styles of the students, they can adapt . . . the implementation of the curriculum more to the student needs" (37). More (1989) warns against stereotyping native students through an overemphasis on learning style differences. He has the following recommendation for teachers of native students: "It is more effective with Native children to present new and difficult material in a visual/spatial/perceptual mode rather than a verbal mode" (24).

A consistent picture emerges of the American Indian learner as one who prefers that mathematics be presented through physical or visual stimuli. In the context of the discussion of Indian learning styles, we should not overlook the caution sounded by Diessner and Walker (1989) that to be competitive in pluralistic America, Indian students need to increase their English language and basic information achievement. This attention to American Indian learning styles is viewed not as an explanation for Indian students' failure to learn abstract mathematics but as an opportunity to accomplish this goal.

The elementary mathematics curriculum emphasizes competence in work with numbers and operations involving them, and geometry assumes a less prominent place. Chapters in geometry are usually near the end of mathematics textbooks and sometimes treat the subject in a superficial manner. Geometry is the one branch of mathematics that stresses spatial rather than analytical approaches to mathematics. Success in geometry is related to a kinesthetic processing of the environment. For example, I found that when given the geometric attribute pieces containing the primary colors, four shapes, and two sizes, non-Indians classify primarily by color first, while Crow Indian students I studied mostly classify by shape first. This observation supports the notion that these Indian students' preferred style of mathematical processing is essentially kinesthetic.

Few curricular efforts have been devoted to addressing different learning styles in mathematics. Perhaps the best-known approach to primary mathematics stressing tactile methods is found in Mary Baratta-Lorton's (1976) *Mathematics Their Way.* This program is activity-oriented; students learn mathematical ideas by working with familiar objects. While the program is intended to help all primary students learn mathematics, its emphasis is such that minority students now have a chance to learn mathematics in an understandable way. The program has been particularly successful with American Indian students who benefit from its more hands-on approach.

Another project dealing with the way native students learn mathematics is Math and the Mind's Eye, a National Science Foundation–funded project directed by Gene Maier in Portland, Oregon. Maier (1985) points out that many people, in the non-Indian as well as in the American Indian culture, find mathematics devoid of meaning—nothing more than jargon and symbol manipulation. The result is mathematics underachievement, anxiety, and aversion. Many of the people who do succeed in post-school mathematics use sensory perception, models, and imagery. This is very different from the views of school mathematics described above. Maier's project stresses the use of manipulatives and activity methods in the middle grades as well as in the primary grades. Certainly, an emphasis on a hands-on approach to mathematics learning would help Indian students make more sense of the way mathematics is presented.

Curriculum designers are being made aware that not all students learn mathematics in the same way. Materials that emphasize the use of hands-on activities will help students whose primary learning mode is kinesthetic rather than abstract, though it can be argued that for real subject matter understanding all students need to learn first from concrete experiences before they move to more abstract representations of those experiences. The use of an activity-centered approach in working with Indian students is one way of responding to their different learning styles. There is a clear suggestion that these students will be more successful when the presentation of mathematics material responds to their learning styles by being less abstract and more visual and tactile. This observation is supported by Indian students' preference for geometric tasks and suggests that these students can succeed in English language mathematics so long as it makes sense in terms of the way they process information. Initially, the use of the native language is important as an aid to learning English language terminology; the continued successful learning of mathematics depends on students being able to process the ideas in a meaningful way. Accordingly, a more visual- or sensory-oriented teaching style would seem to be essential.

Rock Point Community School in Arizona provides an example of a mathematics curriculum for Indian students that incorporates the extensive use of manipulatives in the early grades. Students first use special counting blocks that come both individually and pregrouped in sets of two through ten to perform mathematical calculations. Only after being talked through the block problems in both Navajo and English do the students advance to pictures of blocks on worksheets, and only after using these visual representations of blocks do they move on to abstract calculations using numbers alone. The Rock Point curriculum is based on the now out-of-print Stern Mathematics program that was published by Houghton Mifflin (see also Stern 1949). The success of this multisensory approach is seen in the mathematical knowledge of Rock Point seniors who, on average, score at or above national averages on the mathematics portion of the California Test of Basic Skills (Reyhner 1990).

Current Studies

In more recent work, seventh- and eighth-grade students were provided experiences to help overcome mathematics deficiencies. Students were introduced to a manipulative approach to fractions and logic activities and had to describe these tactile experiences in writing. In addition, assigned activities included creating related story problems and having them solved by their peers. Most of the students responded positively to this approach. One noteworthy exception was the student with the highest mathematics achievement; he disliked using manipulatives and would not take the writing activities seriously because they required a type of reasoning that was difficult for him. He was deficient in language skills and his mathematics test scores were alleged to be a reflection of memory skill. Serious questions are raised whether this student and many others with satisfactory mathematics test scores possess the capabilities—the real understanding of mathematics processes—credited to them. There may be many minority language students who mask deficiencies in mathematical understanding by performing adequately on mathematics tests that focus on computational skills.

Indian students who do well with addition, subtraction, multiplication, and division often fail when it comes to solving story problems, which add a reading or language dimension to mathematics. This is one explanation of the downward trend in Indian students' standardized test scores in the upper elementary grades, where solving story problems becomes more important. Having students start in the primary grades to write their own story problems relevant to their world will help them understand what story problems are all about, will help develop their language skills and, in addition, will give them an understanding of the real world applications of mathematics. A teacher can ask each student to write and illustrate a story problem individually or in groups to fit a given problem, such as $5 - 3 = 2$, and then ask each student to read and solve the story problem for the rest of the class. One Billings, Montana, teacher then had her students glue their sheets together on a bulletin board in such a way that at the end of the school year each student had his or her own math story book to take home for review during the summer. This integration of mathematics, reading, writing, speaking, and listening activities fits the Whole Language approach to instruction currently being advocated by a number of educators for all children (see chapter 12).

In another year-long study, seventh- and eighth-grade Chapter I and resource room students were assigned writing tasks in mathematics—journal writing, descriptions, and explanations of procedures used, and creation of problems. Analysis of observational data indicated that these students, who were reluctant writers, were now more willing to write. Their performance in both language and mathematics improved: in language because they were writing more, and in mathematics because they showed some understanding of the processes they were studying (Davison and Pearce, in press).

The focus of the above studies is to determine how familiar situations and tactile or visual approaches, integrated with systematic language activities, help students improve both their level of language functioning and mathematics performance. An ethnomathematics solution to the problem calls for the use of the familiar to help students learn the mathematics needed for success in our society and be motivated to work to accomplish that goal.

Summary

American Indian students' capacity to learn mathematics is influenced by language, culture, and learning style. However, the methods by which mathematics is typically presented do not take into consideration these factors. Textbooks are typically written for white middle-class American students and present mathematics as an essentially abstract subject. While many textbook series now refer to the use of tactile and visual aids, few teachers present mathematics in other than an abstract manner. To learn mathematics successfully, many American Indian students need a more multisensory approach to mathematics than is usually encountered in schools.

The abstract, decontextualized teaching of mathematics has affected many American Indian students' school success. Students who speak Indian languages should have a chance to learn mathematics terminology in their native language and then to relate this knowledge to the English language mathematics vocabulary. Wherever possible, mathematics concepts should be presented in a culturally relevant manner, using situations that the students find interesting and familiar. Above all, the presentation of mathematical ideas needs to be consistent with how students learn. The use of a tactile or visual approach assists students to form meaningful images. Progress in these three areas will contribute to more successful learning of mathematics by American Indian students.

18

Physical Education

ROBERT W. GRUENINGER

We had games—games that brought good health and sound bodies. Why not put these in your schools?

—Grand Council Fire, December 1989

American Indians helped develop many popular contemporary sports and games and can take sole credit for originating many recreation items and other sports. Ancestral forms of field hockey, ice hockey, soccer, and football were played in the Americas of long ago, as in other parts of the world. Canoes, sleds, snowshoes, moccasins, hammocks, kayaks, ponchos, toboggans, parkas, stilts, swings, tops, and, in fact, rubber balls are Indian inventions (Brescia 1981; Josephy 1968; Lavine 1974). Most are aware that lacrosse is an Indian game.

Indian sports, games, and recreation served the cultural role of perpetuating the values and skills needed for survival. Activities often simulated hunting, food gathering, tepee building, relaying vital messages, and fighting (Wise 1976). Skills emphasized were throwing spears, shooting arrows, riding horses, and running. Games developed and tested the strength, stamina, speed, pain tolerance, and courage required for life.

This chapter focuses on the more common active games, sports, and contests that provided physical fitness. Although many activities are no longer practiced, some are still enjoyed by Indian children and adults. Tribal dancing is omitted, since it thrives both as an exercise and an art form apart from any additional effort needed to preserve it. Also excluded is discussion of the many guessing games and games of chance. Suffice it to say that gambling was associated with games of all types.

Children's Games

Indian children's games mimicked adult activities (Lakota Woskate 1972). Girls would put up miniature tepees and boys would bring rabbits, imitating the hunt. Stilts were fashioned for Hopi, Shoshoni, Crow, Zuni, and Mayan children, to mention but a few. Swings were enjoyed by Pawnee and Teton Sioux youngsters. During the winter, children in the north country would spin conical tops on ice (Lowie 1954). Children also liked to imitate the motions of animals (MacFarlan 1958). Tag games were popular, as were other running and relay games. Games similar to Blind Man's Bluff, Prisoner's Base, Crack the Whip, Hide and Seek, and Follow the Leader were common (Whitney 1977). Some recreational activities suitable for playing in schools today include Fish Trap, Hoop Race, Corncob Darts, and Dodge Ball.

Indian youth of the Northwest Coast played Fish Trap, a tag game played by between four to twelve "fishers" and one to three "fish". The fishers held hands simulating a net and would attempt to catch the fish. If the fish were touched by any part of the net, they were considered caught. The game continued until all of the fish were netted (Ross and Fernandes 1979).

The Beaver Clan of the Seneca Nation enjoyed Hoop Race, a circle relay in which each child passed a hoop twenty-four inches in diameter over the head, body, and legs and back again in reverse sequence (step in the hoop, over the trunk, and off over the head). The first team to complete the circle by passing the hoop, without missing a person or step, was the winner.

Another game involved darts made of shelled corncobs and feathers. The darts were thrown for various distances at a circular target drawn on the ground. Twenty feet was an average distance, although the target was moved nearer or farther depending upon the skill level of the players.

Mandan, Pawnee, and other prairie tribes played a form of Dodge Ball in which a batter would toss up and bat a rawhide ball with a four-foot-long hardwood stick. If any of eight or so fielders encircling the batter caught the ball, the fielder would throw it from that spot at the batter. The batter had to dodge the ball while staying inside a four-foot-diameter circle. If hit, the batter became the fielder, and the thrower became the batter (Whitney 1977).

Bowling

In Georgia, archaeologists discovered several twenty-foot-long bowling alleys built by the Cherokee. The alleys were made of hardened clay. Stones were pitched at clay pins or clubs. But a more prevalent Cherokee game was Chunkgee, in which a discus-shaped stone was rolled and contestants threw poles to land at the estimated final resting place of the stone. Chunkgee yards were a predominant feature of Cherokee villages; centrally located, the yards consisted of an acre of cleared space (Malone 1952).

In the Southwest, corncob targets were knocked down by rolling wooden balls. In Louisiana and Arkansas, however, the Caddo Indians played an interesting team game not unlike what is now known as Pin Guard. A field about thirty by seventy feet was marked out, and six clay "Indian clubs" were placed side by side along each end line. Two teams of seven players competed, with each team confined to its own half of the field. The object was to throw a basketball-sized ball filled with seed so that it would knock down the pins. Play continued until one team had knocked over all the pins on the other team's end line (Whitney 1977).

Football

Games played with the feet ranged from foot catch to soccer to kick-stick races. Foot catch was played by tribeswomen who balanced a small deerskin ball on top of the foot, kicked it into the air, and caught it again on the foot. Pretty Shield described a kicking ball made for her by her older sister: "The thin skin that is over a buffalo's heart is taken off and stuffed with antelope hair. My ball was a very fine one, painted red and blue" (Linderman [1932] 1972, 32). She describes the game as follows:

This happened at The-hollow-rock near The-big-drop. The leaves on the trees were nearly grown. Several of us girls were playing at kicking the ball. In this game, we choose sides. A girl places the ball upon her foot, and kicks it up, keeps doing this until she misses, and the ball falls to the ground. It is then the other side's turn to kick the ball, each girl taking her turn until all have kicked. The side that keeps the ball from falling the longest time, the greatest number of kicks, wins the game; and always the winners touch the foreheads of the losers with their hands. (111)

Among the Eskimos, the ball was one-and-a-half to two inches in diameter, made of buckskin, and somewhat like the hackeysack now possessed by countless American teenagers. By comparison, the soft leather hackeysack also measures about one and a half inches in diameter, or almost five inches in circumference.

There were many versions of ball-kicking games, the earliest having been recorded in 1583. For instance, the Eskimos had a game similar to line soccer. Yakima men and women played football on a field, counting one point per goal and allowing a goalie to block the ball. The Paiutes played Wat Si Mo on a fifty-yard field, with two teams of four players each, using a three-inch-wide buckskin ball (Brescia 1981). Most tribes disallowed use of the hands, although some games employed both feet and hands. The Moquelumnan of California had an elaborate football-handball game in which men had to use their feet, while women were permitted to throw the ball. Another California tribe, the Nisenan, played with a twelve-inch oblong ball, with eight players to a team. While reading Dr. Hudson's description of the Nisenan game, reflect on the present popularity of "eight-a-side" football at small, rural high schools: "One ball is used. The goals consist of pairs of poles, three feet apart, at the ends of a one-thousand foot course. Rough play is the rule, as a player is allowed to run with the ball in his hands, and interference is permissible" (Culin 1975, 703).

Tek'mu Pu'ku means, in Moquelumnan tribal language, "to kick little dog," and was the name of one of many kick-ball and kick-stick races enjoyed by American Indians. Two parallel lines were marked six inches apart, and posts were placed at the end of the lines. The object was to keep the small, buckskin ball between the lines while foot racing; if the ball went out of bounds, it was restarted from that point (Brescia 1981).

Intertribal kick-ball races were common, such as between the Tohono O'odham (formerly Papago) and Pima. The Tohono O'odham played *Wuchuta,* a team relay in which a wooden ball was kicked from one player to another as four teammates raced down a course to score a goal (Woodruff 1939). Other tribes of the Southwest also played kick-ball and kick-stick games. While the Navajo were reputed to have the fastest runners, the Zuni would always win at kick-stick races, kicking a stick along and racing to catch it only to repeat the process for many miles (Nabokov 1981).

Hoop and Pole Games

Sports implements often were derived from weapons used in hunting or in war. Thus in the hoop and pole game, the shield became a hoop and the spear became the pole. In *Gamago,* the Iroquois hoop and pole game, a five-and-a-half-foot spear of maple was thrust at an eight-inch-diameter hoop. Two teams, each of fifteen to thirty players, lined up several feet apart and the hoop was rolled in between. After the hoop was speared, the opposite team tried to throw its spears to hit inside the hoop. Any player who missed lost his spear (Brescia 1981).

Sometimes arrows or darts were thrown at a rolling webbed target hoop that had been divided into different point values according to difficulty. Blackfeet warriors shot arrows at the hoop as it rolled past a specified point. Most tribes restricted participation to men, although some tribes, such as the Yurok, allowed women to participate. Pawnees used darts, and the Sauk and the Fox used arrows (Lavine 1974).

A variation of the game as played on the prairie involved two competitors who slid eight-foot-long poles after the rolling hoop so the hoop would fall over one when it ran out of momentum. If the hoop fell on any part of the pole, the thrower was given one point, if the hoop fell on the butt end of the pole, the thrower received two points. If the hoop fell on the point of the pole, the thrower got three points (Whitney 1977).

Lacrosse

While Indians had their own types of bowling, hockey, baseball, wrestling, and football, primitive forms of these activities have been found in other parts of the world as well. Lacrosse, however, is uniquely American Indian. In 1564, the French explorer René Goulaine de Laudonnière recorded the game in what is now Mississippi, among the Choctaws. The game was called *Kabocca.* The ball used was the size of a golf ball, and most commonly was made of wood (Lavine 1974; Culin 1975). There were as many as seven hundred players on one team! Each player had two sticks with a cup-shaped end to catch and throw the ball. Goal posts were a mile apart. The score could run to one hundred points, and a game could take four to five days, or longer. The Choctaws played *Kabocca* against the Creeks and the Chickasaws to earn hunting privileges, settle disputes, or determine the best warriors. A Cherokee tradition maintained that a huge tract of North Georgia land had been won by their tribe through a ball game victory over the Creeks (Malone 1952).

Kabocca was played by men of the Algonquian and Iroquoian tribes of the Atlantic Coast and Great Lakes, the Teton Sioux to the west, the Muskhogean tribes of the South, and by the Chinooks and the Salish in the Northwest, though different tribes had different names for the game. The Iroquois called it *Tokonhon,* the "little brother of war." French settlers, observing that the curved sticks used by the Senecas resembled the bishop's staff they called *la crossier,* named the game lacrosse.

Lacrosse was a violent, active sport, with much running, quick starts, and frequent injuries (Anderson 1983). Shawnees, Santee Sioux, and Teton Sioux permitted women to play. Cherokees, Choctaws, Muskogees, and Seminoles used two rackets; the other tribes mentioned used one. The Cherokee game was played with a deerskin ball, thrown or carried using two-foot-long sticks with a netting of animal hide strips on one end. Twelve or more players were on a team. Players covered their bodies with oil, to slip by an opponent (Malone 1952). James Mooney described a game he witnessed among the Eastern Cherokees in 1889 as "a very exciting game, as well as a very rough one, and in its general features is a combination of baseball, football, and the old-fashioned shinney" (as quoted in Culin 1975, 586). The rules have been refined through the years. Teams were limited to thirty or so per side, at first, and then to the current ten per side for men and twelve per side for women. The field has decreased to the size of a soccer pitch. Rules of safety and protective equipment have been added (Anderson 1983).

Modern lacrosse is played widely in Canada and the United States (Whitney 1977). A variation, box lacrosse, is played in iceless hockey rinks, adopting rules from ice hockey, lacrosse, and Murder Ball (Lavine 1974).

Shinny

Shinny was the forerunner of both ice and field hockey, and was popular from Canada to Mexico, from the Atlantic to the Pacific.

Although the ice version was played by men and women, the land game was engaged in primarily by women. Field length varied from four hundred feet to one-quarter mile long. Teams competed by defending goals located at opposite ends of the field or by taking turns and counting the number of strokes that it took to score a goal by hitting the ball along the ground with the stick. Indian Agent Albert Kneale gave this account of a version of the game as played on the Crow Reservation:

> The Crows played a game somewhat similar to shinny, and what a game it was! The field was possibly five miles in length and there were no side lines. The goal lines were marked off by an array of vehicles and saddle horses belonging to the contestants, and a few individuals who for some reason were incapacitated. There was no limit to the number of players. It was district versus district. (1950, 188)

The game was more defined among the Blackfeet, whose women had an impartial method of choosing their teams. Each player would place her individually carved stick on a pile, and a blindfolded person would choose the sticks two at a time, dividing them into two piles that then formed the teams (Lavine 1974; Whitney 1977).

Double Ball was a variation of shinny in which two baseball-sized balls were tied together with a six-inch leather thong. The double ball was carried or thrown with a hooked stick from two to six feet long. The game was popular among Pawnee and Pima women as well as with females of many other tribes, but was hardly ever played by men. Menominee women played double ball on a hundred-yard-long field, with a three-foot stick and from six to ten players on a team. The game started with a ball toss at midfield. Then players would pick up, run with, and pass the ball until a goal was scored. It was permissible to tackle the ball carrier, but was not okay to touch the ball with the hands (Brescia 1981). MacFarlan (1958) advises against playing the game because of the considerable risk of injury from the stick.

Winter Sports

Eastern tribespeople slid objects along the ice in contests for distance. The objects, called snow snakes, consisted of sticks, arrows, feathered darts made of animal ribs, horn-tipped saplings, antler pieces, or unstrung bows (Lowie 1954). The snow snake game among northern tribes employed flat or round rods as long as ten feet, which were hurled across crusted snow or smooth ice.

Snow boat apparently was an Indian predecessor of today's Cub Scouts' Pinewood Derby. Today, Cub Scouts make pinewood cars and race them down ramps. Indian children whittled canoes out of hardwood and raced them down iced chutes. A small keel kept the boats from flipping over and off the track (Lavine 1974).

The Teton Sioux made sleds using the ribs of buffalo as runners and cherrywood for the body of the sled. The ribs were tied on with rawhide, and a buffalo head decorated the front of the sled (Wolfe 1982). Koyukon, Cree, and Chippewa youngsters raced both on snow shoes and in toboggans (Whitney 1977).

The most interesting winter game was ice shinny, found among numerous Northern tribes. Early North American white settlers were accustomed to the sight of a brave running across the ice pushing a puck with a curved stick. Shinny was played with crooked sticks similar to the ice hockey sticks of today. In fact, ice shinny may be considered a precursor of ice hockey, although skates were not used. Teams competed in attempting to score goals against the opponents by hitting a ball through a goal with the stick (Lavine 1974). Among the Blackfeet, two upright logs were the goal posts, placed on end lines about one-quarter mile apart. The puck was either a knot of wood covered with rawhide or a stone. A game consisted of seven points. As many as fifty players were on a team.

Running

For many tribes, running was and still is an important part of life. According to Mails (1972), "Boys ten or more years of age were compelled to take long runs, to go without food and water for long periods of time, to roll in the snow, to dive into icy water, and to stay awake and alert for hours on end." Alfonso Ortiz's grandfather told him, "Keep your eye on the mountain top as you run, and in time you'll feel as if you can jump over houses and treetops and across a river" (Ortiz 1990, 78). Hopi children and adults would get up before dawn and run to the fields to cultivate, as far as thirty-five miles, and then back again by nightfall (Brescia 1981). Each season had its running races, such as corn planting in the spring, when the Zunis and Keres would run races to bring rain, and harvesting in the fall, when races were run to please the gods and ensure a rich crop (Lavine 1974). Russell describes a relay race of a southwestern tribe:

> The relay races of the Pimas did not differ materially from those among the Pueblo tribes of the Rio Grande or the Apaches and others of the Southwest. . . . [Y]oung men ran in groups of four or five. There were forty or fifty runners in each village, and he who proved to be the swiftest was recognized as the leader who should run first in the final contest. It was not necessary that each village should enter the same number of men in the race; a man might run any number of times that his endurance permitted. When the final race began each village stationed half its runners at each end of the track, then a crier called three times for the leaders, and as the last call . . . closed the starter shouted "Tâ'wai!" and they were off on the first relay. . . . Sometimes a race was ended by one party admitting that it was tired out, but it usually was decided when the winners were so far ahead that their runner met the other at the center. (quoted in Culin 1975, 806)

A similar shuttle relay was observed at the Papago Fair around 1924. Ten men lined up in teams at opposite ends of the race course. On the signal rattle, the race started with two runners sprinting around the course in opposite directions. Where the players met was marked by sticks—two sticks, as they met twice each lap. Although the race was to have been continued until the two sticks met at the middle, the sticks were not together at the end of twenty minutes. Therefore, the prize went to the team that was leading (Woodruff 1939).

Nabokov (1981) provides a detailed narrative of the August 1980 Tricentennial Run commemorating the Pueblo Indians' 1680 revolt against the Spaniards. The success of the revolt was due in large part to ceremonial runners who spread word of the plan for the rebellion. The 1980 reenactment spanned over 375 miles and took six days! Nabokov digresses in covering the race to discuss the history and accomplishments of Indian runners, from kickstick racers to log runners, messengers, and finally, Olympians. He also mentions the Carlisle Indian School, famous for winning football games against the most prestigious universities in the East and for football coach Pop Warner's distinctive contribution to the sport (Howell and Howell 1978; Warner 1927).

Archery

Indians preferred to hold their bows horizontally rather than vertically, and many would step with the release, as when delivering a punch. Archery contests developed from standing and shooting at a stationary target to standing and shooting at a moving target, such as a ball of yucca (Navajo); standing and shooting at a buffalo hide being dragged by rawhide; trying to have more arrows in the air at one time than did your opponent, using a rapid-fire technique; launching a piece of straw into the air and trying to hit it with an arrow—an activity similar to trapshooting (Crow); and riding and shooting at a grass target (Lavine 1974). Targets varied, depending in part on region: yucca in New Mexico, corncobs in other parts of the Southwest, and sapling branches in California. The Shawnees rolled a hoop made of grapevine along the ground as a target (Clark 1977). According to Wooden Leg (Marquis 1931), a customary target among Cheyennes was an erect image of a man. The contests allowed four successive shots and scored both accuracy and penetration.

The Blackfeet played an ancestral form of archery golf consisting of shooting an arrow into the ground and then shooting a second arrow at the first. Where the first arrow landed became the "tee" for the next shot. The Pawnee variation consisted of shooting an arrow so that it would land flat about fifty yards ahead. Other archers then attempted to shoot so their arrows would come to rest across the first (Whitney 1977).

During the early nineteenth century, Cherokees practiced their archery skill through "stalk shooting." Rules varied, but generally an archer shot at a small corn shock or a stack of several corn stalks some one hundred and fifty yards distant. Points were awarded according to the number of stalks pierced (Malone 1952).

Suggestions for Physical Education

An Ontario task force on American Indian education (Summary Report 1976) recommended that physical education emphasize culturally relevant activities that also promote physical fitness. Furthermore, they recommended that Indian students design their own recreation programs.

In light of the unique aspects of the native experience, physical education instructors should consider introducing primary-level Indian students to games of low organization that are from Indian cultures or can be adapted to the students' cultural setting. Fish Trap, Hoop Race, corncob darts, Dodge Ball, Blind Man's Bluff,

Follow the Leader, Hide and Seek, and Crack the Whip are a few possibilities for the early grades.

In the middle and upper grades, when introducing lead-up games and sports, the physical educator is encouraged to incorporate those that have roots in Indian culture, or at least to explain the extent to which a game was part of the American Indian experience. Pin Guard, line soccer, Dodge Ball, and the Hoop and Pole game may be appropriately adapted for upper elementary and intermediate students.

The Buffalo Hunt game of the Oklahoma area is the version of the Hoop and Pole game preferred for the elementary school. The objective is to throw a blunt spear through a ten-inch-diameter ring made of green branches wrapped with rawhide. Hoops made of plastic or of rubber hose joined with a wooden dowel and tape could substitute for the traditional wooden hoops. Since Indians continually made the best use of what they could find in their environment (such as by using iron for arrow tips and spearheads when it became available), it would not seem impure to use synthetics, plastics, or even manufactured equipment in contemporary versions of physical activities in the nineties that came into existence centuries ago (Adrian Heidenreich, personal communication, July 11, 1986).

In the Buffalo Hunt contest, children are divided into groups so as to make the best use of available equipment and allow maximum participation consistent with good safety practices. The groups may be subdivided into throwers and retrievers. The last person in line rolls the hoop, and the first throws the pole at it. Each child is given five trials. Throwers become retrievers, retrievers join the throwing line as rollers, and so forth. Close supervision is advised, to prevent someone from being hit by a pole (Wise 1976).

For the intermediate and secondary grades, team sports such as field hockey, soccer, lacrosse, box lacrosse, and flag football are excellent activities, demanding skill and fitness while teaching cooperation as well as competitiveness. Bowling and archery are activities that can be introduced at any grade, with size-appropriate equipment and space modifications. Running and other track and field events can be taught, and ought to be, throughout the years.

Again, when introducing a game, sport, or activity, a physical educator can give background information that links current participation with that of Indian ancestors. Teachers and youth leaders are encouraged to remind children of abilities and positive qualities utilized by Indians in their traditional activities, including powers of observation, meditation, courage, patience, humor, self-reliance, strength, and stamina.

For the modern Indian youth in search of a hero, one might mention Jim Thorpe (Sauk and Fox, and Potawatomi), a Carlisle alumnus who was one of the greatest running backs football has ever known and winner of the Olympic decathlon in 1912. William Lonestar Dietz was a football player at Carlisle and a very successful football coach in the pre–World War II years. Dietz coached Washington State College at the first Tournament of Roses football game in 1916 and later became coach at Stanford University. Billy Mills (Oglala Sioux) stumbled during the ten-thousand-meter finals in the 1964 Tokyo Olympic Games, but recovered to win the race and the gold medal.

For evaluating physical fitness, the Physical Best battery available from the American Alliance for Health, Physical Education, Recreation, and Dance (AAHPERD) is recommended. This test allows computer scoring and tracking of data, producing an individualized report specific to the results and goals of each student. It is recommended that the teacher also relate test results to locally or regionally established norms. This may mean computing new norms from the test data at a particular school or area. A student may find these more meaningful than standards based on a larger population with little or no Indian representation. For the AAHPERD Youth Fitness Test, for example, Beckford (1976) constructed norms for fourteen-, fifteen-, and sixteen-year-old girls from seven high schools on the Navajo Reservation.

With all children, give positive feedback. A study in Medford, Oregon, showed that a 4:1 ratio of positive to negative feedback was most beneficial to student achievement in the elementary grades. This means that for every negative comment or result, a student should receive four positive comments, spaced properly and given with sincerity.

Think how games may be adapted to be more inclusive and less exclusive. Torbert and Schneider (1986) suggest that a game such as musical chairs, for example, can be changed from a "me first" approach to a sharing experience. As the music stops and chairs are removed, more children have to sit on fewer and fewer chairs. Perhaps such games identify winners, but also, no losers—if the game is stopped at its proper point and another is introduced. The idea is to encourage cooperation and acceptance of differences, avoid failure, and redefine winning.

Swisher and Swisher (1986) reviewed literature on cooperation versus competition in learning styles and found that Cherokee and Blackfeet children studied were more cooperative and less competitive than non-Indian children. The Blackfeet method of choosing sides described previously is a beautiful, although time-consuming, way of avoiding the humiliation that otherwise might result from being chosen last.

Parents should be involved in the education process to gain their support and create a supportive home atmosphere. Open houses and sports festivals are two ways to increase parental participation.

Here are some other recommendations, based on *Effective Practices in Indian Education: A Teacher's Monograph* (Pepper and Coburn 1985):

Recognize that both Indians and non-Indians can be effective teachers of Indian children.

Realize that Indian children are taught to be accountable for their own actions, and that discipline is handled differently than in non-Indian culture.

Appreciate that there are deep-seated cultural differences—some of which can be traced back as much as fifty thousand years—between Indian and non-Indian children.

Since children are not the same physically, socially, or culturally, everyone should not be treated identically. Some adaptations are necessary both for cultural survival and for individuals to receive optimal educational benefits through physical education.

For Further Information

Black Elk, N. and Brown, J. D. 1953. *Tapa Wanka Yap: The Throwing of the Ball*. Baltimore: Penguin Books. Has an excellent discussion of the religious aspects of the Sioux ball game.

Culin, S. 1975. *Games of the North American Indians*. New York: Dover. (Originally published as *Games of the North American Indians* in the Twenty-Fourth Annual Report of the Bureau of American Ethnology to the Secretary of the Smithsonian Institution 1902–03, by W. H. Holmes, Chief, and published by the U.S. Government Printing Office,

1907.) Compiled as a project of the Smithsonian Institution, this is the most complete study of Indian games. The Dover paperback is well illustrated, with a tabular index to tribes and games. This 810-page book is an invaluable resource.

Hunt, W. B. 1973. *The Complete How to Book of Indiancraft.* New York: Collier Books. Contains instructions for making lacrosse sticks, Crow throwing arrows, and hoops.

On Indian Contributions to Sports

Poatgieter, H. 1981. *Indian Legacy: Native American Influences on World Life and Culture.* New York: Julian Messner.

Pope, S. T. 1918. Yahi Archery. *University of California Publications in American Archaeology and Ethnology* 13:103–52.

For the Modern Youth in Search of Sports Heroes

Oxendine, Joseph B. 1988. *American Indian Sports Heritage.* Champaign, IL: Human Kinetics Books. An outstanding, comprehensive text including a history and description of Indian games and an extensive list with short biographies of Indian sports figures.

Schoor, G. 1951. *The Jim Thorpe Story.* New York: Julian Messner.

Shunk, H. 1971. World of Sports Enriched by 61 American Indian Athletes. *Journal of American Indian Education* 10(3): 30–31.

Tefft, V. 1971. Using Physical Education in English Language Practice. *Journal of American Indian Education* 11(1): 1–6. Discusses the use of physical activities to support language instruction and learning.

Warner, G. S. 1927. *Football for Coaches and Players.* Palo Alto: Stanford University Press. Pop Warner's classic text based on his years of coaching football at the Carlisle Indian School.

American Indians Today: Population and Education Statistics

The preliminary 1990 census count reports that 1,959,234 Americans (about .8 percent of the total population) identify themselves as American Indians, Eskimos, or Aleuts (Johnson 1991). This is a half million more people than in 1980 and more than double the figure for 1970. The 1980 census reported that one-fourth of all American Indians lived on reservations, one-half in rural areas including reservations, and 21 percent in central cities. California, Oklahoma, Arizona, and New Mexico each have over 100,000 American Indians. The greatest tribal affiliation reported is the Cherokee, while the largest reservation population is Navajo. The Los Angeles metropolitan area has the largest urban Indian population.

Although the American Indian and Alaska Native population is climbing rapidly, the reservation land base of American Indians has changed little since the post–World War II termination era, when a few tribes lost their federal protection. In 1974 there were 170 Alaska Native villages, 258 Indian reservations and Indian trust areas, plus 27 federally recognized tribes with trust areas in Oklahoma (*Federal and State Indian Reservations* 1974). These figures have changed little over the past eighteen years. Figure A.1 shows the concentration of these reservations in the western half of the United States.

The 1980 census reported that of the Indian adults over 25 years old, 57 percent had not graduated from high school and 16 percent had completed less than five years of school. The most recent studies on dropouts show that between 29 and 36 percent of American Indian students both on and off reservations are leaving high school before graduating (Reyhner in press). Twenty-eight percent of reservation Indians over 15 are unemployed (Bureau of the Census 1985, 68), 45 percent live below the poverty level (p. 77), 21 percent have homes without piped water (p. 86), and 16 percent are without electricity (p. 86). As of 1980, about a third of the Indian population—a half million—were enrolled in school (Bureau

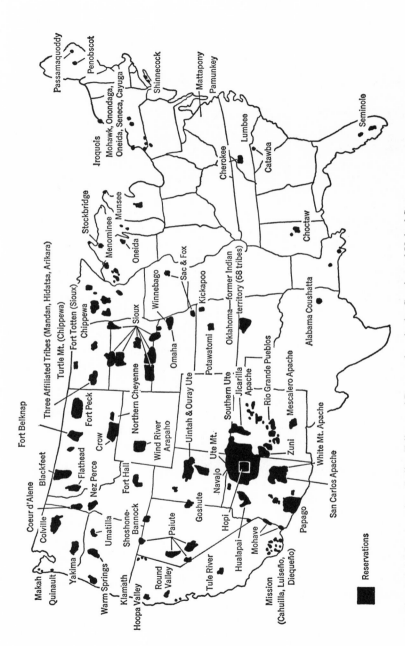

FIGURE A.1 Major American Indian Tribes and Reservations in the Continental United States

Source: From *To Live on This Earth* by Estelle Fuchs and Robert J. Havighurst. Copyright © 1972 by Estelle Fuchs and Robert J. Havighurst. Reprinted by permission of Doubleday & Company, Inc.

of the Census 1984, 98), a half million were employed, and 76,865 were unemployed (p. 100). The mean household income for whites was $21,173 but for American Indians it was $15,418 (pp. 111–12), even though the average Indian household size was 3.3 persons compared to 2.7 persons for the average white household (pp. 129–30). The *Chronicle of Higher Education* (Evangelauf 1990) reported 93,000 Indians enrolled in U.S. colleges and universities for 1988, the lowest figure for any U.S. minority group reported but almost a 20 percent increase from ten years ago. American Indians represent approximately .8 percent of the United States population and .7 percent of the enrollment in higher education. About 42 percent of those enrolled were men, and 7,000 of the total were in graduate or professional schools. In another article, the *Chronicle of Higher Education* (Mooney 1990) reported that 93 American Indians received doctorates in 1989—an increase of almost 15 percent from ten years ago and .4 percent of the total doctorates earned by U.S. citizens.

Education reforms in Indian and minority education seem to have had some effect. The average Scholastic Aptitude Test (SAT) verbal score of American Indians has risen four points between 1976 and 1985 while the corresponding score for white Americans dropped two points. However, Indians still have an average score 57 points below white Americans, although the average scores for blacks, Mexican Americans, and Puerto Ricans are even lower than the score for Indians. The number of Indians taking the SAT test has increased 2 percent over the past five years compared to a 5 percent drop for blacks, a 48 percent increase for Asian Americans, an 11 percent increase for Puerto Ricans, and a 26 percent increase for Mexican Americans ("Number of Blacks Taking SAT" 1986, 108).

One hundred thousand Indian children between the ages of five and seventeen live on reservations, and about one-third of these children attend Bureau of Indian Affairs schools. In 1988 there were 57 BIA-operated day schools (17,589 students), 46 BIA-operated boarding schools (9,126 students), 54 Indian-controlled contract day schools (9,064 students) and 11 Indian-controlled contract boarding schools (2,138 students). While the number of students in contract schools continues to increase, the number of students in BIA-operated schools has decreased by 4,518 students since 1984 (Bureau of Indian Affairs 1988b). Over 80 percent of the 15,729 BIA employees are American Indians, constituting approximately 2.5 percent of all employed Indians (Bureau of the Census 1985, 14). Almost 14,000 American Indians are teachers, librarians, or counselors (representing about 2.7 percent of the work force) whereas 3.5 percent of the white work force are teachers (Bureau of the Census 1984, 138).

Besides operating elementary and secondary schools, the BIA also operates three postsecondary schools and funds twenty tribally con-

trolled community colleges (Bureau of Indian Affairs 1988a). While Indian students were once excluded from many public schools, now some
state departments of education have done extensive work to provide supplemental curriculum about and for Indians in their schools. Oklahoma
and California are especially to be noted for their efforts. Most Indian
students (about 90 percent in 1986) now attend public schools.

A number of good sources exist for data on American Indian demo-
graphics. Two recent books are Russell Thornton's *American Indian
Holocaust and Survival: A Population History since 1492* (1987) and
C. Matthew Snipp's *American Indians: The First of This Land* (1989).
Recent short monographs on American Indian population include *The
Demographics of American Indians: One Percent of the People, Fifty
Percent of the Diversity* (Hodgkinson, Outtz, and Obarakpor 1990) and
"Native American Education at a Turning Point: Current Demographics
and Trends" (Hillabrant, Romano, and Stang in press).

Sources and Recommendations for Indian Children's Literature

Chapters 11 and 14 discuss Indian children's literature. The list of Indian children's books below was compiled from books rated by teachers as excellent. Stories were selected on the basis of how much they might motivate Indian students to read more than on their cultural authenticity. All but the most recent appear in the 1989–90 edition of *Books in Print*. This list concentrates on more recent books; Gilliland's *Indian Children's Books* (1980) and Stensland's *Literature by and About Native Americans: An Annotated Bibliography* (1979) are recommended for their comprehensive listing and ratings of older books. After the list of books is a short list of organizations supplying Indian children's books followed by a list of organizations that evaluate and/or help promote the distribution of Indian children's books.

Selected Native American Children's Books

Picture Books (Primary)

Andrews, Jan. 1986. *Very Last First Time*. New York: MacMillan. (Inuit)

Baylor, Byrd. [1972] 1987. *When Clay Sings*. New York: MacMillan. (Caldecott Medal winner)

Behrens, June. 1983. *Powwow*. Chicago: Children's Press.

Benchley, Nathaniel. 1972. *Small Wolf*. New York: Harper & Row. A story of Indian-White contact. Other books by the same author include the primary story *Running Owl the Hunter* and the junior high novel *Only the Earth and Sky Last Forever*. (Southern Cheyenne/Sioux)

Brother Eagle, Sister Sky: A Message from Chief Seattle. 1991. New York: Dial Books.

Cohen, Caron Lee. 1988. *The Mud Pony*. New York: Scholastic. (adaptation of a traditional Skidi Pawnee story)

Esbensen, Barbara. 1988. *Star Maiden*. Boston: Little, Brown. (Ojibwa tale)

Goble, Paul. 1984. *Buffalo Woman*. New York: Bradbury Press. Retelling of a Plains Indian traditional story. Other stories by the same author include *Inktomi and the Boulder: A Plains Indian Story, Beyond the Ridge, Her Seven Brothers, Dream Wolf, The Great Race of the Birds and Animals, Star Boy, The Girl Who Loved Wild Horses, Death of the Iron Horse, The Friendly Wolf,* and *The Gift of the Sacred Dog*. Two other books are written with Dorothy Goble: *Lone Bull's Horse Raid* and *Red Hawk's Account of Custer's Last Battle*. All are beautifully illustrated.

Luenn, Nancy. 1990. *Nessa's Fish*. New York: Atheneum. (Eskimo)

Morgan, William. 1989. *Navajo Coyote Tales*. Santa Fe, NM: Ancient City.

Moroney, Lynn. 1989. *Baby Rattlesnake*. San Francisco: Children's Book Press.

Parish, Peggy. 1988. *Good Hunting, Blue Sky*. New York: Harper & Row.

Sneve, Virginia Driving Hawk, ed. 1989. *Dancing Teepees*. New York: Holiday House. (Poetry, intertribal)

Van Laan, Nancy. 1989. *Rainbow Crow*. New York: Knopf. (Lenape)

Intermediate/Junior High Books

Many of these books are suitable for reading to younger students.

Armer, Laura Adams. 1931. *Waterless Mountain*. New York: David McKay. Newberry Award–winning story of a Navajo boy.

George, Jean Craighead. [1983] 1987. *The Talking Earth*. New York: Harper Trophy. Contemporary Seminole story with an environmentalist theme.

Girion, Barbara. 1990. *Indian Summer*. New York: Scholastic. A white doctor and daughter spend summer on Indian reservation, where the daughter learns about Indians. (Iroquois)

Hobbs, Will. 1989. *Bearstone*. New York: Atheneum. Orphan Indian boy learns about traditional and white cultures as he grows up. (Navajo/Ute)

Houston, James. 1989. *The White Dawn: An Eskimo Saga*. New York: Atheneum.

Levin, Betty. 1990. *Brother Moose*. New York: Greenwillow. White orphans learn about Indians firsthand.

McDermott, Gerald. 1974. *Arrow to the Sun: A Pueblo Indian Tale*. New York: Penguin.

Morris, Neil, and Morris, Ting. 1984. *Feather Boy and the Buffalo*. Morristown, NJ: Silver Burdette. Also by the same authors: *Little Bear and the White Horse, Morning Sun and the Lost Girl*, and *Taku and the Fishing Canoe*.

O'Dell, Scott. 1970. *Sing Down the Moon*. New York: Dell. A story of the Navajo Long Walk. Also by the same author: *Black Star, Bright Dawn* (Alaskan story of the Iditarod sled race), *Streams to the River, River to the Sea: A Novel of Sacagawea, Island of the Blue Dolphins, The Serpent Never Sleeps: A Novel of Jamestown and Pocahontas*, and *Zia*.

Pitts, Paul. 1988. *Racing the Sun*. New York: Avon Camelot. An assimilated urban Navajo boy goes to live with his traditional grandfather on the reservation, forcing him to compare the different lifeways of his parents and his grandfather.

Roop, Peter. 1984. *Little Blaze and the Buffalo Jump*. Billings, MT: Council for Indian Education. Also by the same author: *Sik-ki-mi* and *Natosi: Strong Medicine*. All are stories about the Blackfeet.

Rudolph, Stormy. 1984. *Quest for Courage*. Billings, MT: Council for Indian Education. (Blackfeet)

Ryniker, Alice. 1980. *Eagle Feather for a Crow*. Oklahoma City: Lowell.

Speare, Elizabeth George. 1983. *The Sign of the Beaver*. New York: Dell.

Tall Bull, Henry, and Weist, Tom. 1973. *Northern Cheyenne Fire Fighters*. Billings, MT: Council for Indian Education. Also by the same authors: *Grandfather and the Popping Machine*, a humorous story about a Northern Cheyenne getting his first car.

Thomasma, K. 1983. *Naya Nuki: Girl Who Ran*. Grand Rapids, MI: Baker Book House. (Shoshoni). Also by the same author: *Soun Tatoken: Nez Perce Boy, Kunu: Escape in the Missouri*, and *Om-kas-toe of the Blackfeet*.

Trimble, Stephen. 1989. *The Village of Blue Stone*. New York: MacMillan. (Anasazi/Pueblo)

High School Books

Important works not in this list by American Indian authors such as Charles Eastman, James Welch, D'Arcy McNickle, and N. Scott Momaday are discussed and listed in chapter 14.

Borland, Hal. 1984. *When the Legends Die*. New York: Bantam. One of the best novels about Indians written by a non-Indian. (Ute)

Carter, Forrest. [1976] 1986. *The Education of Little Tree*. Albuquerque: University of New Mexico Press. Parts are suitable for reading to younger children. Story of an orphaned boy who is educated at home by his Cherokee grandparents in the 1930s.

Erdoes, Richard, and Ortiz, Alfonso. 1985. *American Indian Myths and Legends*. New York: Pantheon.

Hillerman, Tony. [1975] 1989. *Dance Hall of the Dead*. New York: Harper & Row. Also by the same author: *A Thief of Time, The Blessing Way, The Ghostway, Listening Woman, Talking God, People of Darkness,* and *Skinwalkers*. All are murder mysteries that are solved by Navajo tribal policemen. Also of interest is *The Boy Who Made Dragonfly: A Zuni Myth.*

Kinsella, W. P. 1977. *Dance Me Outside: More Tales from the Ermineskin Reserve*. Boston: Godine. Also by the same author: *The Moccasin Telegraph and Other Stories, The Fencepost Chronicles*. Humorous short stories of living on an Alberta Indian reserve. Some stories might not be considered suitable for classroom use.

LaFarge, Oliver. [1929] 1971. *Laughing Boy*. New York: New American Library. This Pulitzer Prize–winning classic about the conflicts between traditional Navajo and modern life is still highly readable though it contains adult themes. LaFarge's out-of-print *The Enemy Gods* about education in boarding schools is also worth reading.

L'Amour, Louis. 1986. *The Last of the Breed*. New York: Bantam. A Sioux test pilot is captured by the USSR and escapes.

Linderman, Frank B. [1932] 1974. *Pretty Shield: Medicine Woman of the Crows*. Lincoln: University of Nebraska Press. An "as told to" biography, this book is suitable for reading to elementary students. Also of interest by the same author is *Plenty-coups, Chief of the Crows.*

Richter, Conrad. 1984. *The Light in the Forest*. New York: Bantam. White boy captured by Indians in eighteenth century begins to identify with his captors. (Lenape)

Organizations Supplying Indian Children's Books

Council for Indian Education (P.O. Box 31215, Billings, MT 59101) has over fifty children's books in print, representing more than eleven different tribes.

Fitzhenry & Whiteside (195 Allstate Parkway, Markham, Ontario L3R 4T8, Canada; phone 416-477-0030). Publishes the CIRCLE program, an integrated beginning ESL language arts program for Native children, developed by the Modern Language Centre of the Ontario Institute for Studies in Education. This program includes a number of storybooks with tapes that tell both traditional and contemporary stories. They also publish a number of other books by and about Indians. Catalog available.

Gabriel Dumont Institute (121 Broadway Avenue E, Regina, Saskatchewan S4N 0Z6, Canada). Publishes about the Metis and Cree in Canada. Catalog available.

Navajo Community College Press (Tsaile, AZ 86556; phone 602-724-3311). Publishes *Navajo Stories of the Long Walk Period, Stories of Traditional Navajo Life and Culture,* and many other books. Suitable for students in high school and above. Catalog available.

Navajo Curriculum Center, Rough Rock Demonstration School (Rough Rock, AZ 86503; phone 602-728-3311). Publishes a number of Navajo stories for children including *Grandfather Stories of the Navajo People* (also in Navajo language edition), *Coyote Stories of the Navajo People,* and a two-volume *Teaching Guide for Indian Literature* that provides chapter-by-chapter questions on and activities for twenty-one American Indian books, mostly novels, at both the elementary and secondary level. Catalog available.

Random House School Division (Dept. 9278, 400 Hahn Road, Westminster, MD 21157; phone 800-733-3000). Has videotapes and sound filmstrips to go with Jean Craighead George's *Julie of the Wolves* (Eskimo), Jamake Highwater's *Anpao: An American Indian Odyssey,* Eloise Jarvis McGraw's *Moccasin Trail* (Crow), Miska Miles's *Annie and the Old One* (Navajo), Scott O'Dell's *Sing Down the Moon* (Navajo), Olaf Baker's *Where the Buffaloes Begin* (Plains), and Paul Goble's *The Girl Who Loved Wild Horses* (Plains). Also has filmstrips with cassettes of "Tales of the Plains Indians" (grades 3–5), "Read-Along American Indian Legends" (grades 2–4), "American Indian Folk Legends" (grades 3–6), and "American Indian Legends" (grades 3–5). Catalog available.

San Juan District Media Center (28 West 200 North, Blanding, UT 84511). Publishes twenty-four Navajo Experience Stories, twelve Cultural Readers, and ten Navajo Cultural Movies, among other materials. Many of these materials include both Navajo and English versions and many of the booklets come with cassettes. Catalog available.

Saskatchewan Indian Cultural Center (120 33rd Street East, Saskatoon, Saskatchewan S7K 0S2, Canada). Specializes in books about Canadian Indians and Canadian Indian languages. Catalog available.

Tipi Press, P.O. Box 98, Chamberlain, SD 57326. Publishes a number of nicely illustrated elementary-level books in English and Lakota including an American Heritage Series.

Sources for Evaluating Indian Children's Literature

Council on Interracial Books for Children (1841 Broadway, New York, NY 10023). Publishes a number of booklets on stereotyping, racism, and sexism. Of special interest is *Unlearning "Indian" Stereotypes: A Teach-*

ing Unit for Teachers and Children's Librarians (1981). Also available is an associated sound filmstrip narrated by New York City Indian children and suitable for use in the intermediate grades. Another useful booklet is *Guidelines for Selecting Bias-Free Textbooks and Storybooks* (1980). Native American stereotypes are dealt with on pages 56–58. They also publish a bulletin.

Slapin, Beverly, and Seale, Doris, eds. 1988. *Books Without Bias: Through Indian Eyes.* Available from Oyate (2702 Mathews Street, Berkeley, CA 94702). Contains a number of essays on Native American children's literature and related topics, plus publishers' addresses and critical reviews of a number of Indian children's books.

Literacy Promotion

Reading Is FUNdamental (600 Maryland Ave. S.W., Room 500, Smithsonian Institution, Washington, DC 20560; phone 202-287-3220). The RIF program provides assistance, including some matching funds, to groups wishing to give books away to children in order to promote literacy in the home. Membership is free; members can purchase books at discount for free distribution to children and receive the RIF newsletter.

Resources for Teaching Social Studies

The 1977 American Indian Policy Review Commission began its final report with the statement that "A history, once thought ancient and dead, has risen to challenge this generation of Americans." It is important that Indian children get an Indian point of view in their classrooms, as this perspective may differ greatly from the non-Indian view. For instance, traditionally oriented Indians do not believe their ancestors came from Asia over the Bering Strait, many geographic sites were known by Indian names before they were renamed by whites, Indians have little to be thankful for on Thanksgiving, and Indian heroes such as Tecumseh, Geronimo, and Chief Joseph were often the white man's enemies. Some of the best sources for information on Native Americans are the writings of the many Native American scholars, such as Francis LaFlesche (Omaha), Luther Standing Bear (Teton Sioux), Ella Deloria (Yankton Sioux), D'Arcy McNickle (Salish), Bea Medicine (Yankton Sioux), Edward Dozier (Santa Clara Pueblo), Jack Forbes (Powhatan), Alfonso Ortiz (Tewa), and Vine Deloria, Jr. (Yankton Sioux). Chapter 3 gives historical background and sources for American Indian history. The resources listed below have been found useful in teaching social studies.

General Resource Books on Indians for Teachers

America's Fascinating Indian Heritage. 1978. Pleasantville, NY: Reader's Digest.

Barreiro, Jose, ed. 1988. *Indian Roots of American Democracy* (special issue of the *Northeast Indian Quarterly,* published by American Indian Program, 400 Caldwell Hall, Cornell University, Ithaca, NY 14853). This special issue contains articles about ways in which Benjamin Franklin and the other Founding Fathers were influenced by American Indian tribal democracy.

Brown, Dee. 1970. *Bury My Heart at Wounded Knee: An Indian History of the American West.* New York. Holt, Rinehart & Winston.

Debo, Angie. 1970. *A History of the Indians of the United States*. Norman: University of Oklahoma Press.

Josephy, Alvin M. 1961. *The Patriot Chiefs*. New York: Viking.

Kehoe, Alice B. 1981. *North American Indians: A Comprehensive Account*. Englewood Cliffs, NJ: Prentice-Hall.

Vogel, Virgil. 1972. *This Country Was Ours: A Documentary History of the American Indian*. New York: Harper & Row. While this book is dated, it contains much useful information, including a list of famous Americans of Indian descent past and present.

Weatherford, Jack. 1988. *Indian Givers: How the Indians of the Americas Transformed the World*. New York: Fawcett, Columbine. This book describes the various contributions Indians have made to our modern civilization.

Children's Books and Series

American Indian Stories Series, Raintree (310 W. Wisconsin Avenue, Milwaukee, WI 53203; phone 800-558-7264). New intermediate-level biographical series with twelve titles, including biographies of Geronimo, Wilma Mankiller, John Ross, Sarah Winemucca, and Plenty Coup.

Childrens Press (5440 North Cumberland Avenue, Chicago, IL 60656). Publishes a New True Book series of reference books for the primary grades that includes *The Apache, Aztec Indians, The Cherokee, The Cheyenne, The Chippewa, The Choctaw, The Hopi, The Inca, Indians, The Mandans, The Maya, The Navajo, The Nez Perce, The Pawnee, The Seminole, The Shoshoni, The Sioux*, and *The Tlingit*. These books are illustrated with authentic photographs. At the same level they also publish *Black Elk: A Man with a Vision* and, at a slightly higher level (grades 3–6), *Wounded Knee, Geronimo*, and *The Blackhawk War*.

Freeman, Russell. 1988. *Buffalo Hunt*. New York: Holiday House. Also by the same author: *Indian Chiefs* (intermediate).

Heroes and Warriors Series, Sterling (387 Park Ave. S., New York, NY 10016-8810; phone 800-367-9692). New intermediate/junior high–level series of five books: *American Indian Warrior Chiefs, Crazy Horse: Sacred Warrior of the Sioux, Chief Joseph: Guardian of the Nez Perce, Geronimo: Last Renegade of the Apache*, and *Tecumseh: Chief the Shawnee*.

Hirschfelder, Arlene. 1987. *Happily May I Walk: American Indians and Alaska Natives Today*. New York: Scribners (intermediate).

Indians of North America, Chelsea House (1974 Sproul Road, Suite 400, Broomall, PA 19008-0914; phone 800-848-2665). A series of fifty-three titles for ages ten and up, starting with *The Abenaki: Northeast, Subarctic* and *American Indian Literature* and ending with *The Yankton*

Sioux: Great Plains and *The Yuma: California.* Varying from 94 to 144 pages, these are well-illustrated books. Titles also include *Federal Indian Policy* and *Urban Indians.*

Katz, William Loren. 1986. *Black Indians: A Hidden Heritage.* New York: Atheneum. Describes the history of mixed black-Indian Americans. (high school)

Luling, Virginia. 1978. *Indians of the North American Plains.* Morristown, NJ: Silver Burdette. (junior high)

Marrin, Albert. 1984. *War Clouds in the West: Indians and Cavalrymen 1860–1890.* New York: Atheneum. (junior high and above)

Native American Series, Silver Burdette Press (P.O. Box 1226, Westwood, NJ 07675-1226; phone 800-848-9500). Edited by Alvin Josephy, this series of six titles includes biographies of Geronimo, Tecumseh, Sequoyah, Hiawatha, Sitting Bull, and King Phillip. (intermediate)

Ortiz, Simon. 1988. *The People Shall Continue.* Rev. ed. San Francisco: Children's Book Press. A very simple history for primary children of American Indian survival.

Payne, Elizabeth. 1965. *Meet the North American Indian.* New York: Random House. (primary to intermediate)

Yue, David, and Yue, Charlotte. 1984. *The Tipi: A Center of Native American Life.* New York: Knopf. (intermediate)

Other Topics

Coe, Ralph T. 1977. *Sacred Circles: Two Thousand Years of North American Indian Art.* Kansas City, MO: Nelson-Atkins Museum of Art.

Hanson, James A. 1975. *Metal Weapons, Tools, and Ornaments of the Teton Dakota Indians.* Lincoln: University of Nebraska Press.

Hunt, W. Ben. 1973. *The Complete How-To Book of Indiancraft.* New York: Collier Books.

Western Trading Post catalog (32 Broadway, Denver, CO 80209).

Pictures, Maps, and Other Graphics

Dunn, Dorothy. 1968. *American Indian Painting of the Southwest and Plains Areas.* Albuquerque: University of New Mexico Press.

Rickman, David. 1983. *Plains Indians Coloring Book.* New York: Dover.

Wade, Edwin L., and Strickland, Rennard. 1981. *Magic Images: Contemporary Native American Art.* Norman: Philbrook Art Center and University of Oklahoma Press.

Waldman, Carl. 1985. *Atlas of the North American Indian.* Illustrated by Molly Braun. New York: Facts on File.

Films, Videotapes, and Posters

Children of the Long-Beaked Bird (Bullfrog Films, Oley, PA 19547; phone 215-779-8226). Videotape of the daily life of a contemporary Crow boy.

The Conquest of Indian America (Historic Indian Publishers, 1404 Sunset Drive, P.O. Box 16074, Salt Lake City, UT 84116-0074; phone 801-328-0458). A set of eighty-four maps and charts. Color brochure available.

I Will Fight No More Forever (Congress Video Group, South Plainfield, NJ 07080). Feature film about flight of Chief Joseph and the Nez Perce from Idaho to Montana.

More Than Bows and Arrows (Camera One Productions, 8024 11th Ave. N.E., Seattle, WA 98115; phone 206-524-5326). Film about Indians' contributions to world culture.

The Trial of Standing Bear (Nebraska ETV Network, P.O. Box 83111, Lincoln, NE 68501; phone 402-472-3611). Film about a Ponca chief's flight from Oklahoma and his subsequent trial for leaving his reservation without permission. A viewers' guide and book are available.

Bibliographies and Directories

Hirschfelder, Arlene B., Byler, Mary G., and Dorris, Michael A. 1983. *Guide to Research on North American Indians.* Chicago: American Library Association.

Native American Directory. 1982. San Carlos, AZ: National Native American Cooperative. Includes tribes, museums, organizations, events, and stores.

Weatherford, Elizabeth, and Seubert, Emelia. 1981. *Native Americans on Film and Video,* 2 vols. New York: Museum of the American Indian. An annotated listing of about four hundred films.

Teaching Guides and Resources

American Indian Cultural Lessons. 1989. Norman: American Indian Institute, University of Oklahoma.

American Indian Education Handbook. 2nd ed. 1990. Sacramento: California State Department of Education.

Native Peoples of the Southwest (Cloud Associates, P.O. Box 39016, Phoenix, AZ 85069; phone 800-888-7820 or 602-866-7820). A multimedia set for grades 2–6 of instructional materials on southwestern Indian tribes. Brochure available.

Oklahoma's Indian People: Images of Yesterday, Today, and Tomorrow. 1983. Oklahoma City: Oklahoma State Department of Education.

Project REACH: Respecting Our Ethnic and Cultural Heritage (Reach Center, 239 North McLeod, Arlington, WA 98233).

Unlearning "Indian" Stereotypes: A Teaching Unit for Elementary and Children's Librarians. 1981. New York: Council on Interracial Books for Children.

APPENDIX D

Other Resources

Periodicals for Student Use

Daybreak Star (1945 Yale Place E., Seattle, WA 98102; phone 206-325-0070). An elementary newsprint magazine for Indian children written by children. Subscribers are encouraged to submit material.

Native Peoples (Media Concepts Group, Inc., 5333 North Seventh St., Phoenix, AZ 85014). According to the publisher, this glossy color photo-journal magazine "is dedicated to the sensitive portrayal of the arts and lifeways of native peoples" and includes articles on Indian education. A curriculum guide for teachers is available for each issue. Suitable for upper-elementary and secondary students.

Professional Organizations

American Educational Research Association (AERA; 1230 17th St., Washington, DC 20036-3078). Includes an American Indian special interest group.

Association for the Study of American Indian Literatures (ASAIL; Department of English, Fort Lewis College, Durango, CO 81301). Publishes *ASAIL Notes*.

Coalition for Indian Education (3620 Wyoming Blvd, N.E., Suite 206, Albuquerque, NM 87111; phone 505-275-9788).

Council on Anthropology and Education (CAE; 1703 New Hampshire Ave., N.W., Washington, DC 20009). Publishes *Anthropology and Education*.

International Reading Association (IRA; 800 Barksdale Rd., P.O. Box 8139, Newark, DE 19714-8139; phone 302-731-1600). Publishes the *Reading Teacher* for elementary teachers and the *Journal of Reading* for secondary teachers.

Joint National Committee for Languages (JNCL; 300 Eye Street, N.E., Washington, DC 20002; phone 202-546-7855). Founded by major language associations in 1976 to promote language study. Meets annually.

National Association for Bilingual Education (NABE; 1220 L Street, N.W., Suite 605, Washington, DC 20005; phone 202-898-1829). NABE holds annual meetings with workshops for teachers and publishes the *NABE Journal* three times a year and *NABE NEWS* eight times a year. Many state-affiliate organizations also meet annually.

National Council of Teachers of English (NCTE; 1111 Kenyon Rd., Urbana, IL 61801). Publishes *Language Arts.*

Native American Language Issues (NALI; P.O. Box 963, Choctaw, OK 73020). NALI holds annual institutes with workshops for teachers and publishes an annual proceedings.

Teachers of English to Speakers of Other Languages (TESOL; 1600 Cameron Street, Suite 300, Alexandria, VI 22314-2705; phone 703-836-0774). TESOL publishes a journal, *TESOL QUARTERLY,* and a newsletter and has annual meetings. State-affiliate organizations also hold annual state and even regional meetings and publish newsletters.

Society for Applied Anthropology (SfAA; 124 E. Sheridan, Suite 100, Oklahoma City, OK 73104).

Journals

Some journals are listed above, with their sponsoring organization.

The Aboriginal Child at School: A National Journal for Teachers of Aborigines (c/o Department of Education, University of Queensland, St. Lucia, Queensland, Australia).

American Indian Quarterly (Native American Studies, University of Nebraska Press, 901 North 17th Street, Lincoln, NE 68588-0520).

Arizona Quarterly (University of Arizona, Tucson, AZ 85721).

American Indian Culture and Research Journal (American Indian Studies Center, 3220 Campbell Hall, University of California, Los Angeles, CA 90024).

Canadian Journal of Native Education (First Nations House of Learning, 6365 Biological Sciences Road, University of British Columbia, Vancouver, B.C. V6T 1Z4, Canada).

Cultural Survival Quarterly (Cultural Survival, 11 Divinity Avenue, Cambridge, MA 02138).

Educational Leadership (125 N. West St., Alexandria, VA 22314-2798; phone 703-549-9110).

Equity and Excellence (formerly *Integrateducation;* University of Massachusetts School of Education Quarterly, 130 Furcolo, University of Massachusetts, Amherst, MA 01003).

Harvard Educational Review (Longfellow Hall, 13 Appian Way, Cambridge, MA 02138-3752).

Journal of American Folklore (1703 New Hampshire Ave., N.W., Washington, DC 20009).

Journal of Navajo Education (Kayenta Unified School District, P.O. Box 337, Kayenta, AZ 86033-0337).

Journal of Ethnic Studies (Western Washington University, Bellingham, WA, 98225).

Journal of American Indian Education (Center for Indian Education, College of Education, Arizona State University, Tempe, AZ 85287-1311).

Multicultural Education Journal (Barnett House, 11010 142nd St., Edmonton, Alberta T5N 2R1, Canada).

Northeast Indian Quarterly (American Indian Program, 300 Caldwell Hall, Cornell University, Ithaca, NY 14853).

Studies in American Indian Literature (c/o Robert M. Nelson, Department of English, University of Richmond, Richmond, VI 23173).

Teacher Magazine (Suite 250, 4301 Connecticut Ave., N.W., Washington, DC 20008; phone 202-364-4114).

Tribal College: Journal of American Indian Higher Education (P.O. Box 898, Chestertown, MD 21620).

The Wicazo Sa Review, Indian Studies Journal (Route 8, Box 510, Dakota Meadows, Rapid City, SD 57702).

Western American Literature (Department of English, UMC 32, Utah State University, Logan, UT 84322). The annual bibliography in each February issue is especially useful.

Winds of Change: A Magazine for American Indians (American Indian Science and Engineering Society, 1630 Thirtieth St., Suite 301, Boulder, CO 80301).

Curriculum Materials

Hualapai Bilingual Academic Excellence Program (P.O. Box 138, Peach Springs, AZ 86434; phone 602-769-2202).

Navajo Curriculum Center, Rough Rock Demonstration School (Chinle, AZ 86503; phone 602-728-3311).

Publishers and Audio-Visual Distributors

Canyon Records (4143 N. 16th St., Phoenix, AZ 85066; phone 602-266-4823).

Four Winds Press (703 W. Ninth, P.O. Box 156, Austin, TX 78767).

Heinemann Educational Books, Inc. (70 Court St., Portsmouth, NH 03801).

Multilingual Matters (Banke House, 8a Hill Rd., Clevedon, Avon, England B5217HH). Also publishes journals.

Clearinghouses, Libraries, and Other Teaching Resources

American Indian Language Development Institute (American Indian Studies, University of Arizona, Tucson, AZ 85721; phone 602-621-7108/1311).

American Indian Library Association (50 E. Huron St., Chicago, IL 60611).

Council for Establishing Dialogue in Teaching and Learning (CED; P.O. Box 25170, Tempe, AZ 85282).

D'Arcy McNickle Center for the History of the American Indian (Newberry Library, 60 W. Walton St., Chicago, IL 60610).

ERIC Clearinghouse on Rural Education and Small Schools (ERIC/CRESS; Appalachia Educational Laboratory, P.O. Box 1348, Charleston, WV 25325; phone 800-624-9120). Publishes free digests on Indian education, including "Unbiased Teaching about American Indians and Alaska Natives in Elementary Schools" by Floy C. Pepper (1990), "Supporting Emergent Literacy Among Young American Indian Students" by William Ross McEachern (1990), and "Changes in American Indian Education: A Historical Retrospective for Educators in the United States" by Jon Reyhner (1989). ERIC/CRESS also publishes bibliographies and resource guides for American Indian education.

ERIC Clearinghouse on Languages and Linguistics (ERIC/CLL; Center for Applied Linguistics, 3520 Prospect St., N.W., Washington, DC 20007). Publishes free digests.

Minority Publishers Exchange (P.O. Box 9869, Madison, WI 53715).

National Clearinghouse for Bilingual Education (NCBE; 1118 22nd St., N.W., Room 217, Washington, DC 20037; phone 800-321-6223). Publishes *NCBE Forum*.

Native American Research Information Service (American Indian Institute, 555 Constitution Ave., Norman, OK 73037).

References

Ada, A. F. 1988. "The Pajaro Valley Experiences Working with Spanish Speaking Parents to Develop Children's Reading and Writing Skills Through the Use of Children's Literature." In *Minority Education: From Shame to Struggle,* edited by T. Skutnabb-Kangas and Jim Cummins. Clevedon, England: Multicultural Matters.

Adler, M. 1982. *Paideia Proposal.* New York: Collier Books.

Ahenakew, Freda. 1986. Text Based Grammars in Cree Language Education. In *Sixth Annual International Native American Language Issues Institute Proceedings: Selected Papers and Biographics,* edited by Suzanne Weryackwe, 1–4. Choctaw, OK: Native American Language Issues.

Aichele, Douglas, and Downing, Carl. 1985. Increasing the Participation of Native Americans in Higher Mathematics. Project funded by the National Science Foundation.

Allen, Minerva, ed. 1986. *Assiniboine/English Bilingual Reading Series.* Hays, MT: Hays/Lodge Pole Schools.

Allen, Paula Gunn. 1983. *Studies in American Indian Literature: Critical Essays and Course Designs.* New York: Modern Language Association.

———, ed. 1989. *Spider Woman's Granddaughters: Traditional Tales and Contemporary Writing by Native American Women.* Boston: Beacon.

Allen, R. V., and Allen C. 1982. *Language Experience Activities.* Boston: Houghton Mifflin.

Allen, T. D. 1982. *Writing to Create Ourselves: New Approaches for Teachers, Students, and Writers.* Norman: University of Oklahoma Press.

Alverman, D. E., Dillon, D. R., and O'Brien, D. G. 1987. *Using Discussion to Promote Reading Comprehension.* Newark, DE: International Reading Association.

Ammons, R. 1987. Social Studies with Trade Books. Tempe, AZ: Jan V Productions.

Anderson, J., ed. 1983. *A Choctaw Anthology.* Philadelphia: Choctaw Heritage.

Anderson, R. C., and Freebody, P. 1981. "Vocabulary Knowledge." In *Comprehension and Teaching: Research Reviews,* edited by J. T. Guthrie, 77–117. Newark, DE: International Reading Association.

Appleton, N. 1983. *Cultural Pluralism in Education.* New York: Longman.

Armstrong, O. K. 1945. Set the American Indians Free! *The Reader's Digest* 47 (August): 47–52.

Armstrong, Virginia I., ed. 1971. *I Have Spoken: American History Through the Voices of the Indians.* Chicago: Swallow.

Asher, James. 1986. *Learning Another Language Through Actions: The Complete Teacher's Guidebook.* Los Gatos, CA: Sky Oaks Productions. (ERIC Document Reproduction Service no. ED 191 314)

Ashton-Warner, Sylvia. 1963. *Teacher.* New York: Simon & Schuster.

Atkins, J. D. C. 1885. *Annual Report of the Commissioner of Indian Affairs to the Secretary of the Interior for the Year 1885.* Washington, DC: Government Printing Office.

–––––––. 1887. *Annual Report of the Commissioner of Indian Affairs to the Secretary of the Interior for the Year 1887.* Washington, DC: Government Printing Office

Atwell, N. 1987. *In the Middle: Writing, Reading, and Learning with Adolescents.* Portsmouth, NH: Heinemann.

–––––––, ed. 1989. *Workshop 1 by and for Teachers: Writing and Literature.* Portsmouth, NH: Heinemann.

–––––––, ed. 1990. *Workshop 2 by and for Teachers: Beyond the Basal.* Portsmouth, NH: Heinemann.

Aukerman, Robert C. 1981. *The Basal Reader Approach to Reading.* New York: John Wiley.

Austin, M. C., and Morrison, C. 1963. *The First R: The Harvard Report on Reading in the Elementary Schools.* New York: Macmillan.

Baker, Colin. 1988. *Key Issues in Bilingualism and Bilingual Education.* Philadelphia: Multilingual Matters.

Banks, James. 1987. *Teaching Strategies For Ethnic Studies.* 4th ed. Boston: Allyn & Bacon.

–––––––. 1988. *Multiethnic Education: Theory and Practice.* 2nd ed. Boston: Allyn & Bacon.

Banks, James, with Clegg, Ambrose. 1977. *Teaching Strategies for the Social Studies*. 2nd ed. Reading, MA: Addison-Wesley.

Baratta-Lorton, Mary. 1976. *Mathematics Their Way*. Menlo Park, CA: Addison-Wesley.

Barfield, Owen, 1965. *Saving the Appearances: A Study in Idolatry*. New York: Harcourt, Brace & World.

Barnes, D. 1976. *From Communication to Curriculum*. Harmondsworth: Penguin.

Barr, Robert, Barth, James, and Shermis, S. Samuel. 1977. *Defining the Social Studies*. Bulletin no. 51. Washington, DC: National Council for the Social Studies.

————. 1978. *The Nature of the Social Studies*. Palm Springs, CA: ETC Publications.

Barrett, T. C. 1972. *A Taxonomy of Reading Comprehension*. Lexington, MA: Ginn.

Bartelt, Guillermo, Jasper, Susan Penfield, and Hoffer, Bates, eds. 1982. *Essays in Native American English*. San Antonio: Trinity University Press.

Bataille, Gretchen M., and Sands, Kathleen Mullen, eds. 1987. *American Indian Women: Telling Their Lives*. Lincoln: University of Nebraska Press.

Beckford, P. A. 1976. A Normative Study of the Physical Fitness of Fourteen, Fifteen, and Sixteen-Year-Old Navajo Girls Using the AAHPERD Youth Fitness Test. Master's thesis, North Texas State University.

Bennett, C. I. 1985. *Comprehensive Multicultural Education: Theory and Practice*. Boston: Allyn & Bacon.

Bennett, William. J. 1986. *First Lessons: A Report on Elementary Education in America*. Washington, DC: Department of Education.

Bettelheim, Bruno. 1961. The Decision to Fail. *School Review* 69 (4): 377–412.

————. 1977. *The Uses of Enchantment: The Meaning and Importance of Fairy Tales*. New York: Vintage.

Bettelheim, Bruno, and Zelan, K. 1982. *On Learning to Read: The Child's Fascination with Meaning*. New York: Knopf.

Bingham, S. and Bingham, J. 1979. *Navajo Farming*. Rock Point, AZ: Rock Point Community School.

————, eds. 1984. *Between Sacred Mountains: Navajo Stories and Lessons from the Land*. Tucson: University of Arizona Press.

Biscaye, Elizabeth, and Pepper, Mary. 1990. The Dene Standardization Project. In *Effective Language Education Practices and Native Language Survival* (Proceedings of the Eighth Annual Native American Language Issues Conference), ed. Jon Reyhner, 23–29. Choctaw, OK: Native American Language Issues.

Blom, G. E., Waite, R. R., and Zimet, S. 1968. Content of First Grade Reading Books. *The Reading Teacher* 21:514–18.

Blondin, Georgina. 1989. The Development of the Zahahti Koe Slavey Language Program. *Canadian Journal of Native Education* 16(2): 89–106.

Bloom, Benjamin. 1981. *All Our Children Learning.* New York: McGraw-Hill.

Board of Indian Commissioners, U.S. Department of the Interior. 1870. *Report of the Board of Indian Commissioners.* Washington, DC: Government Printing Office.

————. 1879. *Eleventh Annual Report of the Board of Indian Commissioners for 1879.* Washington, DC: Government Printing Office.

Boas, Franz. 1911. *The Mind of Primitive Man.* New York: Macmillan.

Bordeaux, Lionel. 1991. "Higher Education from the Tribal College Perspective." In *Opening the Montana Pipeline: American Indian Higher Education in the Nineties,* edited by Deborah Wetsit LaCounte and Patrick Weasel Head. Sacramento: Tribal College.

Bouvier, L. F., and Gardner, R. W. 1986. Immigration to the U.S.: The Unfinished Story. *Population Bulletin* 41(4): 3–50.

Bowler, M. 1978. Textbook Publishers Try to Please All, But First They Woo the Heart of Texas. *The Reading Teacher* 31:514–18.

Boyer, Paul. 1989. *Tribal Colleges: Shaping the Future of Native America.* Princeton, NJ: Carnegie Foundation for the Advancement of Teaching.

Bradley, Claudette. 1984. Issues in Mathematics Education for Native Americans and Directions for Research. *Journal for Research in Mathematics Education* 15:96–106.

Brandt, Elizabeth A., and Ayoungman, Vivian. 1989. Language Renewal and Language Maintenance: A Practical Guide. *Canadian Journal of Native Education* 16(2): 42–77.

Brescia, B. 1981. *A'Una (Let's Go!).* Seattle: Daybreak Star.

Brewer, A. 1977. On Indian Education. *Integrateducation* 15:21–23.

Brown, Anthony D. 1977. An Examination of Age, Sex and Cross-cultural Differences in Cooperation and Competition, and the Relationship of the Two Variables to School Achievement. Ph. D. diss., City University of New York.

————. 1979. "The Cross-over Effect: A Legitimate Issue in Indian Education?" In *Multicultural Education and the American Indian,* 93–113. American Indian Studies Center, University of California, Los Angeles.

Brown, Estelle A. 1952. *Stubborn Fool: A Narrative.* Caldwell, ID: Caxton.

Brumble, H. David, III, ed. 1981. *An Annotated Bibliography of American Indian and Eskimo Autobiographies.* Lincoln: University of Nebraska Press.

Bruner, Jerome. 1960. *The Process of Education.* Cambridge, MA: Harvard University Press.

Bryan, W. 1985. *Montana's Indians: Yesterday and Today.* Helena: Montana Magazine.

Bullock Report. 1975. *A Language for Life: Report of the Committee of Inquiry Appointed by the Secretary of state for Education and science Under the Chairmanship of Sir Allan Bullock.* London: Her Majesty's Stationery Office.

Bureau of the Census, U.S. Department of Commerce. 1984. *General Social and Economic Characteristics, United States Summary, 1980 Census of Population* (PC80-1-C1). Washington, DC.

————. 1985. *American Indians, Eskimos and Aleuts on Identified Reservations and in the Historic Areas of Oklahoma (Excluding Urbanized Areas): 1980 Census of Population, Part 1* (PC80-2-ID). Washington, DC.

————. 1988. *We the First Americans.* Washington, DC: Government Printing Office.

Bureau of Indian Affairs, US Department of the Interior. 1985. *Comprehensive School Report.* Washington, DC.

————. 1988a. *Education Directory.* Washington, DC.

————. 1988b. *Report on BIA Education: Excellence in Indian Education Through the Effective School Process, Final Review Draft.* Washington, DC. Office of Indian Education Programs, BIA. (ERIC Document Reproduction Service no. ED 297 899)

Burgess, B. 1978. "Native American Learning Styles." In *Extracting Learning Styles for Social/Cultural Diversity,* Southwest Teacher Corps Network. Washington, DC: Office of Education.

Burnette, Robert, and Koster, John. 1974. *The Road to Wounded Knee.* New York: Bantam.

Byars, Betsy. 1969. *Trouble River.* New York: Viking.

Byler, M. G. 1973. *American Indian Authors for Young Readers.* New York: Association on American Indian Affairs.

Caduto, M. J., and Bruchac. 1988. *Keepers of the Earth: Native American Stories and Environmental Activities for Children.* Golden, CO: Fulcrum.

Cajete, G. 1986. *Ethnoscience: A Native American Perspective.* Phoenix, AZ: Native American Science Education Association Conference, November 14–15, 1985.

Campbell, D. 1983. *Teaching Guide for Indian Literature.* 2 vols. Rough Rock, AZ: Navajo Curriculum Center.

Cantieni, Graham, and Tremblay, Roger. 1979. "The Use of Concrete Mathematical Situations in Learning a Second Language." In *Bilingual Multicultural Education and the Professional: From Theory to Practice,* edited by Henry T. Trueba and Carol Barnett-Mizrahi, 246–55. Rowley, MA: Newbury House.

Carnegie Forum Task Force on Teaching as a Profession. 1986. As excerpted in *Chronicle of Higher Education,* (May 21): 43–54.

Carter, Forrest. [1976] 1986. *The Education of Little Tree.* Albuquerque: University of New Mexico Press.

Cazden, C. B. 1982. "Four Comments." In *Children in and out of School,* edited by P. Gilmore and A. Glatthkorn. Washington, DC: Center for Applied Linguistics.

Cazden, C. B., and John, V. P. 1971. "Learning in American Indian Children." In *Anthropological Perspectives on Education,* edited by M. L. Wax, S. Diamond, and F. Gearing, 253–72. New York: Basic Books.

Cazden, C. B., and Leggett, E. L. 1981. "Culturally Responsive Education: Recommendations for Achieving Lau Remedies II." In *Culture and the Bilingual Classroom,* edited by H. Trueba, G. Guthrie, and K. Au. Rowley, MA: Newbury House.

Chamot, Anna Uhl. 1981. Applications of Second Language Acquisition Research to the Bilingual Classroom. *National Clearinghouse for Bilingual Education FOCUS* 8.

Chamot, Anna Uhl, and O'Malley, J. Michael. 1985. Using Learning Strategies to Understand Secondary Science Presentations. In *Delivering Academic Excellence to Culturally Diverse Populations,* 33–34. Teaneck, NJ: Fairleigh Dickinson University Press.

———. 1986. *A Cognitive Academic Language Learning Approach: An ESL Content-based Curriculum.* Rosslyn, VA: National Clearinghouse for Bilingual Education.

Chamot, Anna Uhl, and Stewner-Manzanares, G. 1985. *A Synthesis of Current Literature on English as a Second Language*. Rosslyn, VA: National Clearinghouse for Bilingual Education. (ERIC Document Reproduction Service no. ED 261 537)

Child, I. L., Potter, E. H., and Levine, E. M. 1946. Children's Textbooks and Personality Development: An Exploration in the Social Psychology of Education. *Psychological Monographs* 60:1–54.

Chomsky, C. 1981. "Write Now, Read Later." In *Language in Early Childhood Education,* 2nd ed., edited by Courtney Cazden. Washington, DC: National Association for the Education of Young Children.

Clark, J. E. 1977. *The Shawnee*. Lexington: University of Kentucky Press.

Cohen, M. C., and Cohen, S. W. 1982. *Games and Activities for Teaching English as a Second Language*. Berkeley: Bilingual Media Productions.

Cohen, R. A. 1969. Conceptual Styles, Cultural Conflict, and Nonverbal Tests of Intelligence. *American Anthropologist* 71:828–56.

Cole, M., John-Steiner, V., Scribner, S., and Souberman, E., eds. 1978. *L. S. Vygotsky, Mind in Society: The Development of Higher Psychological Processes*. Cambridge, MA: Harvard University Press.

Cole, M., and Scribner, S. 1974. *Culture and Thought: A Psychological Introduction*. New York: John Wiley.

Coleman, James S., Campbell, Ernest Q., Hobson, Carol J., McPartland, James, Mood, Alexander M., Weinfeld, Frederic D., and York, Robert L. 1966. *Equality of Educational Opportunity*. Washington, DC: Government Printing Office.

Collier, John. 1947. *The Indians of the Americas*. New York: Norton.

Collier, Virginia P. 1989. How Long? A Synthesis of Research on Academic Achievement in a Second Language. *TESOL Quarterly 23*: 509–31.

Colonese, Tom, and Owen, Louis. 1985. *American Indian Novelists: An Annotated Bibliography*. New York: Garland.

Congress Video Group. 1985. *I Will Fight No More Forever*. South Plainfield, NJ. (videotape)

Cooper, J. D. 1986. *Improving Reading Comprehension*. Boston: Houghton Mifflin.

Copple, C., Sigel, I., and Saunders, R. 1979. *Educating the Young Thinker: Classroom Strategies for Cognitive Growth*. New York: Van Nostrand.

Costo, Rupert. 1970. *Textbooks and the American Indian*. San Francisco: Indian Historian Press.

Council for Interracial Books for Children. 1981. *Unlearning "Indian" Stereotypes: A Teaching Unit for Teachers and Children's Librarians.* New York.

Cox, B. G., and Ramirez, M., III. 1981. "Cognitive Styles: Implications for Multiethnic Education." In *Education in the 80's: Multiethnic Education,* edited by James A. Banks, 61–71. Washington, DC: National Education Association.

Crawford, James. 1989. *Bilingual Education: History, Politics, Theory and Practice.* Boston: Crane.

Cronback, Lee J., ed. 1955. *Text Materials in Modern Education.* Urbana: University of Illinois Press.

Culin, S. 1975. *Games of the North American Indians.* New York: Dover.

Cullinan, B. E. 1987. *Children's Literature in the Reading Program.* Newark, DE: International Reading Association.

Cummins, Jim. 1981. "The Role of Primary Language Development in Promoting Educational Success for Language Minority Students." In California State Department of Education, *Schooling and Language Minority Students,* 3–49. Los Angeles: Evaluation, Dissemination and Assessment Center, California State University, Los Angeles.

———. 1984. *Bilingualism and Special Education: Issues in Assessment and Pedagogy.* San Diego, CA: College Hill.

———. 1985. Theory and Policy in Bilingual Education. Paper developed for the National Seminar on Education in Multicultural Societies, Ljubljana, Yugoslavia, and distributed by the Organization for Economic Co-operation and Development, Paris.

———. 1986. Empowering Minority Students: A Framework for Intervention. *Harvard Educational Review* 56(1): 18–36.

———. 1989. *Empowering Minority Students.* Sacramento: California Association for Bilingual Education.

———. 1990. Language Development Among Aboriginal Children in Northern Communities. Report prepared under contract with the government of the Yukon for presentation at the Circumpolar Education Conference, Umea, Sweden.

Curtis, N. 1923. *The Indian's Book.* New York: Dover.

D'Ambrosio, Ubiratan. 1985. *Socio-cultural Bases for Mathematics Education.* São Paulo, Brazil: Universidade Estadual de Campinas (Unicamp).

Davidson, Karen L. 1989. A Comparison of Native American and White Students' Cognitive Strengths as Measured by the Kaufman Assessment Battery for Children. Master's thesis, Eastern Montana College.

Davis, F. B. 1968. Research in Comprehension in Reading. *Reading Research Quarterly* 7:499–545.

Davison, David M. 1990. An Ethnomathematics Approach to Teaching Language Minority Students. In *Effective Language Education Practices and Native Language Survival* (Proceedings of the Eighth Annual Native American Language Issues Conference), Jon Reyhner, 143–48. Choctaw, OK: Native American Language Issues.

Davison, David M., and Pearce, Daniel L. in press. "The Influence of Writing Activities on the Mathematics Learning of American Indian Students." *Journal of Educational Issues of Language Minority Students.*

Davison, David M., and Schindler, Duane E. 1986. "Mathematics and the Indian student." In *Teaching the Indian child,* edited by Jon Reyhner, 178–86. Billings, MT: Eastern Montana College Press.

———. 1988. "Mathematics for the Native Student." In *Teaching the Native American,* edited by Hap Gilliland, Jon Reyhner, and Rachel Schaffer, 153–57. Dubuque, IA: Kendall/Hunt.

De Avila, Edward A. 1985. "Motivation, Intelligence, and Access: A Theoretical Framework for the Education of Minority Language Students." In *Issues in English Language Development,* National Clearinghouse for Bilingual Education, 21–31. Rosslyn, VA: InterAmerica Research Associates.

———. 1988. Bilingualism, cognitive function, and language minority group membership. In *Linguistic and Cultural Influences on Learning Mathematics,* edited by Rodney R. Cocking and Jose P. Mestre, 101–21. Hillsdale, NJ: Erlbaum.

Deloria, Jr., Vine. 1974. *Behind the Trail of Broken Treaties.* New York: Dell.

Dewey, J. 1916. *Democracy and Education.* New York: Macmillan.

Deyhle, D. 1983. Measuring Success and Failure in the Classroom: Teacher Communications About Tests and the Understandings of Young Navajo Students. In The Transcultural Education of American Indian and Alaska Native Children: Teachers and Students in Transaction, special issue edited by D. McShane. *Peabody Journal of Education* 61:1, 67–85.

Dick, A. 1980. *Village Science.* Iditarod, AK: Iditarod Area School District.

Diessner, Rhett, and Walker, Jacqueline L. 1989. A Cognitive Pattern of the Yakima Indian Students. *Journal of American Indian Education* 28(4):84–88.

Dinges, N. G., and Hollenbeck, A. R. 1978. Field Dependence-Independence in Navajo Children. *International Journal of Psychology* 13:215–20.

Dionisio, M. 1983. Write? Isn't This Reading Class? *Reading Teacher* 36:746–50.

Doebler, L. K., and Mardis, L. J. 1981. Effects of Bilingual Education Program for Native American Children. *NABE Journal* 5(2): 23–28.

Drew, Nancy, and Hamayan, Else. 1979. Math and the Bilingual Student. *Bilingual Education Service Center Newsletter* 7(1): 9–10.

Dulay, H., Burt, M., and Krashen, S. 1982. *Language Two.* New York: Oxford University Press.

Dumont, R. V., and Wax, M. L. 1969. Cherokee School Society and the Intercultural Classroom. *Human Organization* 28:217–26.

Dumont, R. V. 1972. "Learning English and How to Be Silent: Studies in Sioux and Cherokee Classrooms." In *Function of Language in the Classroom,* edited by C. Cazden, V. John, and D. Hymes. New York: Teachers College.

Eastman, Charles [1902] 1971. *Indian Boyhood.* Greenwich: Fawcett.

––––––. [1916] 1977. *From the Deep Woods to Civilization: Chapters in the Autobiography of an Indian.* Lincoln: University of Nebraska Press.

Edmonds, W. D. 1941. *The Matchlock Gun.* New York: Dodd, Mead.

Education Development Center. 1970. *Antler and Fang.* Cambridge, MA.

Efta, M. 1984. "Reading in Silence: A Chance to Read." In *Readings on Reading Instruction,* 3rd ed., edited by A. J. Harris and E. R. Sipay, 387–91. New York: Longman.

Ellis, Arthur. 1981. *Teaching and Learning Elementary Social Studies.* 2nd ed. Boston: Allyn & Bacon.

Emerson, R. W. 1981. *Selected Writings of Emerson.* Edited by Donald McQuade. New York: Modern Library.

Erickson, F., and Mohatt, G. 1982. "Cultural Organization of Participation Structures in Two Classrooms of Indian Students." In *Doing the Ethnography of Schooling,* edited by G. Spindler. New York: Holt, Rinehart & Winston.

Evangelauf, Jean. 1990. 1988 Enrollments of All Racial Groups Hit Record Levels. *Chronicle of Higher Education* 36(30): A1, A36–46.

Evans, G., and Abbey, K. 1979. *Bibliography of Language Arts Materials for Native North Americans: Bilingual, English as a Second Language and Native Language Materials 1975–1976, with Supplemental Entries for 1965–1974.* American Indian Studies Center, University of California, Los Angeles.

Evans, G. Edward, Abbey, K., and Reed, D. 1977. *Bibliography of Language Arts Materials for Native North Americans: Bilingual, En-*

glish as a Second Language and Native Language Materials 1965–1974. American Indian Studies Center, University of California, Los Angeles.

Featherly, Bernadine. 1985. The Relation Between the Oral Language Proficiency and Reading Achievement of First Grade Crow Indian Children. Ph.D. diss., Montana State University, Bozeman.

Federal and State Indian Reservations and Indian Trust Areas. 1974. Washington, DC: Government Printing Office.

Fedullo, Mick. 1990. *It's Like My Heart Pounding: Imaginative Writing for American Indian Students.* Ogden, UT: Mountain West Educational Equity Center, Weber State College.

Fitzgerald, Frances. 1979. *America Revised: History Schoolbooks in the Twentieth Century.* Boston: Atlantic–Little, Brown.

Fleisher, M. S. 1982. "The educational implications of American Indian English." In *Language Renewal Among American Indian Tribes,* edited by Robert St. Clair and William Leap, 141–48. Rosslyn, VA: National Clearinghouse for Bilingual Education.

Fleres, Augie. 1989. Te Kohanga Reo: A Maori Language Renewal Program. *Canadian Journal of Native Education* 16(2): 78–88.

Forbes, Jack D. 1990. Undercounting Native Americans: The 1980 Census and the Manipulation of Racial Identity in the United States. *Wicazo Sa Review* 6(1): 2–26.

Franciscan Fathers. 1910. *An Ethnologic Dictionary of the Navajo Language.* St. Michaels, AZ: St. Michaels Mission. (Reprinted in 1968)

Franklin, Benjamin. 1784. *Two Tracts: Information to Those Who Would Remove to America, and Remarks Concerning the Savages of North America.* Dublin: L. White.

Freeman, Y., and Freeman, D. 1988. Bilingual Learners: How Our Assumptions Limit Their World. Occasional Paper no. 18, Program in Language and Literacy, College of Education, University of Arizona, Tucson.

Freire, Paulo. 1970. *Pedagogy of the Oppressed.* New York: Continuum.

Fries, C. 1962. *Linguistics and Reading.* New York: Holt, Rinehart & Winston.

Fuchs, Estelle, and Havighurst, Robert J. 1972. *To Live on This Earth: American Indian Education.* Garden City, NY: Anchor Books.

Gambrell, L. B. 1985. Dialogue Journals: Reading-Writing Interaction. *Reading Teacher,* 38:512–15.

Garbe, Douglas G. 1985. Mathematics Vocabulary and the Culturally Different Student. *Arithmetic Teacher* 33(2): 39–42.

Garcia, R. 1991. *Teaching in a Pluralistic Society.* 2nd ed. New York: Harper & Row.

Gardner, Howard. 1983. *Frames of Mind: The Theory of Multiple Intelligences.* New York: Basic Books.

Gardner, R. 1959. Cognitive Control: A Study of Individual Consistencies in Cognitive Behavior. *Psychological Issues* 4:22–30.

Gates, Arthur. 1962. The Word Recognition Ability and the Reading Vocabulary of Second- and Third-Grade Children. *Reading Teacher* 15:443–48.

George, Phil. 1975. "Name Giveaway," in *Voices of the Rainbow,* ed. Kenneth Rosen. New York: Viking Press, 160.

Gibson, M. 1976. Approaches to Multicultural Education in the United States. *Anthropology and Education Quarterly* 7(4): 7–18.

Gilliland, Hap. 1980. *Indian Children's Books.* Billings, MT: Council for Indian Education. (ERIC Document Reproduction Service no. ED 232 809)

————. 1982. The New View of Native Americans in Children's Books. *Reading Teacher* 35(8): 912–16.

————. 1983. Modern Indian Stories are Essential to the Success of Modern Indian Children. *Native American Education* (newsletter of the Council for Indian Education) 2(1): 1–2.

————. 1988. Learning Through Cooperation and Sharing. In *Teaching the Native American,* edited by Hap Gilliland, Jon Reyhner, and Rachel Schaffer, 38–46. Dubuque, IA: Kendall/Hunt.

Glock, Charles Y., et al. 1975. *Adolescent Prejudice.* New York: Harper & Row.

Golden, Gertrude. 1954. *Red Moon Called Me: Memoirs of a Schoolteacher in the Government Indian Service.* Edited by Cecil Dryden. San Antonio: Naylor.

Goldhammer, R. 1969. *Clinical supervision: Special Methods for the Supervision of Teachers.* New York: Holt, Rinehart & Winston.

Goodman, Kenneth S. 1986. *What's Whole in Whole Language.* Richmond Hill, Ontario: Scholastic.

Goodman, Kenneth S., and Goodman, Yetta M. 1977. Learning About Psycholinguistic Processes by Analyzing Oral Reading. *Harvard Educational Review* 47:317–33.

Goodman, Kenneth S., Shannon, Patrick, Freeman, Yvonne S., and Murphy, Sharon. 1988. *Report Card on Basals.* Katonah, NY: Richard C. Owen.

Graves, Donald H. 1983. *Writing: Teachers and Children at Work.* Portsmouth, NH: Heinemann.

Gray, W. S., Artley, S., Arbuthnot, M. H., and Gray, L. 1951. *Guidebook to Accompany the New Fun with Dick and Jane.* Chicago: Scott, Foresman.

Green, R., and Brown, J. W. 1976. *Recommendations for the Improvement of Science and Mathematics Education for American Indians.* Washington, DC: American Association for the Advancement of Science.

Gribskov, Margaret. 1973. A Critical Analysis of Textbook Accounts of the Role of Indians in American History. Ph.D. diss., University of Oregon.

Grobe, E. P. n.d. *300 Creative Writing Activities for Composition Classes.* Portland, ME: J. Weston Walch.

Guthridge, G. 1986. Eskimos Solve the Future. *Analog* (April): 67–72.

Gwe Gnaavja. 1985. Supai, AZ: Havasupai School.

Habermas, Jurgen. 1971. *Knowledge and Human Interests.* Translated by Jerey J. Shapiro. Boston: Beacon.

Hakuta, Kenji. 1986. *Mirror of Language: The Debate on Bilingualism.* New York: Basic Books.

Hakuta, K., and Diaz, R. M. 1985. "The Relationship Between Degree of Bilingualism and Cognitive Ability: A Critical Discussion and Some New Longitudinal Data." In *Children's Language,* Vol. 5, edited by K. E. Nelson. Hillsdale, NJ: Erlbaum.

Hale, Janet Campbell. 1974. *Owl Song.* Garden City, NY: Doubleday.

Hale, K. 1980. Linguistics and Local Languages in a Science Curriculum for Bilingual/bicultural Programs. Massachusetts Institute of Technology. (unpublished)

Hardy, G. E. 1891. The Function of Literature in Elementary Schools. *Education Review* 2(July): 140–50.

Harjo, Joy. 1983. *She Had Some Horses.* New York: Thunder's Mouth Press.

Harris, Louise Dyer, and Harris, Norman Dyer. 1960. *Slim Green.* Boston: Little, Brown.

Harris, Marvin. 1975. *Culture, People, Nature: An Introduction to General Anthropology.* 2nd ed. New York: Thomas Y. Crowell.

Harvey, Karen D., Harjo, Lisa D., and Jackson, Jane K. 1990. *Teaching About Native Americans.* Bulletin no. 84. Washington, DC: National Council for the Social Studies.

Havighurst, Robert J. 1970. *National Study of American Indian Education*. Washington, DC: Office of Education.

Heath, S. B. 1982. "Questioning at Home and at School: A Comparative Study." In *Doing the Ethnography of Schooling,* edited by G. Spindler. New York: Holt, Rinehart & Winston.

————. 1983. *Ways with Words.* Cambridge: Cambridge University Press.

Henry, J. 1961. Reading for what? In *Claremont Reading Conference, 25th Yearbook,* 19–35. Claremont, CA: Claremont Reading Conference.

Herber, H. L. 1978. *Teaching Reading in Content Areas.* 2nd ed. Englewood Cliffs, NJ: Prentice Hall.

Herber, H. L., and Nelson, J. B. 1975. Questioning Is Not the Answer. *Journal of Reading* 18:512–17.

Hillabrant, Walter, Romano, Mike, and Stang, David. In press. "Native American Education at a Turning Point: Current Demographics and Trends." In *Indian Nations at Risk: Solutions for the 1990s* (supplement volume), edited by G. Mike Charleston. Washington, DC: Indian Nations at Risk Task Force, Department of Education.

Hirsch, E. D., Jr. 1987. *Cultural Literacy: What Every American Needs to Know.* Boston: Houghton Mifflin.

Hirst, Lois. 1986. Native Language Promotes Student Achievement. In *Sixth Annual International Native American Language Issues Institute Proceedings: Selected Papers and Biographics,* ed. Suzanne Weryackwe, 47–50. Choctaw, OK: Native American Language Issues.

Hirst, L. A., and Slavik, C. 1990. Cooperative Approaches to Language Learning. In *Effective Language Education Practices and Native Language Survival: Proceedings of the Ninth Annual Native American Language Issues Institute,* ed. Jon Reyhner, 133–42. Choctaw, OK: Native American Language Issues.

Hman Qaj Gwe Fnuudja (Havasupai Poetry by Havasupai Elementary School Students). 1985. Supai, AZ: Havasupai Bilingual Program.

Hodgkinson, Harold L., Outtz, Janice Hamilton, and Obarakpor, Anita M. 1990. The Demographics of American Indians: One Percent of the People, Fifty Percent of the Diversity. Washington, DC: Institute for Educational Leadership, Center for Demographic Policy.

Hoeveler, Diane Long. 1988. "Text and Context: Teaching Native American Literature." *English Journal* 77(Sept.): 20–24.

Holdaway, D. 1979. *Foundations of Literacy.* New York: Ashton Scholastic.

Holm, Wayne. 1985. Community School Charts Achievements. *Indian Affairs* 108(February): 2–3.

Holt, B. 1977. *Science with Young Children*. Washington, DC: National Association for the Education of Young Children.

Howard, Oliver O. 1907. *My Life and Experiences Among Our Hostile Indians*. Hartford, CT: Worthington.

Howell, R. A., and Howell, M. L. 1978. The Myth of Pop Warner: Carlisle Revisited. *Quest Monograph* 30(Summer): 19–27.

Hoxie, Frederick E. 1984. *A Final Promise: The Campaign to Assimilate the Indians, 1880–1920*. Lincoln: University of Nebraska Press.

Hudelson, S. 1989. *Write On: Children Writing in ESL*. Englewood Cliffs, NJ: Center for Applied Linguistics and Prentice Hall Regents.

Huey, Edmund B. [1908] 1918. *The Psychology and Pedagogy of Reading*. New York: Macmillan.

Hunter, D., and Whitten, P. 1976. *Encyclopedia of Anthropology*. New York: Harper & Row.

Indian Education: America's Unpaid Debt (the eighth annual report to the Congress of the United States by the National Advisory Council on Indian Education). 1982. Washington, DC: Government Printing Office.

Jackson, Helen Hunt. [1881] 1886. *A Century of Dishonor: A Sketch of the United States Governments Dealings with Some of the Indian Tribes*. Boston: Roberts Brothers.

Jahoda, M. 1960. *Race Relations and Mental Health*. Paris: UNESCO.

James, George Wharton. 1908. *What the White Race May Learn from the Indian*. Chicago: Forbes.

John, V. P. 1972. "Styles of Learning—Styles of Teaching: Reflections on the Education of Navajo Children." In *Functions of Language in the Classroom,* edited by C. Cazden, D. Hymes, and V. P. John. New York: Teachers College Press.

John-Steiner, V. P., and Osterreich, H. 1975. Learning Styles Among Pueblo Children. Department of Educational Foundations, University of New Mexico. (unpublished)

Johnson, Broderick, H., ed. 1975. *Navajo Stories of the Long Walk Period*. Tsaile, AZ: Navajo Community College.

———. 1977. *Stories of Traditional Navajo Live and Culture by Twenty-two Navajo Men and Women*. Tsaile, AZ: Navajo Community College.

Johnson, D. 1991, March 11. 1990 Census: National and State Population Counts for American Indians, Eskimos, and Aleuts. Washington, DC: U.S. Department of Commerce, Bureau of the Census.

Johnson, D., Johnson, R., and Holubec, E. 1986. *Circles of Learning: Cooperation in the Classroom.* Edina, MN: Interaction.

Johnson, D., and Pearson, P. D. 1984. *Teaching Reading Vocabulary,* 2nd ed. New York: Holt, Rinehart & Winston.

Johnson, Willis N. 1975. Teaching Mathematics in a Multicultural Setting: Some Considerations When Teachers and Students Are of Differing Cultural Backgrounds. (ERIC Document Reproduction Service no. ED 183 414)

Jones, A. 1983. *Nauriat Niginaqtuat: Plants that We Eat.* Kotzebue, AK: Northwest Arctic School District.

Jordan, Cathy. 1984. Cultural Compatibility and the Education of Hawaiian Children: Implications for Mainland Educators. *Educational Research Quarterly* 8(4): 59–71.

Josephy, A. M. 1968. *The Indian Heritage of America.* New York: Knopf.

Kagan, J. 1966. Reflection-Impulsivity: The Generality and Dynamics of Conceptual Tempo. *Journal of Abnormal Psychology* 71:17–24.

Kari, P. R. 1977. *Dena'ina K'et'una: Tanaina Plantlore.* Anchorage, AK: Adult Literacy Laboratory, Anchorage Community College.

Kates, E. C., and Matthews, H. 1980. *Crow Language Learning Guide.* Crow Agency, MT: Bilingual Materials Development Center.

Kazemek, F. E. 1985. Stories of Our Lives: Interviews and Oral Histories for Language Development. *Journal of Reading* 29:211–18.

King, Dorothy F. 1990. Toward Excellence in Educating Navajo Students One School's Journey: An Interview with Helen Zongolowicz. *Journal of Navajo Education* 7(2): 22–27.

Kleinfeld, Judith. S. 1979a. *Eskimo School on the Adreafsky: A Study of Effective Bicultural Education.* New York: Praeger.

————. 1979b. Effective Teachers of Eskimo and Indian Students. *School Review* 2:335.

————. 1973. Intellectual Strengths in Culturally Different Groups: An Eskimo Illustration. *Review of Educational Research* 43:341–59.

Kleinfeld, Judith S., McDiarmid, G. W., and Parrett W. 1983. Doing Research on Effective Cross-cultural Teaching: The Teacher Tale. In The Transcultural Education of American Indian and Alaska Native Children: Teachers and Students in Transaction, special issue edited by D. McShane. *Peabody Journal of Education* 6(1): 86–108.

Klineberg, Otto. 1963. Life Is Fun in a Smiling, Fair-skinned World. *Saturday Review* (February 16): 75–77, 87.

Kluckhohn, Clyde. 1962. *Culture and Behavior.* New York: Free Press of Glencoe.

Kluckhohn, Clyde, and Leighton, Dorothy. 1962. *The Navaho.* Rev. ed. New York: Doubleday.

Kneale, Albert H. 1950. *Indian Agent.* Caldwell, ID: Caxton.

Kogan, N. 1971. "Educational Implications of Cognitive Styles." In *Psychology and Educational Practice,* edited by G. S. Lesser. Glenview, IL: Scott, Foresman.

Krashen, Stephen D. 1981. "Bilingual Education and Second Language Acquisition Theory." In California State Department of Education, *Schooling and Language Minority Students,* 52–79. Los Angeles: Evaluation, Dissemination and Assessment Center, California State University, Los Angeles.

———. 1982. "Theory Versus Practice in Language Training." In *Innovative Approaches to Language Teaching,* edited by R. W. Blair, 15–30. Rowley, MA: Newbury House.

———. 1983. "Newmark's 'Ignorance Hypothesis' and Current Second Language Acquisition Theory." In *Language Transfer in Language Learning,* edited by S. Gass and L. Selinker. 135–53. Rowley, MA: Newbury House.

———. 1984. *Writing: Research, Theory and Applications.* New York: Pergamon.

———. 1985. *Inquiries and Insights: Selected Essays.* Haywood, CA: Alemany.

———. In press. *Comic Book Reading and Language Development.* Victoria, British Columbia: Abel.

Krashen, Stephen D., and Biber, Douglas. 1988. *On Course: Bilingual Education's Success in California.* Sacramento: California Association for Bilingual Education.

Krashen, Stephen D., and Terrell, Tracy D. 1983. *The Natural Approach: Language Acquisition in the Classroom.* Hayward, CA: Alemany.

Kwachka, Patricia. 1989. Oral and Written English of the Koyukon Athabaskan Area: A Preliminary Analysis. Nenana, AK: Yukon-Koyukon School District.

La Farge, Oliver. [1929] 1971. *Laughing Boy.* New York: New American Library.

———. 1937. *The Enemy Gods.* Cambridge, MA: Riverside Press.

La Flesche, Francis [1900] 1963. *The Middle Five: Indian Schoolboys of the Omaha Tribe.* Madison: University of Wisconsin Press.

Lakota Woskate. 1972. *Curriculum Materials Resource Unit 6*. Washington, DC: National Center for Educational Research and Development.

Lambert, W. E. 1975. "Culture and Language as Factors in Learning and Education." In *Education of Immigrant Students*, edited by A. Wolfgang. Toronto: Ontario Institute for Studies in Education.

———. 1984. An Overview of Issues in Immersion Education. In California State Department of Education, *Studies on Immersion Education: A Collection for U.S. Educators*, 8–30. Sacramento, CA.

Lankford, R., and Riley, J. D. 1986. Native American Reading Disability. *Journal of American Indian Education* 25(3): 1–11.

Latham, Glenn I. 1989. Thirteen Most Common Needs of American Education in BIA Schools. *Journal of American Indian Education* 29(1): 1–11.

Lavine, S. A. 1974. *The Games the Indian Played*. New York: Dodd. Mead.

Lawson, R. 1940. *They Were Strong and Good*. New York: Viking.

Layman, Martha Elizabeth. 1942. A History of Indian Education in the United States. Ph. D. diss., University of Minnesota.

Leacock, E. 1976. "The Concept of Culture and Its Significance for School Counselors." In *Schooling in the Cultural Context*, edited by J. I. Roberts and S. K. Akinsany. New York: David McKay.

Leap, William L. 1978. "American Indian English and Its Implications for Bilingual Education." In *International Dimensions of Bilingual Education*, edited by James Alatis, 657–69. Washington, DC: Georgetown University Press.

———. 1982a. "Roles for the Linguist in Indian Bilingual Education." In *Language Renewal among American Indian Tribes: Issues, Problems, and Prospects*, edited by Robert St. Clair and William Leap. Rosslyn, VA: National Clearinghouse for Bilingual Education.

———. 1982b. "Semilingualism as a Form of Linguistic Proficiency." In *Language Renewal Among American Indian Tribes: Issues, Problems and Prospects*, edited by Robert St. Clair and William Leap, 149–59. Rosslyn, VA: National Clearinghouse for Bilingual Education.

———. 1988. "Assumptions and Strategies Guiding Mathematics Word Problem-solving by Ute Indian Students." In *Linguistic and Cultural Influences on Learning Mathematics*, edited by Rodney Cocking and Jose Mestre, 161–86. Hillsdale, NJ: Erlbaum.

———. 1989. "Snakes never sleep": The Significance of Ute English Non Sequitur Responses to Standard English Questions. In *The Pro-*

ceedings of the Eighth Annual Native American Language Issues Institute. Choctaw, OK: Native American Language Issues.

————. 1990. Written Ute English: Texture, Construction, and Point of View. In *Effective Language Education Practices and Native Language Survival* (Proceedings of the Eighth Annual Native American Language Issues Conference), edited by Jon Reyhner, 39–52. Choctaw, OK: Native American Language Issues.

————. 1991. Pathways and Barriers to Indian Language Literacy Building on the Northern Ute Reservation. *Anthropology and Education Quarterly* 22:21–41.

————. Forthcoming. "Educational Implications of American Indian English." In *American Indian English.* Berlin: Mouton-De Gruyter.

————, ed. 1977. *Studies in Southwestern Indian English.* San Antonio: Trinity University Press.

Lin, Ruey-Lin. 1985. The Promise and Problems of the Native American Student. *Journal of American Indian Education* 25(1): 6—16.

————. 1990. Perception of Family Background and Personal Characteristis Among Indian College Students. *Journal of American Indian Education* 29(3): 19–28.

Lincoln, Kenneth. 1983. *Native American Renaissance.* Berkeley: University of California Press.

Linderman, F. B. [1932] 1972. *Pretty Shield; Medicine Woman of the Crows* (originally titled *Red Mother*). Lincoln: University of Nebraska.

Lindfors, Judith W. 1985. "Oral Language Learning: Understanding the Development of Language Structure." In *Observing the Language Learner,* edited by A. Jagger and M. Trika Smith-Burke, 41–72. Newark, DE: International Reading Association.

————. 1987. *Children's Language and Learning.* 2nd ed. Englewood Cliffs, NJ: Prentice Hall.

————. 1989. "The Classroom: A Good Environment for Language Learning." In *When They Don't All Speak English: Integrating the ESL Student into the Regular Classroom,* edited by P. Rigg and V. G. Allen, 39–54. Urbana, IL: National Council of Teachers of English.

Littlebear, Dick. 1990. Keynote Address. In *Effective Language Education Practices and Native Language Survival* (Proceedings of the Eighth Annual Native American Language Issues Conference), edited by Jon Reyhner, 1–8. Choctaw, OK: Native American Language Issues.

Livingston, M. C. 1974. Children's Literature: In Chaos a Creative Weapon. *Reading Teacher* 27:534–39.

Longstreet, E. 1978. *Aspects of Ethnicity*. New York: Teachers College Press.

Lower Kuskokwim School District Bilingual/Bicultural Department. 1983. *Pitengnaqsaraq: Yup'ik Eskimo Subsistence Board Game*. Lower Kuskokwim, AK: Author.

Lowie, R. H. 1954. *Indians of the Plains*. Lincoln: University of Nebraska Press.

McCarty, T. L. 1989. School as Community: The Rough Rock Demonstration. *Harvard Education Review* 59:484–503.

McEachern, William R., and Luther, Frances. 1989. The Relationship Between Culturally Relevant Materials and Listening Comprehension of Canadian Native Indian Children. *Language Culture and Curriculum* 2(1): 55–60.

MacFarlan, A. A. 1958. *Book of American Indian Games*. New York: Association.

McFee, Malcolm. 1968. the 150 Percent Man, a Product of Blackfeet Acculturation. *American Anthropologist* 70(6): 1096–1107.

MacGregor, Gordon. 1946. *Warriors Without Weapons*. Chicago: University of Chicago Press.

McKenna, F. R. 1981. The Myth of Multiculturalism and the Reality of American Indians in Contemporary America. *Journal of American Indian Education* 21(1): 19.

McLaughlin, Barry. 1987. *Theories of Second-Language Learning*. New York: Edward Arnold.

McLaughlin, Daniel. 1989. Sociolinguistics of Navajo Literacy. *Anthropology and Education Quarterly* 20:275–90.

———. In press. *When Literacy Empowers: An Ethnography of Uses of English and Navajo Print*. Albuquerque: University of New Mexico Press.

McLoughlin, William. 1984. *Cherokees and Missionaries*. New Haven: Yale University Press.

McNeil, J. D. 1987. *Reading comprehension: New directions for classroom practice*. 2nd ed. Glenview, IL: Scott, Foresman.

McNickle, D'Arcy. [1936] 1978. *The Surrounded*. Albuquerque: University of New Mexico Press.

———. 1954. *Runner in the Sun*. New York: Holt.

Mahan, J. M., and Criger, M. K. 1977. Culturally Oriented Instruction for Native American Students. *Integrateducation* 15:9–13.

Maier, Gene. 1985. Math and the Mind's Eye. Project funded by the National Science Foundation.

Mails, T. E. 1972. *The Mystic Warriors of the Plains*. Garden City, NY: Doubleday.

Malone, H. T. 1952. A Social History of the Eastern Cherokee Indians from the Revolution to the Removal. Ph.D. diss., Emory University.

Manuel-Dupont, Sonia. 1990. Narrative Literacy Patterns of Northern Ute Adolescent Students. In *Effective Language Education Practices and Native Language Survival* (Proceedings of the Eighth Annual Native American Language Issues Conference), edited by Jon Reyhner, 53–94. Choctaw, OK: Native American Language Issues.

Manzo, A. V. 1969. The Request Procedure. *Journal of Reading* 11: 123–26.

———. 1975. Guided Reading Procedure. *Journal of Reading* 18: 287–91.

Marquis, T. B., interpreter. 1931. *Wooden Leg: A Warrior Who Fought Custer*. Lincoln: University of Nebraska Press.

Mathews, John Joseph. [1934] 1979. *Sundown*. Boston: Gregg.

Medicine, Beatrice. 1981. Speaking Indian: Parameters on language use among American Indians. *Focus 6* (March).

Meeker, L. L. 1901. *Ogalala Games*. Philadelphia: Department of Archaeology, University of Pennsylvania. (Reprinted from the *Bulletin of the Free Museum of Science and Art*.)

Mehan, H. 1981. "Ethnography of Bilingual Education." In *Culture and the Bilingual Classroom,* edited by H. Trueba, G. Guthrie, and K. Au. Rowley, MA: Newbury House.

Mercer, J. 1973. *Labeling the Mentally Retarded*. Berkeley: University of California Press.

Meriam, Lewis, ed. 1928. *The Problem of Indian Administration*. Baltimore: Johns Hopkins University Press.

Miller, A. G., and Thomas, R. 1972. Cooperation and Competition among Blackfoot Indian and Urban Canadian Children. *Child Development* 43: 1104–10.

Miller, Mary Rita. 1977. *Children of the Salt River: First and Second Language Acquisition Among Pima Children*. Language Science Monographs no. 16. Bloomington: Indiana University Press.

Mitchell, Emerson Black Horse. 1967. *Miracle Hill*. Norman: University of Oklahoma Press.

Mohan, B. A. 1986. Language and Content Learning: Finding Common Ground. *ERIC/CLL News Bulletin* 9:1, 3–4.

Mohatt, G., and Erickson, F. 1981. "Cultural Differences in Teaching Styles in an Odawa school: A Sociolinguistic Approach." In *Culture and the Bilingual Classroom,* edited by H. Trueba, G. Guthrie, and K. Au, 105–19. Rowley, MA: Newbury House.

Moll, L. C., and Diaz, S. 1987. Change as the Goal of Educational Research. *Anthropology and Education Quarterly* 18:300–11.

Momaday, N. Scott. 1968. *House Made of Dawn.* New York: Harper & Row.

Montagu, A. 1974. *Man's Most Dangerous Myth.* New York: Oxford University Press.

Mooney, Carolyn J. 1990. Universities Awarded Record Number of Doctorates Last Year. *Chronicle of Higher Education* 36(32): A1, A11.

Moore, D. W., Readence, J. E., and Rickelman, R. J. 1988. *Prereading Activities for Content Area Reading and Learning.* 2nd ed. Newark, DE: International Reading Association.

More, Arthur J. 1989. Native Indian Learning Styles: A Review for Researchers and Teachers. *Journal of American Indian Education* 28(4): 15–28.

Morey, Sylvester M., and Gilliam, Olivia, L. 1974. *Respect for Life: The Traditional Upbringing of American Indian Children.* Garden City, NY: Waldorf.

Mourning Dove. [1927] 1981. *Co-ge-we-a.* Lincoln: University of Nebraska Press.

Nabokov, Peter. 1981. *Indian Running.* Santa Barbara, CA: Capra.

Nader, Ralph. 1969. "Statement of Ralph Nader, Author, Lecturer." In *Indian Education, 1969,* pt. 1, 47–55. Hearings before the Subcommittee on Indian Education of the Committee on Labor and Public Welfare. U.S. Senate, 91st Cong., 1st sess. Washington, DC: Government Printing Office.

Nagy, W. E. 1988. *Teaching Vocabulary to Improve Reading Comprehension.* Newark, DE: International Reading Association.

National Association for the Advancement of Colored People, Legal Defense and Educational Fund, Inc. 1971. *An Even Chance.* Annandale, VA: Graphics 4.

Navajo Division of Education. 1985. *Navajo Nation: Educational Policies.* Window Rock, AZ: Navajo Division of Education.

Neihardt, John G., ed. [1932] 1961. *Black Elk Speaks.* Lincoln: University of Nebraska Press.

Nicholson, Rangi. 1990. Maori Total Immersion Courses for Adults in *Aoteaora*/New Zealand. In *Effective Language Education Practices and Native Language Survival* (Proceedings of the Eighth Annual Native Language Issues Conference), edited by Jon Reyhner, 107–20. Choctaw, OK: Native American Language Issues.

Noll, J., and S. Kelley. 1970. *Foundations of Education in America.* New York: Harper & Row.

North Slope Borough School District. 1981. *Ulgunigmiut: People of Wainwright, Vol. 1,* Wainwright, AK: Author.

Northern Ute tribe. 1985. Ute Language Policy. *Cultural Survival Quarterly* 9(2): 16–19.

Number of Blacks Taking SAT Drops 5 Pct. in 5 Years. 1986, *Chronicle of Higher Education* (September 3): 108.

Oberly, John H. 1885. In *Annual Report of the Commissioner of Indian Affairs to the Secretary of the Interior for the year 1885,* lxxv–ccxxv. Washington, DC: Government Printing Office.

O'Dell, Scott. 1970. *Sing Down the Moon.* Boston: Houghton Mifflin.

Office of Inspector General, U.S. Department of the Interior. 1991. Audit Report: Implementation of the Education Amendments of 1978, Bureau of Indian Affairs, Report no. 91-I-941.

Ogbu, J. U. 1978. *Minority Education and Caste: The American System in Cross-cultural Perspective.* New York: Academic Press.

————. Variability in Minority School Performance: A Problem in Search of an Explanation. *Anthropology and Education Quarterly* 18(4): 312–34.

O'Neil, Floyd. 1979. "Multiple Sources and Resources for the Development of Social Studies Curriculum for the American Indian." In *Multicultural Education and the American Indian,* 153–56. American Indian Studies Center, University of California, Los Angeles.

Ortiz, A. A., and Yates, J. R. 1983. Incidence of exceptionality among Hispanics: Implications for Manpower Planning. *NABE Journal* 7: 41–54.

Ortiz, Alfonso. 1990. Interview. *Omni* (March).

Ortiz-Franco, Luis. 1981. Suggestions for Increasing the Participation of Minorities in Scientific Research. (ERIC Document Reproduction Service no. ED 210 152)

Otto, P. B., and Eagle Staff, R., eds. 1980. *Science Lessons for Native Americans.* Vermillion: School of Education, University of South Dakota.

Ovando, Carlos J., and Collier, Virginia P. 1985. *Bilingual and ESL Classrooms.* New York: McGraw-Hill.

Padover, S. 1946. *Thomas Jefferson on Democracy.* New York: Penguin.

Parsons, Jackie. 1980. *The Educational Movement of the Blackfeet Indians 1840–1979.* Browning, MT: Blackfeet Heritage Program; Browning Public Schools.

Pascua Yaqui Tribal Council. 1984. *Yaqui Language Policy for the Pascua Yaqui Tribe: Policy Declaration.* Tucson, AZ: Tucson Unified School District.

Pearson, P. D. 1982. *Asking Questions About Stories.* Ginn Occasional Paper no. 15. Columbus, OH: Ginn.

———. 1985. *Six Essential Changes in Reading Comprehension.* Ginn Occasional Paper no. 20. Columbus, OH: Ginn.

Penfield-Jasper, Susan. 1980. Selected Grammatical Characteristics of Mohave English. Ph.D. diss. Tucson: University of Arizona.

Pepper, Floy C. 1971. "Teaching the American Indian Child in mainstream settings." In *Mainstreaming and the Minority Child,* edited by R. C. Jones, 133–58. Reston, VA: Council for Exceptional Education.

Pepper, Floy C., and Coburn, Joseph. 1985. *Effective Practices in Indian Education: A Teacher's Monograph.* Portland, OR: Northwest Regional Educational Laboratory.

Pettitt, George Albert. 1946. *Primitive Education in North America.* Berkeley: University of California Press.

Philion, W. E., and Galloway, C. E. 1969. Indian Children and the Reading Program. *Journal of Reading* 12:553–60, 598–602.

Philips, Susan U. 1972. "Participant Structures and Communicative Competence: Warm Springs Children in Community and Classroom." In *Functions of Language in the Classroom,* edited by Courtney B. Cazden, Vera P. John, and Dell Hymes, 370–94. New York: Teachers College Press.

———. 1983. *The Invisible Culture: Communication in Classroom and Community on the Warm Springs Indian Reservation.* New York: Longman.

Piaget, J. 1954. *The Construction of Reality in the Child.* New York: Basic Books.

———. 1966. *The Origins of Intelligence in Children.* New York: International Universities Press.

Platero, D. 1973. "Cultural Pluralism." In *Cultural Pluralism in Education: A Mandate for Change,* edited by W. Stent and H. Rivilin. New York: Prentice Hall, Appleton-Century-Crofts.

Platero, Juanita and Miller, Siyowin. 1973. "Chee's Daughter," in *Literature of the American Indian*, edited by Thomas Sanders and William E. Peek. New York: Glencoe.

Platero Paperwork, Inc. 1986. *Executive Summary: Navajo Area Student Dropout Study*. Window Rock, AZ: Navajo Nation, Navajo Division of Education.

Porter, Rosalie Pedalino. 1990. *Forked Tongue: The Politics of Bilingual Education*. New York: Basic Books.

Postovsky, V. 1982. "Delayed Oral Practice." In *Innovative Approaches to Language Teaching*, edited by R. W. Blair, 67–76. Rowley, MA: Newbury House.

Prucha, Francis Paul. 1973. *Americanizing the American Indians*. Cambridge, MA: Harvard University Press.

————. 1976. *American Indian Policy in Crisis: Christian Reformers and the Indian, 1865–1900*. Norman: University of Oklahoma Press.

————. 1985. *The Indians in American Society: From the Revolutionary War to the Present*. Berkeley: University of California Press.

Qoyawayma, Polingaysi (Elizabeth White). 1964. *No Turning Back: A Hopi Indian Woman's Struggle to Live in Two Worlds*. Albuquerque: University of New Mexico Press.

Ramirez III, Manuel, and Castaneda, Alfredo. 1974. *Cultural Democracy, Bicognitive Development, and Education*. New York: Academic Press.

Read, John Arthur Stanley. 1978. A Sociolinguistic Study of Crow Language Maintenance. Ph.D. diss., University of New Mexico, Albuquerque.

Report of the Board of Indian Commissioners. 1880. Eleventh Annual Report for 1879. Washington, DC: Government Printing Office.

Report of the Indian Peace Commission. 1868. House Executive Doct. no. 97, 40th Cong., 2d sess., serial 1337.

Report on Indian Education, Task Force Five: Final Report to the Indian Policy Review Commission. 1976. Washington, DC: Government Printing Office.

Reyhner, Jon. 1984a. *Heart Butte: A Blackfeet Indian Community*. Billings, MT: Council for Indian Education. (ERIC Document Reproduction Service no. ED 250 115)

————. 1986. Native Americans in Basal Readers: Are There Enough? *Journal of American Indian Education* 26(1): 14–22.

————. 1989. Review of *Fools Crow*. *Journal of Navajo Education* 6(2): 59–60.

————. 1990. A Description of the Rock Point Community School Bilingual Education Program. In *Effective Language Education Practices and Native Language Survival* (Proceedings of the Eighth Annual Native American Language Issues Conference), edited by Jon Reyhner, 95–106. Choctaw, OK: Native American Language Issues.

————. In press. "Plans for Dropout Prevention and Special School Support Services for American Indian and Alaska Native Students." In *Indian Nations at Risk: Solutions for the 1990s* (supplement volume), edited by G. Mike Charleston. Washington, DC: Department of Education Indian Nations at Risk Task Force.

————, ed. 1984b. *Stories of Our Blackfeet Grandmothers*. Billings, MT: Council for Indian Education.

———— ed. 1984c. *Famine Winter*. Billings, MT: Council for Indian Education. (ERIC Document Reproduction Service no. ED 252 326)

Reyhner, Jon, and Eder, Jeanne. 1989. *A History of Indian Education*. Billings, MT: Eastern Montana College.

Rhodes, Robert W. 1990. Measurements of Navajo and Hopi Brain Dominance and Learning Styles. *Journal of American Indian Education* 29(3): 29–40.

Richard-Amato, P. A. 1988. *Making It Happen*. New York: Longman.

Richardson, James D., ed. 1910. *A Compilation of the Messages and Papers of the Presidents*. Washington, DC: Bureau of National Literature and Art.

Richardson, J. S., and Morgan, R. F. 1990. *Reading to Learn in the Content Areas*. Belmont, CA: Wadsworth.

Richau, D. 1981. *Introduce Science to Students Using the Environment*. Pre-College Teacher Development Programs, Northern Arizona University and University of South Dakota.

Rietz-Weems, Sandra A., LaCounte, Marlene, and Streeter, Sandra K. 1990. Educational Facilities Master Plan. Prepared for the Mississippi Band of Choctaw Indians and the Office of Construction Management of the Bureau of Indian Affairs, United States Department of the Interior.

Rigg, P. 1985. "Desert Wind": A Fresh Breeze in Indian Education. *Journal of Reading* 28:393–97.

Riggs, Stephen R. 1880. *Mary and I: Forty Years with the Sioux*. Chicago: W. G. Holmes.

Roessel, Robert, Jr. 1962. *Handbook for Indian Education*. Los Angeles: Amerindian.

Rohner, R. P. 1965. Factors Influencing the Academic Performance of Kwakiutl Children in Canada. *Comparative Education Review* 9: 331–40.

Rosier, Paul, and Holm, Wayne. 1980. *Bilingual Education Series: 8; The Rock Point Experience: A Longitudinal Study of a Navajo School Program (Saad Naaki Bee Na'nitin).* Washington, DC: Center for Applied Linguistics.

Ross, C., and Fernandes, R. 1979. *Coastal Culture Area.* Native American curriculum series. Seattle: Curriculum Associates.

Routman, Regie. 1988. *Transitions: From Literature to Literacy.* Portsmouth: NH: Heinemann.

Ruoff, A. LaVonne Brown, and Kroeber, Karl. 1983. *American Indian Literature in the United States: A Basic Bibliography for Teachers.* New York: Association for Study of American Indian Literatures.

Salisbury, Neal. 1974. The "Praying Indians" of Massachusetts Bay and John Eliot. *William and Mary Quarterly* 3(January): 27–54.

————. 1986. "Red Puritans: The 'Praying Indians' of Massachusetts Bay and John Eliot." In *The American Indian: Past and Present,* 3rd ed., edited by R. L. Nichols, 73–88. New York: Knopf.

Sandoz, Mari. 1961. *These Were the Sioux.* Lincoln: University of Nebraska Press.

Sauer, Carl. 1975. *Man in Nature: America Before the Days of the Whiteman.* Berkeley, CA: Turtle Island Foundation.

Savage, D. G. 1987. Why Chapter 1 Hasn't Made Much Difference. *Phi Delta Kappan* 68: 581–84.

Savignon, S. J. 1983. *Communicative Competence: Theory and Classroom Practice.* Reading, MA: Addison-Wesley.

Sawyer, D. 1988. The Writing Process and Native Students. *Canadian Journal of Native Education* 15(2): 15–21.

Saxe, Geoffrey B. 1982. "Culture and the development of numerical cognition: Studies among the Oksapmin of Papua New Guinea." In *Children's Logical and Mathematical Cognition,* edited by Charles J. Brainerd, 157–76. New York: Springer-Verlag.

Schindler, Duane E., and Davison, David M. 1985. Language, culture, and the mathematics concepts of American Indian learners. *Journal of American Indian Education* 24(3): 27–34.

Scott, Colin. 1908. *Social Education.* New York: Ginn.

Scribner, S., and Cole, M. 1973. Cognitive Consequences of Formal and Informal Education. *Science* 182: 553–58.

Shafer, R. E., and Staab, C. 1983. *Language Functions and School Success*. Glenview, IL: Scott, Foresman.

Shaver, James P., Davis, O. L., Jr., and Helburn, Suzanne W. 1979. The Status of Social Studies Education: Impressions from Three NSF Studies. *Social Education* 43:150–53.

Short, K. G., and Pierce, K. M. 1990. *Talking About Books: Creating Literate Communities*. Portsmouth, NH: Heinemann.

Silko, Leslie. 1977. *Ceremony*. New York: Viking Press.

Simpson-Tyson, Audrey K. 1978. Are Native American First Graders Ready to Read? *Reading Teacher* 31:798–801.

Sion, C., ed. 1985. *Recipes for Tired Teachers*. Reading, MA: Addison-Wesley.

Skinner, L. 1986. *Star Stories*. Washington, DC: Native American Science Education Association.

Skutnabb-Kangas, T. 1984. *Bilingualism or Not: The Education of Minorities*. Clevedon, England: Multilingual Matters.

Slavin, R. 1983. *Cooperative Learning*. New York: Longman.

Smith, Frank. 1978. *Understanding Reading*. 2nd ed. New York: Holt, Rinehart & Winston.

———. 1983. *Essays into Literacy*. London: Heinemann.

———. 1988. *Joining the Literacy Club: Further Essays into Education*. Portsmouth, NH: Heinemann.

Smith, K. L. 1972. The Role of Games, Sports, and Dance in Iroquois Life. Master's thesis, University of Maryland.

Snipp, C. Matthew. 1989. *American Indians: The First of This Land*. New York: Russell Sage Foundation.

Spolsky, Bernard. 1973. The Development of Navajo Bilingual Education. (ERIC Document Reproduction Service no. ED 094 559)

———. 1978. "American Indian Bilingual Education." In *Case Studies in Bilingual Education*, edited by Bernard Spolsky and Robert L. Cooper, 332–61. Rowley, MA: Newbury House.

———. 1980. "Forward." In *The Rock Point Experience: A Longitudinal Study of a Navajo School Program (Saad Naaki Bee Na'nitin)*, edited by Paul Rosier and Wayne Holm, v–vi. Bilingual Education Series: 8. Washington, DC: Center for Applied Linguistics.

St. Clair, Robert N. 1982. "What Is Language Renewal?" In *Language Renewal Among American Indian Tribes: Issues, Problems, and Prospects,* edited by Robert St. Clair and William Leap, 3–17. Rosslyn, VA: National Clearinghouse for Bilingual Education.

St. Clair, Robert, and Leap, William L., eds. 1982. *Language Renewal Among American Indian Tribes*. Rosslyn, VA: National Clearinghouse for Bilingual Education.

Standing Bear, Luther. 1928. *My People the Sioux*. Edited by E. A. Brininstool. Boston: Houghton Mifflin.

Stauffer, Russell G. 1976. *Teaching Reading as a Thinking Process*. New York: Harper & Row.

————. 1980. *The Language Experience Approach to the Teaching of Reading*. New York: Harper & Row.

Stensland, Anna Lee. 1979. *Literature by and About the American Indian: An Annotated Bibliography*. 2nd ed. Urbana, IL: National Council of Teachers of English.

Stern, Catherine. 1949. *Children Discover Arithmetic: An Introduction to Structured Arithmetic*. New York: Harper.

Stokes, D. W. 1976. *A Guide to Nature in Winter*. Boston: Little, Brown.

Stout, Steven O. 1979. Sociolinguistic Aspects of English Diversity among Elementary-Aged Students from Laguna Pueblo. Ph.D. diss., American University.

Studies in Immersion Education: A Collection for United States Educators. 1984. Sacramento: California State Department of Education.

Suina, Joseph H. 1988. "Epilogue: And Then I Went to School." In *Linguistic and Cultural Influences on Learning Mathematics*, edited by Rodney Cocking and Jose P. Mestre, 295–99. Hillsdale, NJ: Erlbaum.

Sullivan, J. O. 1845, December. Editorial. New York: *Morning News*.

Summary Report of the Task Force on the Educational Needs of Native Peoples of Ontario. 1976. (ERIC Document Reproduction Service no. ED 154 947)

Sutman, F., Allen, V., and Shoemaker, F. 1986. *Learning English Through Science*. Washington, DC: National Science Teachers Association.

Sutman, F., and Bilotta, C. 1986. *Integrating Methodologies of Science/math and Language*. Teaneck, NJ: Fairleigh Dickinson University.

Swann, Brian, and Krupat, Arnold, eds. 1989. *I Tell You Now: Autobiographies and Essays by Native American Writers*. Lincoln: University of Nebraska Press.

Swisher, Karen. 1984. Comparison of Attitudes of Reservation Parents and Teachers Toward Multicultural Education. *Journal of American Indian Education* 23(3): 1–10.

Swisher, Karen, and Swisher, C. 1986, September. A Multicultural

Physical Education Approach: An Attitude. *Journal of Physical Education, Recreation and Dance* (September): 35–39.

Szasz, Margaret Connell. 1977. *Education and the American Indian: The Road to Self-Determination Since 1928.* 2nd ed. Albuquerque: University of New Mexico Press.

———. 1988. *Indian Education in the American Colonies, 1607–1783.* Albuquerque: University of New Mexico Press.

Task Force Five: Indian Education. 1976. *Report on Indian Education: Final Report to the American Indian Policy Review Commission.* Washington, DC: Government Printing Office.

Tharp, Roland G. 1982. The Effective Instruction of Comprehension: Results and Description of the Kamehameha Early Education Program. *Reading Research Quarterly* 17:503–27.

Thornton, Russell. 1987. *American Indian Holocaust and Survival: A Population History Since 1492.* Norman: University of Oklahoma Press.

Tikunoff, R. 1984. An Emerging Description of Successful Bilingual Instruction. Executive Summary of Part I of the Significant Bilingual Instructional Features Study. San Francisco: Far West Laboratory.

Tizard, J., Schofield, W. N., and Hewison, J. 1982. Collaboration Between Teachers and Parents in Assisting Children's Reading. *British Journal of Educational Psychology* 52:1–15.

Tocqueville, Alexis de. [1835] 1966. *Democracy in America.* Translated by George Lawrence. New York: Harper & Row.

Torbert, M., and Schneider, L. B. 1986. Positive Multicultural Interaction: Using Low Organized Games. *Journal of Physical Education, Recreation and Dance* (September): 40–44.

Triplett, Frank. 1883. *Conquering the Wilderness.* New York: N. D. Thompson.

Trueba, Henry T. 1979. "Bilingual-Education Models: Types and Designs." In *Bilingual Multicultural Education and the Professional: From Theory to Practice,* edited by Henry T. Trueba and Carol Barnett-Mizrahi, 54–73. Rowley, MA: Newbury House.

Twain, Mark [Samuel L. Clemens]. [1876] 1958. *The Adventures of Tom Sawyer.* New York: Dodd, Mead.

Underhill, Ruth M. 1940. *Hawk Over Whirlpools.* New York: J. J. Augustin.

U.S. Department of Education. 1986. *What Works: Research About Teaching and Learning.* Washington, DC: Author.

U.S. Senate. Committee on Labor and Public Welfare. Special Subcommittee on Indian Education. 1969. *Indian Education: A National Trag-*

edy, A National Challenge. Senate Report 80, 91st Congress, 1st sess. (commonly known as the Kennedy Report).

U.S. Senate. Special Committee on Investigations of the Select Committee on Indian Affairs. 1989, November. *Final Report and Legislative Recommendations.* Washington, DC: Government Printing Office.

Utley, Robert M. 1984. *The Indian Frontier of the American West 1846–1890.* Albuquerque: University of New Mexico Press.

Vacca, R. T., and Vacca, J. L. 1989. *Content Area Reading.* 3rd ed. Glenview, IL: Scott, Foresman.

Van Ness, Howard. 1981. "Social Control and Social Organization in an Alaskan Athabaskan Classroom: A Microethnography of 'Getting Ready' for Reading." In *Culture and the Bilingual Classroom,* edited by H. T. Trueba, G. P. Guthrie, and K. Hu-Pei Au, 120–38. Rowley, MA: Newbury House.

Veit, R. 1986. *Discoverying English Grammar.* Boston: Houghton Mifflin.

Vogel, Virgil J. 1972. *This Country Was Ours: A Documentary History of the American Indian.* New York: Harper & Row.

Vygotsky, L. S. 1978. *Mind in Society.* Cambridge, MA: Harvard University Press.

Walters, J., and Gardiner, H. 1984. "The Development and Education of Intelligences." A paper presented to the Bernard Van Leer Foundation, The Hague, Netherlands. (ERIC Document Reproduction Service no. ED 254 545)

Warner, G. S. 1927. *Football for Coaches and Players.* Palo Alto: Stanford University Press.

Watahomigie, Lucille, Powskey, M., and Bender, J. 1982. *Ethnobotany of the Hualapai.* Peach Springs, AZ: Hualapai Bilingual Program, Peach Springs School District No. 8.

Watahomigie, Lucille, Powskey, M. Bender, J., Uqualla, J., and Watahomigie, P. Sr. 1983. *Waksi: Wich Hualapai Cattle Ranching.* Peach Springs, AZ: Hualapai Bilingual Program, Peach Springs School District No. 8.

Watahomigie, Lucille J., and Yamamoto, Akira Y. 1987. Linguistics in action: The Hualapai bilingual/bicultural education program. In *Collaborative research and social change: Applied Anthropology in Action,* edited by Donald D. Stull and Jean J. Schensul, 77–98. Boulder, CO: Westview.

Waters, Frank. [1941] 1971. *The Man Who Killed the Deer.* New York: Pocket Books.

Wauters, Joan K., Bruce, Janet Merrill, Black, David R., and Hocker, Phillip N. 1989. Learning Styles: A study of Alaska Native and Non-Native Students. *Journal of American Indian Education* 28(4): 53–62.

Wax, Murray L. 1971. *Indian Americans: Unity and Diversity*. Englewood Cliffs, NJ: Prentice Hall.

Wax, Murray L., Wax R. H., and Dumont, R. V., Jr. 1964. Formal Education in an American Indian Community. *Social Problems* 11(suppl.): 95–96.

Wax, Rosalie, and Wax, Murray. 1968. "Indian Education for What?" In *The American Indian Today*, edited by Stuart Levine and Nancy O. Lurie, 257–67. Baltimore: Penguin.

Welch, James. 1986. *Fools Crow*. New York: Viking.

Wells, G. 1982. "Language, Learning and Curriculum." In *Language, Learning and Education*, edited by G. Wells. Bristol, England: Centre for the Study of Language and Communication, University of Bristol.

———. 1986. *The Meaning Makers: Children Learning Language and Using Language to Learn*. Portsmouth, NH: Heinemann.

Werner, O., and Begishe, K. 1968. Styles of Learning: The Evidence for Navajo. Paper presented for conference on styles of learning in American Indian children, Stanford University, Stanford, California.

Whitney, A. 1977. *Sports and Games the Indians Gave Us*. New York: David McKay.

Wiget, Andrew. 1985. *Native American Literature*. Boston: G. K. Hall, Twayne Publishers.

Wilder, Laura Ingalls. [1935] 1971. *Little House on the Prairie*. New York: Harper & Row.

Winograd, Peter, N. 1989. "Introduction: Understanding Reading Instruction." In *Improving Basal Reading Instruction*, edited by Peter N. Winograd, Karen K. Wison, and Marjorie Y. Lipson, 1–20. New York: Teachers College Press.

Wise, L. C., ed. 1976. *Indian Education Curriculum Guidelines*. Oklahoma City: Oklahoma State Department of Education.

Wolcott, H. 1976. *A Kwakiutl Village and School*. Chicago: Holt, Rinehart & Winston.

Wolfe, K. 1982. "Things to Do." In *Classroom Activities for the Middle Grades*. Olympia, WA: Office of the State Superintendent of Public Instruction.

Woodruff, J. 1939. *Indian Oasis*. Caldwell, ID: Caxton.

Woodward, G. S. 1963. *The Cherokees*. Norman: University of Oklahoma Press.

Yarington, David. J. 1978. *The Great American Reading Machine*. Rochele Park, NJ: Hayden.

Yava, Albert. [1978] 1981. *Big Falling Snow: A Tewa-Hopi Indian's Life and Times and the History and Traditions of His People*. Albuquerque: University of New Mexico Press.

Yukon-Koyukuk School District of Alaska. 1981a. *Madeline Solomon, Koyukuk: A Biography*. Blaine, WA: Hancock House.

———. 1981b. *John Honeal, Ruby: A Biography*. Blaine, WA: Hancock House.

Zintz, Miles V. 1984. *The Reading Process: The Teacher and the Learner*. Dubuque, IA: Wm. C. Brown.

The Contributors

Janet Goldenstein Ahler is Associate Professor of Education at the University of North Dakota. She is an educational anthropologist and multicultural educator who has spent more than twenty years working with Indian students and schools throughout the United States.

Elected in 1987, **Ben Nighthorse Campbell** represents the third district of Colorado in the U.S. House of Representatives. He was a member of the Advisory Committee for the White House Conference on Indian Education. He is Northern Cheyenne.

Jim Cummins is Professor and Head of the Modern Language Centre of the Ontario Institute for Studies in Education. He has written extensively in the field of bilingual education, including such works as *Bilingualism and Special Education: Issues in Assessment and Pedagogy* (College-Hill, 1984) and *Empowering Minority Students* (California Association for Bilingual Education, 1989). His research interests include language planning, patterns of language acquisition and academic development among minority students, and the effects of teaching practices on the development of language and literacy. He has worked with the Baffin Divisional Board of Education in researching the effects of Inukitut-English bilingual education policies and with the government of the Yukon Territory on policy issues in bilingual education.

David M. Davison is Professor of Education in the Department of Curriculum and Instruction at Eastern Montana College, where he has taught for fifteen years. He has worked extensively with the mathematics learning of American Indian students. He has offered a number of workshops and courses for teachers of American Indian students. Most recently he has directed a summer mathematics clinic for Crow Indian students.

Donna Deyhle is an Associate Professor of Anthropology and Education and Native American Studies in the Departments of Educational Studies and Ethnic Studies at the University of Utah. She is a former Spencer Fellow and has published widely on the topic of school success and failure among American Indians and Alaska Natives, with emphasis on Navajos.

Jeanne Eder is Sioux and a former Associate Professor and Coordinator of Native American Studies at Eastern Montana College. She has consulted extensively in the field of Native American Studies and is currently working on a doctorate in history at Washington State University.

Sandra Fox is an Oglala Sioux with twenty-three years of experience in Indian education at all levels. She has worked with both Title V Indian Education Act and Bureau of Indian Affairs programs. She is currently Chief, Branch of Monitoring and Evaluation, for the Bureau of Indian Affairs Education Office in Washington, D.C.

Ricardo L. Garcia is Director of the Division of Teacher Education in the College of Education at the University of Idaho. He has offered workshops and college courses in American Indian communities in Kansas, Oklahoma, Utah, and Montana in the areas of bilingual instruction and countering stereotypes and biases in public school curriculum and textbooks. His book *Teaching in a Pluralistic Society* (Harper & Collins, 1991) is in its second edition.

Robert W. Grueninger is Chair of Health, Physical Education, and Recreation at Morehead State University.

Edwina Hoffman has taught English as a second language to the Micusukee tribe in Florida at all levels for six years and has been honored by both the tribe and the Bureau of Indian Affairs for her work. She has consulted and offered numerous workshops around the country on teaching tribal language, teaching English as a second language, and sensitizing teachers to the special needs of non-English-speaking people.

Marlene F. LaCounte is Associate Professor of Curriculum and Instruction at Eastern Montana College. She is former Chair of the Department of Curriculum and Instruction and has been a consultant to various American Indian tribes.

William L. Leap is Associate Professor of Anthropology at the American University in Washington, D.C. He pioneered the field of Indian English research. He has been active in Indian bilingual education since 1974 and has written numerous articles on the subject. He is currently completing a book on Indian English.

Dick Littlebear is Northern Cheyenne and Director of the Alaska (Bilingual) Multifunctional Resource Center in Anchorage. He is a former Western Regional Representative for the National Association for Bilingual Education, former president of the Montana Association for Bilingual Education, and former secretary of the Alaska Association for Bilingual Education.

T. L. McCarty is Assistant Professor of Language, Reading, and Culture at the University of Arizona, Tucson, where she codirects the American Indian Language Development Institute and teaches courses on bilingual/multicultural and Indian education. She has worked as an Indian student counselor, teacher, and curriculum developer, and in her current position continues to work with American Indian schools and communities throughout the western United States.

Carlos J. Ovando is Professor of Education at Indiana University, where he teaches courses in multicultural education and curriculum and instruction. An internationally recognized expert in the field of multicultural education, he has written extensively on issues of culture, language, and curriculum pertaining to language-minority students. He is senior coauthor of *Bilingual and ESL Classrooms: Teaching in Multicultural Contexts* (McGraw-Hill, 1985). Three of Ovando's most recent publications are "Intermediate and Secondary School Curricula: A Multicultural and Multilingual Framework" (*Clearing House,* March 1990); "Language Diversity and Education" (in *Multicultural Education: Issues and Perspectives,* ed. J. A. Banks and C. M. Banks, 1989); and "Politics and Pedagogy: The Case of Bilingual Education" (*Harvard Educational Review,* August 1990). He has taught previously at Oregon State University, the University of Alaska-Anchorage, and the University of Southern California.

Daniel L. Pearce is Associate Professor of Reading at Northeastern Illinois University. He has given workshops on teaching reading comprehension to Indian students and taught reading courses on a number of Montana reservations.

Jon Reyhner is Associate Professor of Curriculum and Instruction at Eastern Montana College. He has twenty years' experience in Indian education as a teacher and school administrator and has worked on the White Mountain Apache, Blackfeet, Colorado Indian Tribes, Fort Peck, Navajo, Rocky Boy's, and Havasupai Reservations. He has given numerous workshops in the field of Indian education and written extensively on the subject.

James R. Saucerman is Chair of the Department of English at Northwest Missouri State University, where he teaches American literature, including that of American Indians. He has presented conference papers on a number of American writers and has published scholarly articles on western American poetry and American writers such as Emerson, Thoreau, Twain, Ray Young Bear, and Wendy Rose.

Rachel Schaffer, Associate Professor of English, has taught linguistics and composition at Eastern Montana College since 1983. She has tutored Indian students and taught special ESL sections for American Indian students. She has presented and published in the fields of teaching American Indian students and developing culturally relevant classroom materials.

Karen Swisher is an Assistant Professor of Multicultural Education in the Division of Curriculum and Instruction, Arizona State University. She is also Director of the Center for Indian Education and editor of the *Journal of American Indian Education.*

Index

Acculturation, 104, 198; defined, 24
Active teaching strategies, 139–40
Activity-centered mathematics, 247
Adler, Mortimer, 18
Affective filter, 75, 139
Alienation, 195
Allotment, 47, 50
American Board of Foreign Missions, 373
American Indian English, 145
American Indian Movement, 55
Anglo-conformity orientation, 7
Annuities, 46–47
Anthologies, American Indian, 200
Arapaho children, 186
Archery, 259–60
Asher, James, 133
Ashton-Warner, Sylvia, 162–63
Assessment. *See* Testing
Assimilation, 15, 22; coercive, 33; defined, 24; enforced, 105; total, 106
Atkins, J. D. C., 41–43, 45

Background knowledge, 182
Barfield, Owen, 196–98
Basal readers. *See* Textbooks
Bennett, William, 161
Bible: Algonquian, 35; Dakota, 43; translators, 71–72
Bibliographies: Indian literature, 199; native language, 73
Bicultural ambivalence, 4
Biculturalism, 227
Bigotry, 20
Bilingual, education, 109; Education

Act, 63, 72; materials development, 72
Bilingual programs: Choctaw, 229; immersion, 63–66; maintenance, 63–65; Navajo, 67–69; transitional, 63–64, 66
Bilingualism, additive-subtractive, 6, 239
Black Elk, 199
Blackfeet children, 89
Blackfeet Dictionary Project, 72
Black Hills, 45
Blood quantum, 26
Bloods: full, 28; mixed, 28
Bloom, Benjamin, 211
Board of Indian Commissioners, 41, 44
Boarding Schools, 39, 44, 46, 50, 52, 145, 267
Boas, Franz, 48
Books, with Indian themes, 98
Bowling, 253
Brainstorming, 182
Brown v. Board of Education of Topeka, 54
Bruner, Jerome, 212
Buffalo Hunt, 261
Bureau of Indian Affairs, 44
Byler, Mary, 158

Calhoun, John C., 40
Carlisle Indian School, 46, 259
Center for Indian Education, 54
Chamot, Anna, 227–29, 238, 244
Cherokee Nation v. Georgia, 38
Cherokees, 29, 38–39; children, 89; classrooms, 88